After Defeat

Not being of the West; being behind the West; not being modern enough; not being developed or industrialized, secular, civilized, Christian, transparent, or democratic – these descriptions have all served to stigmatize certain states through history. Drawing on constructivism as well as the insights of social theorists and philosophers, *After Defeat* demonstrates that stigmatization in international relations can lead to a sense of national shame, as well as auto-Orientalism and inferior status. Ayşe Zarakol argues that stigmatized states become extra-sensitive to concerns about status, and shape their foreign policy accordingly. The theoretical argument is supported by a detailed historical overview of central examples of the established/outsider dichotomy throughout the evolution of the modern states system, and in-depth studies of Turkey after the First World War, Japan after the Second World War, and Russia after the Cold War.

AYŞE ZARAKOL is an Assistant Professor of Politics at Washington & Lee University. She teaches courses on global politics, international security, and political theory and her research focuses on the social evolution of the international system and the integration of regions outside of the West into the modern international order.

Cambridge Studies in International Relations: 118

After Defeat

Cambridge Studies in International Relations is a joint initiative of Cambridge
University Press and the British International Studies Association (BISA). The
series will include a wide range of material, from undergraduate textbooks and
surveys to research-based monographs and collaborative volumes. The aim of the
series is to publish the best new scholarship in International Studies from Europe,
North America, and the rest of the world.

Cambridge Studies in International Relations

Series list continues after index

After Defeat

How the East Learned to Live
with the West

AYŞE ZARAKOL

CAMBRIDGE
UNIVERSITY PRESS

CAMBRIDGE UNIVERSITY PRESS
Cambridge, New York, Melbourne, Madrid, Cape Town, Singapore,
São Paulo, Delhi, Dubai, Tokyo, Mexico City

Cambridge University Press
The Edinburgh Building, Cambridge CB2 8RU, UK

Published in the United States of America by Cambridge University Press, New York

www.cambridge.org
Information on this title: www.cambridge.org/9780521145565

First published 2011

Printed in the United Kingdom at the University Press, Cambridge

A catalogue record for this publication is available from the British Library

Library of Congress Cataloguing in Publication data
Zarakol, Ayşe.
    After defeat : how the East learned to live with the West / Ayşe Zarakol.
        p.   cm. – (Cambridge studies in international relations ; 118)
    Includes bibliographical references and index.
    ISBN 978-0-521-19182-1 (hardback)
    1. International relations–Social aspects.   2. Inferiority complex–
    Social aspects.   3. Defeat (Psychology)   4. Collective memory.
    5. Military history, Modern–20th century.   6. Turkey–Foreign relations–
    1918–1960.   7. Japan–Foreign relations–1945–1989.   8. Russia
    (Federation)–Foreign relations.   I. Title.   II. Series.
    JZ1251.Z37 2010
    327.1–dc22
                              2010037098

ISBN 978-0-521-19182-1 Hardback
ISBN 978-0-521-14556-5 Paperback

For Michael Barnett and David Leheny

You see, our whole life, from earliest childhood, has been geared to the European mentality. Is it possible that any of us could have prevailed against this influence, this appeal, this pressure? How is it that we have not been regenerated once and for all into Europeans? That we have not been so regenerated I think all will agree, some with joy, others, of course, with anger that *we have not grown up enough* for regeneration. But that is another matter. I am speaking only of the fact that we have not been regenerated even in the presence of such irresistible influences, and I cannot understand this fact.

Fyodor Dostoyevsky,
From *Winter Notes on Summer Impressions* (1863)

Contents

Acknowledgments

This book is about the insecurities created by the manner of incorporation of non-Western actors into the international system and how those insecurities continue to shape fundamental dynamics in world politics. In order to do that argument justice, I have at times traveled out of the more familiar confines of International Relations into social and political theory, comparative history, political sociology, and area studies. I read most of this literature without much guidance, and I sincerely hope specialists in each will forgive me for both omissions and unusual interpretations. While I am certain that in my attempt to paint a broad picture I have overlooked important details, this should not be construed in any way as intentional disrespect. I can only hope that the book's comprehensive vision compensates to some extent for its shortcomings.

This project has descended from a dissertation completed at the University of Wisconsin-Madison, but has become something much larger and bolder since then. Most of the current draft was written at Washington & Lee University, and supported by the generous Glenn and Lenfest summer research grants. Among many great colleagues, Robin LeBlanc and Mark Rush have been especially kind and encouraging during my time at this institution. I am also grateful to the Department of Politics, as well as the Williams School, for all the support I have received for my research agenda.

Back at the University of Wisconsin-Madison, I encountered great role models who always encouraged me to follow what interests me rather than what is in vogue. There is something in this book from almost each class I took in Madison. I would like to thank my professors Michael Barnett, David Leheny, Jason Wittenberg, Jon Pevehouse, Mark Beissinger, Edward Friedman, Bernard Yack, Marion Smiley, Paul Hutchcroft, and Aseema Sinha for their wisdom and support. I should also mention here my undergraduate professors from Middlebury College, most notably Murray Dry, Jeff Cason and Michael Kraus, without whose example I probably would not have become a political scientist. I am also thankful to my classics professors from Middlebury College, especially Jane Chaplin and Eve Adler, for making me realize by their brilliance that a little levity does not hurt at all when talking about history. Part of the research for this book was undertaken when I was a research fellow at Istanbul Bilgi University, and I am especially grateful to İlter Turan for giving me that opportunity.

Over the course of writing, several people have given me tips or feedback which improved the book. I would like to thank Georgi Derluguian, Shogo Suzuki, Brent Steele, Iaonnis Stivachtis, Patrick Thaddeus Jackson, Richard Beardsworth, and Roger Haydon, as well as other individuals who have asked questions at panels and talks where I have presented parts of this work. Parts of this book originally appeared in the article "Ontological (In)security and State Denial of Historical Crimes: Turkey and Japan," *International Relations*, Volume 24, Issue 1 (2010). The original article can be found at http://ire.sagepub.com. I would be remiss if I did not thank the editor of that journal, Ken Booth, as well as the two anonymous reviewers, for their many suggestions about that article, which I have also taken into account here. I am also incredibly grateful to the two anonymous readers from Cambridge University Press for their excellent directions about how to improve this book. In addition, I would like to thank my editors, John Haslam and Carrie Parkinson, for overseeing this project into print. I am especially thankful to John Haslam for taking a chance on me by sending the manuscript out to review.

During the course of writing this book, I have also benefited from a wonderful support network of friends and family. Among many great friends, I am especially thankful to Simanti Lahiri, Jelena Subotic, Patrick Cottrell, Travis Nelson, Demet Lüküslü, Burç Beşgül, Özge Onursal, and Zeynep Gülşah Çapan for their comments on various drafts, for many days and nights of stimulating "nerdy" conversation, as well as for their genuine friendship. I should also mention here friends who kept me grounded by reminding me that there is a world outside of academia. I would like to thank Aylin Ülçer, Arzu Soysal, Ayşin Hattat Vardar, Banu Kutlu, Hürol Ayaz, İrem Çavuşoğlu, Irazca Geray, Liz Amado, Petek Salman, Selin Arat, Sibel Demir, and my brother, Aras Zarakol. I am also grateful to my in-laws Margaret and James Jajich for their patience with me at times when this book project took precedence over family matters. My parents, Necla and

Cihan Zarakol, are, and have always been, the best part about being me, and they continue to inspire me in every way imaginable. Finally, no one has put up with more in service of this project than my wonderful, kind, generous, brilliant husband, Dmitri Jajich, who also took the photograph on the cover image of this book.

I dedicate this book to my mentors, Michael Barnett and David Leheny. I know I would never have finished this book without their unwavering encouragement. All failings in what follows are mine alone, but the credit for what is worthwhile belongs rightly to Michael and Dave.

Introduction

... And from the other side, it is also the case that the most earnest and heartfelt efforts to imitate some foreign model can never entirely succeed in eliminating tell-tale traces of older, traditional local patterns of human interaction. The modern history of Japan, Russia and Turkey should suffice to tell us that.

William McNeill, "A Defence of World History"

In 2006, while I was working on an earlier draft of this book, Turkish novelist Orhan Pamuk won the Nobel Prize for Literature. What should have been a joyous occasion for the writer and for Turkey, however, was instead marked by histrionic public accusations of treachery against Pamuk. He was vilified in the Turkish press. Several months before the announcement of the award, Pamuk had been interviewed by a Swiss newspaper, and in response to the reporter's characterization of Turkey as a country having difficulty in facing its past, he had emphasized his own willingness to discuss the Armenian genocide and the plight of Turkey's Kurdish minority. Even though Pamuk's transparency had been partly motivated by a desire to defend Turkey (against the implied charge that Turkey cannot deal with its problems like an "adult" and therefore does not deserve to join the European Union), when this interview was later covered in the Turkish media, many Turks decided that Pamuk was either a traitor or, at best, a sleaze. Official charges were brought against him for denigrating "Turkishness" (the charges were later dropped). Some even argued that if Pamuk were an honorable man, he would return his prize, which was surely given to him for political reasons. It was suggested that by accepting the Nobel Prize he was playing into the hands of the Westerners, whose sole motivation in their dealings with Turks was to make Turkey look bad.

I suppose everything about this episode looks ridiculous to an outsider. Here is a country that has bent itself out of shape for almost a century to join the Western world, while at the same time holding on to the worst kind of paranoid suspicions about Western intentions. Turks accuse Westerners of portraying Turks always in an unflattering light (and rewarding those native sons, such as Pamuk, for playing along); yet their way of dealing with this perceived injury is to act in the most petulant way imaginable, giving credence to those who like to portray Turks as brutish. Even to sympathetic observers, Turks' general tendency to fly off the handle when confronted by any ugly facet of their country, their strange laws protecting "Turkishness," and their inability to break out of groupthink when it comes to narratives of Turkish history seems like nationalism run amok. And there is some truth to that assessment.

I hope I do not come across as an apologist, however, if I suggest that the exaggerated sense of pride and the persecution complex exhibited by Turkish nationalism today is not an inherent tendency of "Turks," but rather the unfortunate consequence of Turkey's place in the international system. This is not to say that Turks are justified in acting in this manner or cannot help but act in this manner. Nonetheless, however responsible Turks may be for their conduct, the underlying causes of such behavior can be found only in the interactions between Turkey and international society throughout the last century.

Orhan Pamuk is a writer who personifies Turkey's greatest aspirations and anxieties. He was able to achieve a level of international recognition that most Turks believed would never be accorded to a Turkish citizen; but he did this by writing (and speaking) evocatively about things that Turks find embarrassing while simultaneously ridiculing things that Turks lionize. Many Turks believe that Pamuk was rewarded for confirming the West's worst perceptions of Turkey, from the Armenian genocide to the fact that some Turkish women wear headscarves.[1] And they are partly right.

The nationalists are obviously wrong about Pamuk being a traitor, but in all of the misdirected anger at him, there lies the justifiable (or at least understandable) frustration with the fact that Pamuk gets recognition because he often writes about what is different about Turkey.

---

[1] This is one of the subject matters of Pamuk's *Snow*. "'Isn't it bad for us if American readers find out from this book that some Turkish women wear headscarves?' asked a worried boy, who had told me he learned his excellent American English by chatting on the Megadeth fansite. 'Won't they think we're ... like Iran?'" From Gloria Fisk, "Orhan Pamuk and the Turks."

Turks (or, at least, the secular, urban, establishment Turks) want what they cannot get: to be recognized simultaneously for what Turkey has in common with the West (i.e. as an ordinary, "normal" country) and for the super-human effort Turks have put into creating that common ground (i.e. as an extraordinary, "special" country). The realization that the West cares more about what lies beyond the Westernized Turkey Turks have worked so hard and sacrificed so much to create is an existential kick in the gut.

National identity and stigma

Are the nationalist Turks irrational? Perhaps. Their frustration is not that different, however, than that of a blind person who has spent a lifetime developing skills to function as well as a "normal"[2] person, only to find time and time again that people cannot but see him as a blind person, that whatever he does, he cannot shed the label of blindness as the primary marker of his identity. Being rewarded for one's handicap is in some ways worse than being shunned for it – a person is thus deprived also of the righteous indignation of the deliberately victimized and has difficulty justifying his anger.

In their reactions to Pamuk's award as well as in their other seemingly irrational behavior, Turks, as a group, are acting very much like an individual who carries a "stigma" and who is trying to hide it. Erving Goffman describes "stigma" as "a special discrepancy between virtual and actual social identity."[3] If the stigmatized individual assumes that "his differentness is known about already" he is someone who is "*discredited*"; if he assumes that his stigma "is neither known ... nor immediately perceivable" he is someone who is "*discreditable*." Modern Turks continuously live with the fear of becoming discredited; they worry about being forever stuck with their "stigma(s)": Eastern, backward, Asian, Muslim, uncivilized, barbaric, etc.

One of the distinctive features of having to endure life with a stigma is feeling the need to be always "on," "having to be self-conscious and calculating about the impression [one] is making, to a degree and in areas of conduct which [one] assumes others are not."[4] In stigmatized

---

[2] "We and those who do not depart negatively from the particular expectations at issue I shall call the *normals*." Goffman, *Stigma*, p. 5.
[3] *Ibid.*, p. 3.　[4] *Ibid.*, p. 14.

collectives, the same need to be "on" seems to manifest as the emergence of an officially sanctioned group self-narrative that is quite stifling of individual members' ability to express themselves honestly to the outside world. Actions such as Pamuk's are perceived as a betrayal of the highest order, and in some ways they are: by undermining the sanctity of the group narrative, they spoil the identity of the group and therefore threaten its very existence.

One of the underlying arguments in this book is that stigma has the same effect on states that it has on individuals: it colors and therefore motivates every subsequent interaction. Not being of the "West," being behind the "West," not being "modern" enough, not being developed or industrialized or secular or civilized or Christian or democratic enough – these are examples of designations (and, later, self-evaluations) that have essentially functioned as stigmas for states. To treat such labels as if they were only objective assessments of the facts on the ground is to miss entirely the social dynamics of international relations. By drawing attention to the stigma-like properties of seemingly objective assessments in international relations, I want to draw attention to the socially constructed nature of the international system – it is only in a social, comparative, relative setting that various physical conditions become problems to be managed or overcome. After all, it is the norm of sightedness that makes blindness a stigma, something much more than an individual attribute.

Stigma is not at all the same thing as discrimination, although there is considerable overlap between the two in practice. Goffman said that in order to understand stigma we need "a language of relationships, not attributes."[5] Stigma, in essence, is a socially shared ground between the "normals" and those who are being discredited: "The stigmatized individual tends to hold the same beliefs about identity that we do" and "the standards he has incorporated from the wider society equip him to be intimately alive to what others see as his failing, inevitably causing him, if only for moments, to agree that he does indeed fall short of what he ought to be."[6] Stigma, then, is *as much the internalization of a particular normative standard that defines one's own attributes as discreditable*, as it is a label of difference imposed from outside.

[5] *Ibid.*, p. 3.   [6] *Ibid.*, p. 7.

Apart from a few states which have chosen total isolation (and even those may not be completely free), most in the world today still evaluate themselves according to the ideals and ideas of modernity.[7] Many people all around the globe continue to equate modernization with progress, development with improvement, and they hardly ever question that these are the rightful missions of a state. Even if their own particular state does not embody those ideals, most feel that it should, and feel disappointed, and perhaps even humiliated, when it falls short.

This is why Orhan Pamuk's books, which deal with the existential issues of being trapped between the East and the West, resonate with readers in the "East" as much as they fascinate Westerners. In an interview with *The Believer* magazine, Pamuk remarks:

I'll tell you something. I have just come back from Japan, China, Hong Kong, Taipei. And you know what they say? This is very peculiar ... No one thinks his country is completely East. In China, they say, "Yes, Mr. Pamuk, we have the same East/West question here." They think that they are also torn between the East and the West, the way we are here in Turkey. They don't consider themselves in China or in Tokyo completely "East." They think that they have some part of the "West" and "East," you see? ... And they will tell you this, and then they will smile – knowing the strangeness of it. There is no place, perhaps, in humanity, where the subject considers himself completely Eastern.[8]

What sets Turkey apart from the West, much to the consternation of secular Turks who want to pass as ordinary Europeans, unites it in a common fate with the majority of states in the modern international system. Most communities in the world exist in a constant state of identity struggle. While it is extremely difficult to live up to the standards of modernity – which, despite its universal language, has undeniable Western origins and therefore carries certain assumptions about proper social and institutional configurations – without feeling inauthentic, it is also almost impossible to be authentically non-Western.

---

7 See Meyer and Jepperson, "'Actors' of Modern Society," 105, for a further elaboration of this point.
8 Rockingham, "Interview with Orhan Pamuk."

Modernity and the international system

The lack of attention given to the particular cultural and historical origins[9] of the modern international system may just be the most glaring oversight in mainstream International Relations (IR). The emotional price that the majority of peoples around the world have had to pay as a result of joining a system of states with very specific cultural origins – the rules of which they did not create, the norms of which were unfamiliar at best, the major players of which judged and explicitly labeled them as inferior, and the ontology of which convinced them that they indeed were lacking in some way – is swept under the rug as being irrelevant to international affairs.

People who have grown up in countries whose modernity has never been in question may not fully understand how all-consuming[10] the stigma of comparative backwardness may become for a society; how tiring it is to conduct all affairs under the gaze of an imaginary and imagined West, which is simultaneously idealized *and* suspected of the worst kind of designs; or how scary it is to live continuously on the brink of being swallowed by a gaping chasm of "Easternness," which is simultaneously denigrated *and* touted as the more authentic, the more realistic choice. No amount of hostile bravado disguised as nationalist rhetoric of pride can cover up the fear people around the world feel when they think about their place in the international system. Let me turn to Pamuk once again:

What literature needs most to tell and investigate today are humanity's basic fears: the fear of being left outside, and the fear of counting for nothing, and the feelings of worthlessness that come with such fears; the collective humiliations, vulnerabilities, slights, grievances, sensitivities, and imagined insults, and the nationalist boasts and inflations that are their next of kin … We have often witnessed peoples, societies and nations outside the Western world – and I can identify with them easily – succumbing

---

[9] See Salter, *Barbarians and Civilization*, pp. 114–20, as well as Blaney and Inayatullah, *Problem of Difference*, Introduction, for an extended discussion of this critique.

[10] "The awareness of inferiority means that one is unable to keep out of consciousness the formulation of some chronic feeling of the worst sort of insecurity, and this means that one suffers anxiety and perhaps even something worse, if jealousy is really worse than anxiety." Sullivan, as quoted by Goffman, *Stigma*, p. 13.

to fears that sometimes lead them to commit stupidities, all because of their fears of humiliation and their sensitivities. I also know that in the West – a world with which I can identify with the same ease – nations and peoples taking an excessive pride in their wealth, and in their having brought us the Renaissance, the Enlightenment, and Modernism, have, from time to time, succumbed to a self-satisfaction that is almost as stupid.[11]

To be torn between the East and the West as a state, as a society, as a nation, is to exist in the international system with the dilemmas that are faced by stigmatized individuals in everyday interaction. The individual with stigma may accept that he has a stigmatized attribute and try to improve his life within the bounds of that awareness – but that choice implies resigning oneself to second-class status. Bringing oneself to that kind of resignation is extremely difficult, even in cases where it may unavoidable.[12] Or the individual may try to act as if he does not have a stigma or convince himself that it may be overcome with the right measures, but that course of action relegates one to a lifetime of dissonance, and does not necessarily guarantee success.[13]

Just like individuals, some states have coped with potentially stig-matizing labels more calmly than others. Turkey is not one of those countries. The emotional trauma inflicted by the collapse of the Ottoman Empire, which came toward the tail end of the century in which Turks internalized modern standards and their own stigma-tization, has made Turkey, at least thus far, a state that is obsessed with international stature, recognition, and acceptance. Much like an individual who attains a stigma attribute later in life and blames it for everything that goes wrong after that point, modern Turkish identity was constructed around the notion that the only thing keeping Turkey

---

[11] Pamuk, "My Father's Suitcase."

[12] Goffman quotes the account of a newly blind girl visiting an institution for the blind:

Here was the safe, segregated world of the sightless – a completely different world, I was assured by the social worker, from the one I had just left ... I was expected to join this world. To give up my profession and to earn my living making mops. I was to spend the rest of my life making mops with other blind people, eating with other blind people, dancing with other blind people. I became nauseated with fear, as the picture grew in my mind. Never had I come upon such destructive segregation. (*Stigma*, p. 17)

[13] More on this point later, but for now, see also Bauman, *Modernity and Ambivalence*, pp. 77–8, 80.

from regaining its former glory was its identity as a non-Western state. In the reconstructed nationalist narrative of the republic, the failure to modernize, to become Western, is seen as the primary reason for the collapse of the Ottoman Empire. In other words, for Turks, the pain of losing an empire is fused with the feeling of inferiority due to being not Western/modern enough.

Three cases of stigmatization: Turkey, Japan, and Russia

By now, it will probably come as no surprise to the reader if I confess that I started this project with the desire to understand the things I found so frustrating about my native country, Turkey – but also because I thought that there had to be something missing from a body of literature that had almost nothing to say about political actions I observed on an almost daily basis.

Now that I have put some emotional and physical distance between Turkish society and myself, I am able to observe a certain peculiar tendency in friends and family. "Only in Turkey," they will frequently say, "such a thing could only happen in Turkey!" The complaints vary, but the formula remains the same: "if only we were living under a true democracy/in a modern country/among civilized people, then our fellow citizens would behave/dress appropriately/talk politely/have manners/they would not be so religious/or wear headscarves/or try to cut corners/or elect a government like AKP/and so on." Goffman points out that this kind of condescension is a way of putting a distance between oneself and one's "own": "The stigmatized individual exhibits a tendency to stratify his 'own' to the degree to which their stigma is apparent and obtrusive. He can then take up in regard to those who are more evidently stigmatized than himself the attitudes the normals take to him."[14] There is also a parallel narrative about the uniqueness of Turkey. Only Turkey is supposed to be unfairly singled out for discrimination by the West; only Turkey can bridge the East and the West; only Turkey can be a model for Muslim countries; nobody understands Turkey; nobody appreciates Turkey; Turkish society is too complex for ordinary political institutions to work there, etc.

[14] Goffman, *Stigma*, p. 107.

There was a time I would have agreed with them wholeheartedly – after all, I too am shaped by the Turkish national habitus.[15] Growing up in Turkey, I was inclined to think that Tolstoy's maxim about unhappy families applied equally well to nations, and that Turkey was a special bundle of contradictions and problems, the likes of which nobody else had to deal with. Thankfully, I was wrong (misery loves company). As much as Turks would like to believe that they face a unique set of challenges, there are in fact other countries with similar constellations of problems.

The domestic narratives in both Japan and Russia bear a striking resemblance to those in Turkey. All three countries are torn between the East and the West, and in each case this condition is sometimes seen as a weakness that needs to be overcome (by choosing one side over the other) and sometimes as a blessing that needs to be exploited (by acting as either a bridge or a protective gate between the two).[16]

This similarity may be surprising given the differences between these countries' material conditions, but it is no accident. Certain characteristics set these states apart from both the "East" and the "West," and it is no coincidence that William McNeill singled these three countries out as examples of states that were unable to eliminate "tell-tale traces" of older patterns despite their "heartfelt efforts."

Turkey, Japan, and Russia all pre-date the Westphalian system as political entities.[17] As empires, they[18] long sustained social universes capable of producing comprehensive worldviews – in other words, before their incorporation into the Westphalian system these states had their own normative standards by which they defined themselves as "normal" and others as different, abnormal, or inferior.

[15] Habitus is "an active residue or sediment of [the actor's] past that functions within his present, shaping his perception, thought, and action and thereby molding social practice in a regular way." Crossley, "The Phenomenological Habitus," 83.
[16] E.g. Neumann, *Russia and the Idea of Europe*, p. 177; Klien, *Rethinking Japan's Identity*, p. 6.
[17] Obviously, these were not the only states around in the seventeenth century to have missed the beginning of system formation only to join it in some form later. Aspects of my argument apply to states such as Iran, India, China, and Thailand as well, but what distinguishes Turkey, Japan, and Russia is the relative autonomy they were able to retain vis-à-vis Europe.
[18] For system-level arguments, the book follows the IR (and layman's) convention of referring to states *as if* they are capable of expressing purposeful, unitary agency.

Therefore, incorporation into the Westphalian system in the case of these pre-modern empires necessitated giving up a self-affirming position of relative privilege and accepting a self-negating position of an outsider instead. This new position did not square well with self-understandings shaped by centuries of being the masters of their own domains.[19] Furthermore, because they joined the original incarnation of the international system, the European society of states, as autonomous entities, their position of inferiority was not overtly forced on them, as it was in the case of colonized peoples[20] – they came to an awareness about their inferiority, i.e. in the sense of a lack or deficit of modernity, through their own internal discussions.[21] As such, people of these states did not reject outright the values of modernity as a hostile foreign imposition (as is perhaps the case with certain schools of Muslim thought) but, rather, looked upon those values as something to be emulated; believed Westernization to be a goal that a state could achieve by trying hard enough, and saw it as a solution that might allow them to recreate their past privileged position in the new normative universe. In the twentieth century, all three countries experimented with revisionist grand strategies with the intent of capturing what they thought was their rightful place in the new international system. However, instead of earning them a seat among the "established" members of the international society, these revisionist policies ended in failure.

As I will demonstrate throughout this book, the aforementioned dynamics between the Western core of the international system and the Eastern latecomers closely resemble the *established-outsider* figuration delineated by the famous sociologist Norbert Elias. According

---

[19] The importance of having a consistent self-understanding for state behavior is stressed in the literature on "ontological security." Ontological security is first and foremost about having a consistent sense of "self." See Zarakol, "Ontological Insecurity," as well as Lebow, *Cultural Theory*, pp. 25–6, for an extended overview of the relevant literature.

[20] Having escaped direct colonization is a significant element of both Turkish and Japanese identity narratives. The Japanese call this a "'parting point in history' (rekishi no wakare)." Klien, *Rethinking Japan's Identity*, p. 11.

[21] This is the case even with Russia. Despite its success in joining the Westphalian system as an equal member after Peter's reforms, Russia maintained an outsider status within this in-group and its differences became more evident after the radical transformations in Western Europe at the turn of the nineteenth century.

to Elias, one of the remarkable aspects of the established-outsider con-figuration is that through *stigmatization* "the 'superior' people may make the less powerful people themselves feel that they lack virtue – that they are inferior in human terms."[22] In the nineteenth century, the elites in these empires came to see themselves and their countries through European eyes, even if they did not necessarily agree on any specific course of action vis-à-vis Europe.

Not only did the defeat of the Ottoman Empire in World War I, Japan in World War II, and the Soviet Union in the Cold War cost the titular nations their empires, it also reinforced the very stigmas these states were trying to escape. It is no accident that the interna-tional community holds the crimes[23] committed by these empires in their pursuit for glory to be especially heinous.[24] This is a reaction very much similar to what Goffman observed in attitudes against the stigmatized: "Further, we may perceive his defensiveness to his situa-tion as a direct expression of his defect, and then see both defect and response as just retribution for something he or his parents or his tribe did, and hence a justification of the way we treat him."[25] This is not to say that the actions of the Ottoman Empire, or Japan, or the Soviet Union were not beyond the pale, but rather to point out the fact that in the case of stigmatized – i.e. "backward," "barbaric," "uncivilized," "authoritarian," "childlike," "warlike" – Eastern states, violence is

---

[22] Elias, "A Theoretical Essay," p. xvi.

[23] E.g. the Armenian genocide, Japanese war crimes, Stalin's actions.

[24] Germany seems an exception here, but it is not. However, due to its more secure place in Europe, Germany is better understood as an "in-group deviant," whose aberrant actions are tolerated much longer than would be the case with an outsider and for whom every door reopens after rehabilitation. See Goffman, *Stigma*, chapter 5. Here is but one example of the differing attitudes against outsiders vs. in-group deviants:

> ... in February 1945, a few weeks after being posted to the Pacific after years of covering the war in Europe, Ernie Pyle, the most admired of American war correspondents, told his millions of readers that "in Europe we felt that our enemies, horrible and deadly were still people. But out here I soon gathered that the Japanese were looked upon as something, subhuman and repulsive, the way some people feel about cockroaches or mice." He went on to describe the Japanese prisoners of war: "They were wrestling and laughing and talking just like normal human beings, and yet they gave me the creeps, and I wanted a mental bath after looking at them." (Matsuda, *Soft Power*, p. 84)

[25] Goffman, *Stigma*, p. 6.

often assumed to be the default response stemming from inherent tendencies and not the aberration it is supposed to be in Europe.[26]

At some point in the twentieth century, then, each of these three countries found itself stigmatized, defeated, *and* stigmatized again because of having fought to overcome a stigma position. Having bet the farm (or the empire) in a quest to regain a privileged "normal" status in the new normative universe of the modern states system, these states emerged from their respective wars even further away from the "established" core. Therefore, even though this book is concerned with the larger questions of international stigmatization and established-outsider dynamics since the inception of the modern states system, the empirical inquiry is limited to post-defeat choices.

Research approach and chapter outline

After Defeat juxtaposes the post-defeat choices of Turkey (1919–39), Japan (1945–74), and Russia (1991–2007) to demonstrate that – for at least some states in the international system – international status, respect, and acceptance[27] are primary motivators in decision-making. I will argue that post-defeat, each country chose a strategy designed explicitly to minimize the social status gap accrued during their outsider pasts and in their unsuccessful military bids for recognition. Such identity-oriented policies were preferred even when there were other viable policies with potentially greater military or material yields.

Especially in the immediate aftermath of defeat, each country has preferred policies that were meant to signal an understanding and acceptance of international norms that stigmatized them – having been charged with a lack of "civilization," Turkey directed all of its efforts to obliterating signs of "Easternness"; Japan swore off its militarist past to embrace pacifism while putting great effort into economic "development"; "enigmatic" Russia set upon a course (albeit temporarily) of transparency and openness to foreign advice. These states dealt with their status deficit by choosing policies intended to

---

[26] Which, of course, is met with defensive posturing from the guilty parties, and seen as further evidence of violent tendencies. For a more extended discussion of Turkish and Japanese attitudes to war crimes, see Zarakol, "Ontological Insecurity."

[27] For an overview of how these concepts have been (mis)handled in the IR literature, see Lebow, *Cultural Theory*, pp. 21–4.

yield social capital, given the norms of international society at the time of their defeat: a secular European model of modernization and nation-building in the case of Turkey, economic development within American parameters in the case of Japan, and a "triple-transition" in the case of the former Soviet Union.

The book is divided into six chapters. The first chapter starts with a discussion of the evolution of the modern international system beginning with its seventeenth-century origins. The dating of the origins of the modern international system to the seventeenth century follows John G. Ruggie in that territorial sovereignty is taken to be the main demarcating principle separating the modern system from previous systems.[28] However, the focus of this chapter is mostly on the nineteenth century, developments during which were extremely critical in shaping countries like Turkey, Japan, and Russia both because nationalist projects (and therefore state identities) have their origins in this period, and because it was the time[29] when the modernist ontology underlying international stigmatization crystallized. Chapter 1 will demonstrate that in the nineteenth century the relationship between the European society of states and non-European states came to resemble the established-outsider figuration outlined by Norbert Elias.

The second chapter analyzes the international system as such an established-outsider figuration and utilizes Goffman's aforementioned stigma theory to enumerate the possible forms of interaction responses available to stigmatized outsider states. The two most realistic choices are either to attempt normalcy (either by "passing" or fixing one's discrediting characteristics) or to embrace one's stigma (but that still leaves the choice between attempting to use it to one's advantage in normal society and withdrawing to one's stigma group). That choice will ultimately depend on both the structure of the international society and domestic considerations. The chapter outlines which configurations of these factors are likely to lead to choosing the existence of a *discreditable* state over a *discredited* one. Underlying this discussion is not only an assumption that states care about their identity (or their "ontological security"), but an argument that such concerns shape international dynamics to a much greater extent than is usually allowed. The second chapter also provides an overview

[28] E.g. Ruggie, "Territoriality and Beyond," 148–51.
[29] See also Reus-Smit, *Moral Purpose*, p. 122.

of the evolution of normative standards in the international system, starting with the nineteenth-century Standard of Civilization up to the present-day discourses about stability and danger.

By wedding Elias's discussion of the established-outsider figuration in social relations with Goffman's explanations of stigma, the theoretical model presented here offers a new way to think about state interaction in the international system. Constructivist IR theories strongly emphasize "social" aspects of international politics, but generally ignore manifestations of social *stratification* within the international system. The constructivist research agenda on norms[30] in the international system has produced many fine examples[31] of scholarship in the last decades, but very few of these works make the power dynamics[32] behind socializing relationships their explicit focus. This is not to say that constructivists (or others who study socialization[33]) deny that there is often a relationship of inequality driving the process of socialization.[34] Yet, to the extent the power disparity behind norm internalization is studied, it is conceptualized as a relatively unproblematic "incentive" driving socialization, and not as something that

---

[30] Defined in this literature often "as a standard of appropriate behavior for actors within a given identity." Finnemore and Sikkink, "International Norm Dynamics," 891. Note that this definition does not diverge far from Goffman's.

[31] See e.g. Klotz, "Norms Reconstituting Interests"; Klotz, "Norms and Sanctions"; Florini, "Evolution of International Norms"; Finnemore, *National Interests*; Sikkink, "Transnational Politics"; Flockhart, "Complex Socialization"; Checkel, "Why Comply?"; Checkel, "Norms, Institutions and National Identity."

[32] One possible exception is Johnston in "Treating International Institutions," 493.

[33] For instance, neorealists tend to view socialization as a mostly automatic process whereby systemic constraints force the weak to emulate the successful states. See e.g. Waltz, *Theory of International Politics*, pp. 118, 128. The best-known neoliberal approach to the study of socialization, Ikenberry's *After Victory*, puts most of the explanatory emphasis on the choices of hegemonic victors. The problem with such approaches is that the power dynamic is thought of as completely independent and *a priori* to the socializing process. Incidentally, constructivist disinterest in the power disparity in socializing relationships may stem from a desire to counter this earlier agenda and its over-emphasis on the role of hegemons in driving normative compliance.

[34] Alderson argues that acknowledging the power dimension is one advantage the socialization literature has over the "learning" approach of neoliberal institutionalism. See "Making Sense," 424.

is possibly constituted or reproduced by the socializing process itself. For instance, Finnemore and Sikkink argue that states may have three possible *motivations* for responding to "peer pressure" to socialize: legitimation, conformity, and esteem.[35] However, because in such studies the focus is on what drives compliance and not what happens to the state's identity after internalization, the distinction between motivation and actual outcome is obscured.[36] In other words, there is little to no consideration of how a relationship of unequals may survive intact even if socialization is successful, much less an acknowledgment that the process of socialization may itself be perpetuating that inequality.[37]

This neglect of the stratifying potential of international norms and socialization in constructivism[38] is unfortunate because in domestic society we know that normative expectations always generate exclusionary figurations and status hierarchies. Even *prima facie* benign social norms generate complications that affect identity. Even if a particular norm – defining, say, a citizen, a worker, or a sovereign state – is couched in universal, abstract, inclusive language, stratification is inevitable. There are pressures to conform, choices to be made, and questions about authenticity, and these constraints are not distributed evenly throughout society. Furthermore, stratification often is a *consequence* of socialization; one becomes aware of the stigmatizing potential of one's attributes (and therefore, one's inferiority) only after internalizing the standards of larger society. Even if stigmatizing attributes can be corrected, correction is not the same as never having had that attribute: "Where such repair is possible, what often results is not the acquisition of fully normal status, but a transformation of self from someone with a particular blemish into someone with a record of having corrected a particular blemish."[39] Norms are essentially tools of power: they reflect the power dynamics in the system

---

[35] Finnemore and Sikkink, "International Norm Dynamics," 902–4.

[36] Even Johnston, who approaches the constructivist norm literature with a relatively critical eye and offers a nuanced theory of socialization, reproduces this pattern. See "Treating International Institutions," 499.

[37] See Bauman's *Modernity and Ambivalence* in its entirety for the most astute articulation of this point.

[38] Obviously, this problem is even more prevalent in neorealism and neoliberal institutionalism, but those approaches are more internally consistent on this point; they do not emphasize the constitutive effects of norms.

[39] Goffman, *Stigma*, p. 9; Bauman, *Modernity and Ambivalence*, p. 77.

and are as likely to perpetuate them as they are to ameliorate them. The flipside of socialization is otherness. Otherness implies the presence of an established-outsider dynamic.

There are several reasons why constructivist work on socialization and norm internalization has failed to draw attention to the stratifying after-effects of these processes. To begin with, especially early on, constructivist work on norms centered around "'hard' cases of moral transformation in which 'good' global norms prevail over the 'bad' local beliefs and practices."[40] Because until recently much empirical work focused on the diffusion of norms that researchers agree with in principle, such as human rights, women's equality, etc., it has been difficult to conceive of such positive "socialization" as having adverse effects on state identity.[41] Furthermore, earlier constructivist work on norm diffusion mechanisms focused almost exclusively on persuasion.[42] Persuasion approaches assume a level of deliberate communication in socializing interactions that is not necessarily commensurate with the historical development of the modern states system. Additionally, such a focus leads to an emphasis on shallower single-issue norms about which one can be demonstrably "persuaded," as opposed to broader shifts and deeper rifts in worldviews. Hence, it is no accident that much of this earlier persuasion/learning literature in constructivism was rather individualist in its methodology[43] and retained the rationalist cost/benefit analysis of previous regime scholarship[44] on norms, as well as its focus on highly institutionalized settings.

At the root of these shortcomings is the presentist bias inherent in the studies of socialization in constructivism. It is only relatively recently in the history of the international system that it has become conceivable to think of all states as actors which may be persuaded by norm entrepreneurs (or other states) to choose from a menu of international norms. That very conceptualization is made possible by a much more structural, homogenizing (and homologizing)

---

[40] Acharya, "How Ideas Spread," 239.
[41] E.g. Sikkink, "Transnational Politics," 520.
[42] Johnston, "Treating International Institutions," 493.
[43] Checkel, "Why Comply?" 557–8.
[44] See e.g. Keohane, *After Hegemony*; Oye, *Cooperation Under Anarchy*; Martin, *Coercive Cooperation*.

normative convergence.[45] This convergence around the norms of modernity[46] is what made it possible to speak of norm diffusion and social learning *as if* they are processes that every state actor can partake in relatively autonomously as a rational agent; *as if* the diffusion of these processes has never been anchored in geography; *as if* international norms have no particular cultural content or an overwhelming ethnocentric bias. Such assumptions are plausible to some extent if we focus only on the present-day international system. As I will discuss in Chapter 2, the international normative order has become relatively more inclusive and less culturally anchored over the course of its history, and states are more similar than ever before.[47] Nevertheless, the present dynamics of the international system continue to be underwritten by the status hierarchies of the past, and socialization into the deep structures of the international system has played a historically significant role in both establishing and perpetuating those hierarchies. The abstract and generalized language about norms and socialization we find in much of constructivism obscures much of that history,[48] and misleads us about the underlying causes of present-day insecurities.[49]

This indifference to the stratifying effects of international norms may be attributed to the divisions within constructivism itself. More "sociologically" oriented constructivists, especially Wendt,[50] have positioned constructivism as a systemic theory in direct competition

---

[45] See for instance Meyer, "World Polity"; Meyer *et al.*, "World Society and the Nation-State"; Meyer *et al.*, "Expansion of Mass Education"; Boli, "World Polity"; see also Finnemore, "Norms, Culture, and World Politics."

[46] See especially Meyer and Jepperson, "'Actors' of Modern Society."

[47] In fact, one could argue that the reason why the international system seems more inclusive today is because there has been such a great degree of convergence around Westphalian norms.

[48] Even Checkel, who urges more caution about causal processes involved in socialization and more attention to domestic agency, is partly guilty of this. For instance, he points out that norm diffusion is more likely when there is a "cultural match" between the systemic norm and the historically constructed domestic norms. See e.g. Checkel, "Norms, Institutions and National Identity." This is an excellent insight, but what is missing from the picture is an acknowledgment that the likelihood of a cultural match is not distributed randomly throughout the international system.

[49] See Zarakol, "Ontological Insecurity."

[50] In fact, Lebow considers Wendt to be "a structural liberal" rather than a constructivist. *Cultural Theory*, p. 3, fn7.

with neorealism.[51] This was arguably a necessary and ultimately successful epistemological strategy, but the trade-off (at least thus far) has been the neglect of processes at a slightly lower level of abstraction that may not apply to all states equally, as well as the particularly uneven history of the expansion of the international system. Wendt's discussion of the self–other dynamic in *Social Theory*,[52] for instance, is rather ahistorical;[53] similarly, Wendt's discussion of recognition in "Why a World State is Inevitable" assumes a degree of uniformity in the distribution of various processes throughout the social system. Constructivists who tend toward what may be called the "psychological" side of the literature, i.e. those scholars who are more sensitive to domestic processes and identity narratives that are generated endogenously, have been traditionally more open to incorporating historical accounts and geographical differences into causal explanations (and as a result, stand closer to new generations of English School scholarship).[54] However, this vein of scholarship generally is less concerned with macro-theorizing.[55]

The theoretical model advanced in this book links these two flanks of constructivism in a novel way. While the theoretical chapters of this book build upon previous constructivist contributions on norms and socialization, my main goal is to advance a more nuanced understanding of the *unevenly experienced* social constraints driving the socialization of states. As noted earlier, I do this first and foremost by borrowing from Elias and Goffman the sociological insights about established-outsider dynamics and stigmatization. The emergence of the established-outsider figuration is a system-level dynamic, but it is one which creates *different* levels of pressures on states depending on the particular social space they are occupying at a given time in history. Stigmatization is also a social process, the presence of which needs to be first explained from a *systemic angle*, but responses to stigmatization can only be understood by paying serious attention to *endogenous dynamics* within societies.

[51] See e.g. Smith, "Wendt's World."
[52] Wendt, *Social Theory.*
[53] See Buzan and Little, "Why International Relations Has Failed."
[54] See e.g. Neumann, *Uses of the Other.*
[55] Lebow's recent *A Cultural Theory of International Relations* is an exception to this generalization. However, as excellent as that book is, it does not address the gap I am discussing here: i.e. the uneven distribution of systemic social constraints.

The application of these sociological frameworks to the international system advances several other literatures as well. The demonstration of the presence of the established-outsider figurations throughout the evolution of the international system builds upon the more historically oriented scholarship in IR and sociology such as the English School,[56] the historical institutionalist variants of constructivism,[57] the World Polity school,[58] but also the more materialist approaches such as World-System theory and macro-realism.[59] Each of these approaches has made invaluable contributions to our understanding of the evolution of the Westphalian state model and the modern states system. However, the account offered in Chapters 1 and 2 concerning the evolution of the modern states system is not an uncritical summary of the aforementioned literatures. What is critically absent from most of these approaches is a theory of society at the international level[60] and an interest in agency in the face of socialization pressures.

While I do not claim to advance a proper theory of international society, there is an *implicit* argument about society underlying the discussions of stigmatization in this book. Contrary to what most of the IR literature would lead us to believe, emulation does not necessarily guarantee that the socialized actor comes automatically to resemble the "normals." Socialization driven by a desire to escape stigmatization can actually perpetuate the established-outsider figuration. However, the presence of the desire to emulate is itself telling because it means that the actor has internalized the judgment of the larger society. In other words, stigmatization points to the presence of shared norms, and as I will argue in Chapter 2, this is a more realistic litmus test for deducing the presence of an "international

---

[56] Especially the more recent generation of scholarship such as Keene, *Beyond Anarchical Society*; Suzuki, *Civilization and Empire*; Hobson and Sharman, "Enduring Place."

[57] What I have in mind here is works such as Reus-Smit's *Moral Purpose*, or Bukovansky, "Altered State"; Blaney and Inayatullah, "Westphalian Deferral"; Ruggie, "Territoriality and Beyond." Obviously, this variant of constructivism is intimately linked with the new generation of English Scholarship mentioned in the previous footnote and vice versa.

[58] See footnotes 40 and 43.

[59] Wallerstein, Chase-Dunn, Derluguian, Tilly, Collins, etc.

[60] Lebow, *Cultural Theory*, pp. 2–4.

society" than the sense of "we-ness," common purpose,[61] or the legal-
istic approaches[62] used in the IR literature.

Realist arguments rejecting the existence of an international society of states (or deem an international society at best a negligible
presence compared with thicker versions of society) have one thing
in common with the English School approaches: too high a standard
of what constitutes "society." There are plenty of domestic societies
where common purpose or a sense of explicit "we-ness" is at best
a remote ideal or simply empty rhetoric, and it is actually the presence of stratification that points to a shared normative ground. The
Brahmin, for instance, does not feel he has anything in common with
the Untouchable; the White Supremacist is antagonistic toward racial
minorities; many Saudi men believe the testimony of four women
equals that of one man. In fact, as Lebow points out, "given the
inequalities of all social orders, and the exclusions, restrictions and
compulsions they entail, it is nothing short of remarkable that most
people in most societies adhere to stipulated practices and rules."[63]
While the people in the examples above presumably live under a common state, that is not the only thing that binds them together in a
society: in all of the examples, the oppressor and the oppressed, the
powerful and the powerless, the insider and the outsider share a common framework, a common habitus, a common ontology (such as

---

[61] E.g. "A society of states (or international society) exists when a group of
states, conscious of certain common interests and common values, form a
society in the sense that they conceive themselves to be bound by a common
set of rules in their relations with one another, and share in the working
of common institutions." Bull, *Anarchical Society*, p. 13. Also see Wight,
"Western Values"; Bull and Watson, *Expansion of International Society*,
p. 1. Buzan, "From International System," provides a review of how
"society" has been conceptualized in the English School.

[62] As Suzuki notes, the legal positivist perspective adopted by English School
scholars "resulted in a belief that when European and non-European states
entered into treaty relations based on normative concepts originating
from European international society, this implied an almost automatic
and reciprocal commitment to the Society's institutions and practices."
Civilization and Empire, p. 16. Earlier generations of the English School
suffered from the same blind spot as to the perverse effects of socialization
that the constructivist scholarship on norms is permeated with; scholars such
as Bull and Watson treated the expansion of European international society
as an overwhelmingly positive development. See O'Hagan, *Conceptualizing
the West*, p. 129; Suzuki, *Civilization and Empire*, p. 15.

[63] Lebow, *Cultural Theory*, p. 4.

faith or ethnicity) of the world, and recognize each other as part of that framework.[64] The international system is not that different: states rely on recognition[65] from other states for their sovereign existence, which implies that there is a shared understanding about what a modern "state" is. There are criteria for recognition as a state: territory, a constituency, a recognizable administrative structure, etc.[66] There is a great deal of homology between domestic structures. Finally, that there is a "society" at the international level becomes obvious when we consider the implicit common ground shared by the states in the modern international system,[67] which is even more remarkable given the absence of a world government. As Chapter 2 will demonstrate, the Standard of Civilization, the distinctions between modernity and barbarism, the obsession with development, etc., are all examples of shared normative ground between *the established* and *the outsiders* of the international system.

Chapter 2 will also address the link between modernity and the projection of the established-outsider dynamic to the international level. Drawing especially upon Hegel and Nietzsche, I will argue that it is no accident that the established-outsider figuration truly manifested on an international scale for the first time in the nineteenth century. While there are good reasons to argue that making distinctions between "us" and "others" is a feature of the human condition,[68] there is no reason to suppose that "us" and "others" will always agree

---

[64] This is also in line with Lebow's argument that societies are bound together by one of four reasons: "fear, interest, honor and habit." *Ibid.*

[65] E.g. Wight, *Systems of States*, p. 153; Clark, "Legitimacy in a Global Order," 84–5.

[66] See for instance Meyer, "World Polity"; Meyer *et al.*, "World Society and the Nation-State"; Meyer *et al.*, "Expansion of Mass Education"; Frank *et al.*, "Rationalization and Organization"; Frank *et al.*, "Nation-State"; Ramirez, "Global Changes"; Schofer, "Science Associations"; Thomas *et al.*, *Institutional Structure*; see also Finnemore, "Norms, Culture, and World Politics."

[67] Bull and Watson note in *Expansion of International Society*, p. 5, that the reciprocity of sovereign recognition is a unique feature of the *modern* international system. We may also recall Giddens's observation that the emergence of international relations is coeval with the origins of the nation state.

[68] See e.g. Tajfel, *Human Groups and Social Categories*. For a more general overview of the literature theorizing the self–Other relationship, see also Neumann, *Uses of the Other*, chapter 1; Salter, *Barbarians and Civilization*; Abizadeh, "Does Collective Identity Presuppose an Other?"

on how they are ranked in relation to each other.[69] The distinction
between "us" and "others" may not be an obstacle to social cohesion[70]
if that distinction is built into the self-understanding of both parties.[71]
This is essentially what distinguishes the "established-outsider" figuration from the more ubiquitous "us–others" dynamic. It is the former,
not the latter, that characterizes relations in the modern international
system, which "does not aim at the 'elimination of enemies but at the
destruction of strangers, or more generally strangehood'."[72] What sets
modernity apart is not "the division into selves and others. Rather, it
is the effect of seeming to exclude the other absolutely from the self, in
a world divided into two."[73] As Bauman has argued, it is this type of
dynamic which creates pressures to assimilate, because in such situations, the burden to resolve the ambivalence created by strangeness,
being on the wrong side of the dichotomy, falls on the stranger, the
outsider.[74]

Finally, Chapter 2 will also explore the available options for modern
international actors who find themselves on the losing end of the
established-outsider dynamic. Being stigmatized as an outsider has
serious costs, and leaves a permanent mark on the national habitus.
I noted above that treatments of socialization in constructivism tend
to focus too much on the present-day international system and suggested that a more historically grounded approach may be needed
to draw attention to the uneven distribution of social constraints in
the modern states system. However, it is possible to err too much on
the opposite end of the spectrum and to seriously underestimate the
agency of stigmatized, outsider, "Eastern" actors.

While the abstract, ahistorical models of socialization one encounters in neorealism, neoliberalism, and certain variants of constructivism mistakenly impute equal maneuvering room to all actors in
the international system, the historically conscious narratives of the
English School literature have traditionally downplayed almost all

---

[69] In other words, what distinguishes the stigmatized "outsider" from the more
generic "other" is that he agrees with the "normal" society to some extent
that his devaluation is deserved.

[70] See Lebow, *Cultural Theory*, p. 8, for a discussion of why this may pose a
threat to social cohesion.

[71] See also Huysmans, "Security!" 242–3.

[72] Bauman, *Modernity and Ambivalence*, p. 153.

[73] Mitchell, *Colonising Egypt*, p. 167.   [74] *Ibid.*, p. 75.

agency at the receiving end. The problem of incorporation is posed from the point of view of the existing international society, in this case the European society states. As a result, there is not enough theoretical conceptualization of the mechanisms driving socialization. Buzan, for instance, relies on the Waltzian logic of anarchy generating like units in order to explain the emergence of international society. His only remark about agency at the other end is his remark that "historical discussions of how non-European states came to terms with what Gong has termed the European Standard of Civilization are *suggestive* of how this process of convergence toward a shared identity works, the most striking case being Japan's conscious reshaping of itself into a Western state during the nineteenth century,"[75] which hardly goes further than acknowledging that some kind of socialization occurs in a competitive system.[76] The World Polity school suffers from a similar weakness. World Polity scholars correctly reject functional depictions of the modern state – as a natural, purposive, and rational actor – inherent in realism, as well as accounts of state formation which are exclusively based in localized national cultural narratives, in favor of a view of the modern bureaucratic state as a cultural construct that is embedded and legitimated by a global culture.[77] Yet they are silent on the mechanisms of socialization,[78] a choice which inevitably downplays the agency of the emulative actors.

This book aims to underline the additional pressures faced by Eastern actors on the one hand and bring their agency in responding to stigmatization to the forefront on the other hand.[79] In keeping with these goals, case studies are used to emphasize the often neglected agency of "Eastern" actors in the international system without losing sight of different systemic pressures such actors face. The theoretical discussion of available stigma-coping strategies presented in Chapter 2 is later matched by detailed historical reconstructions of after-defeat choices in each case presented in the following Chapters 3 to 5. Chapter 3 focuses on the actions of Turkey between 1918 and 1938; Chapter 4 on Japan between 1945 and 1974; and Chapter 5

---

[75] Buzan, "From International System," 335.
[76] A similar functionalism pervades the writings of Bull and Watson as well.
[77] Meyer, "World Polity," pp. 147, 158.
[78] Finnemore, "Norms, Culture, and World Politics," 339.
[79] See also Suzuki, *Civilization and Empire*, pp. 6–15, 26–9, for similar critiques of the English School literature.

on Russia between 1990 and 2007. In each chapter, I demonstrate that the strategy chosen was *deliberately* picked because of *status concerns*, given the international normative standards of the time, and over other strategies that may have been more in line with the predictions of mainstream IR theories. These case studies advance an empirical argument about the significance of status and self-esteem concerns in the international system.

In terms of social scientific approach, this book is located within the historical institutionalist paradigm that is interested in historical dynamics and the complex interaction among social processes. This body of work is most notable for taking into account all fields of human interaction, i.e. economic and social as well as political. Because of this comprehensive interest, this kind of work "require[s] a multiplicity of theoretical tools, [as well as] the painstaking analytical reconstruction of environments in historical and comparative planes."[80] This approach is also in line with the Bhaskarian insight that "structural analysis explains the 'possible' while historical analysis explains the 'actual.'"[81] The research approach undertaken here falls under comparative-historical methodology, primarily expressed through reconstructed historical event and strategy narratives intended to map causal structures suggested by applications of social stratification theories on to the international system.[82] Agency is located within the constraints imposed by the structural space, and variation is explained by contingency of social action on time, space, and context as illustrated in the narrative. Causation is inferred by comparing narratives across cases, and grounded in a macro-historical framework. The approach is neither purely inductive nor purely deductive, but should rather be thought of as layered, moving back and forth between various levels of abstraction, inference, and observability. Social constraints do not lend themselves as easily to measurement

[80] See Derluguian, "Terrorism," 6.
[81] Patomaki, "How to Tell Better Stories," 126.
[82] For other examples of the use of historical narrative for the analysis of causal processes, see Abbott, *Time Matters*; Griffin, "Causal Interpretation in Historical Sociology"; Sewell, "Three Temporalities"; Stryker, "Beyond History versus Theory"; see also Glass and Mackey, *From Clocks to Chaos*; Reisch, "Chaos, History, and Narrative"; Shermer, "Exorcising Laplace's Demon." For a discussion of causation in case studies, see Mahoney, "Comparative-Historical Methodology"; see also Brady and Collier, *Rethinking Social Inquiry*; Paige, "Theory in Macrosocial Inquiry."

as material constraints, but they can nevertheless be conceptualized and observed in their particular manifestations. As Goldstone noted, "the test of the worth of a work of comparative history is whether it identifies and illuminates relationships heretofore unrecognized or misunderstood."[83] Furthermore, as Jackson has argued, it is not necessary (or possible) "to find evidence for 'real motives' driving particular individuals to make particular choices"; rather, it is more sensible to follow Weber's lead in focusing on "the production and reproduction of boundaries of action,"[84] i.e. on the social context out of which policy outcomes arise.

Case studies are therefore a particularly suitable approach to study the *actual* manifestation of the structural conditions. "Given the necessity of reconstructing meaning and of studying the effects of mechanisms in overdetermined, open systems" that social relationships are governed by, explanatory and comparative small-N case studies of empirical events are the only way we can access the underlying structures.[85] The case-study approach benefits from empirical research without being epistemologically empiricist. Empiricism is problematic because it reduces social science to only what is observable, "expressed more often as a vague 'actualism,' that is a stance denying the existence, plausibility, or usefulness of conceiving of underlying structures which determine ... events, and instead locates the succession of cause and effect at the level of events."[86] Critical realism, on the other hand, allows for a layered view of the world, wherein we can distinguish between underlying causal mechanisms and observable phenomena: it "encompasses a theory of *emergence* of ontological levels, and it sketches out the basic lineaments of a specifically *social* ontology, organized around the difference between human agents and social structures and the differences between social and natural mechanisms – specifically, the time, space, concept, and practice dependency of the former."[87] This is the broad approach underlining the analyses of case studies in this book.

---

[83] Goldstone, *Revolution and Rebellion*, p. 60.
[84] Jackson, *Civilizing the Enemy*, p. 22. The broader discussion on Weberian legitimation starts on p. 16.
[85] See Steinmetz, "Odious Comparisons."
[86] Collier, *Critical Realism*, p. 7, as quoted in Steinmetz, "Odious Comparisons," 375.
[87] See *ibid.*, 377; also see Bhaskar, *Reclaiming Reality*.

The final chapter extends the discussion to present-day international dynamics, beginning with the question of why Russia seems to have changed course more quickly than Turkey and Japan. The answer lies both in the historical proximity of Russia to the "established" core of the international system (at least compared to Turkey and Japan), and also in the evolution of international normative order. However, both Turkey and Japan have started signaling a realization that their post-defeat strategies are no longer as viable in the international system. I conclude by returning to the two themes I have introduced here: the impact of international stigmatization on international relations, and the place of the established-outsider figuration in the present-day international system.

PART I

Of gates and keepers in the international system

Before the law sits a gatekeeper. To this gatekeeper comes a man from the country who asks to gain entry into the law. But the gatekeeper says that he cannot grant him entry at the moment. The man thinks about it and then asks if he will be allowed to come in sometime later on. "It is possible," says the gatekeeper, "but not now." ... The gatekeeper gives him a stool and allows him to sit down at the side in front of the gate. There he sits for days and years. He makes many attempts to be let in, and he wears the gatekeeper out with his requests. The gatekeeper often interrogates him briefly, questioning him about his homeland and many other things, but they are indifferent questions, the kind great men put, and at the end he always tells him once more that he cannot let him inside yet. The man, who has equipped himself with many things for his journey, spends everything, no matter how valuable, to win over the gatekeeper. The latter takes it all but, as he does so, says, "I am taking this only so that you do not think you have failed to do anything" ...

Franz Kafka
From *Before the Law* (1925)

1 | *Outsiders and insiders in the international system*

These beleaguered empires traditionally harbored an elevated self-esteem – translated in modern times into a unifying nationalism – and possessed sizable cultural elites capable of superimposing their frustrations onto the grievances of mainly peasant populations, through mechanisms ranging from religious sermonizing to nationalist education and communist propaganda ...

Georgi Derluguian, Bourdieu's Secret Admirer

Introduction

This chapter introduces three political entities – Turkey, Japan, and Russia – that were not part of the original Westphalian system, despite having existed prior to the seventeenth century. In hindsight, this was a costly absence. Some time after the seventeenth century, rulers of Turkey, Japan, and Russia each made a deliberate decision to join the states system emerging from Europe, by accepting its international standards and borrowing a number of the domestic institutions of its major players. This initial decision to emulate "the West"[1] had persistent consequences, not only for the foreign policies of the states in question, but also their domestic affairs. In the intervening centuries, each country went through numerous reforms, restorations, revolutions, reactionary backlashes, and wars, all of which were primarily motivated by the goal of catching up, competing, and standing equal with the core powers of the modern states system. However, even in the best of times, neither Turkey nor Russia, and not even Japan, has been completely able to shed its original "outsider" status and secure

---

[1] "The West" is a term with many connotations – and how it is defined at a given moment is contingent on the processes described in this book. For now, the term should be understood as referring to what the country (or countries) in question thought "the West" to be at the time.

an unambiguous seat among the rule-makers of the modern states system.

This chapter sets up the argument that everything these states have done since joining the international system, from periods of enmity to periods of extreme cooperation with "the West" (and everything in between), is best explained by the ambiguous "insider but outsider" status shared by these three countries. At some point during their nineteenth-century interactions with the West, having to cope with the stigma of this insider–outsider status created great ontological insecurity for these states: a "deep, incapacitating state of not knowing which dangers to confront and which to ignore, i.e. how to get by in the world."[2] Because this ontologically insecure relationship with the West was one of the key ingredients used to forge a "modern sense of self," it has remained ingrained in the identities of these states.

It is often overlooked that these entities, which survived from the "pre-modern"[3] era but were not organic participants in the "modernization" processes taking place in Western Europe, undertook the project of reconstructing themselves as "modern" states in the same period as that of having to come to terms with the "rise of the West." The perceived social, technological, and economic lag vis-à-vis Europe – especially emphasized during formative periods for the construction of the modern, Westphalian, "nation"-state identity in Russia, Turkey, and Japan – created a sustained preoccupation with international stature, a near pathology in the self-conception of these states not in any way healed, but perhaps even exacerbated, by the memories of the near-brushes with great-power status. This common ailment of Turkey, Japan, and Russia is the only thing that explains why the similarities between the political choices of these otherwise very different countries are so striking.

The puzzling socialization of Turkey, Japan, and Russia

Turkey, Japan, and Russia each exhibited the same 180-degree turn in their foreign policy behavior in the twentieth century: Turkey circa

---

[2] Mitzen, "Ontological Security," 341.
[3] Jack Goldstone argues that the term "early-modern" is misleading and Eurocentric; see "Problem Of the 'Early Modern' World."

1923, Japan circa 1945, and Russia circa 1991.[4] Within a relatively short time span, each country stopped fighting with the core Western powers and began not only to cooperate, but also to remake their institutions according to the prevailing (Western) international norms of the time.

Mainstream IR theories dismiss these outcomes as a by-product of competition or as the socialization of the vanquished by the victors. In the mainstream IR literature socialization is often viewed as a rational response by states to systemic constraints or material incentives. Neorealism, for instance, does not even consider socialization "an important policy question because it is so common and inevitable,"[5] and holds that the competitive environment created by the anarchic nature of the international system pushes states to become "like units" or fall by the wayside.[6] Of the three cases mentioned above, this explanation could potentially apply to all, but has been most frequently invoked to explain changes in Russian behavior toward the end of the Cold War, probably because in that case there was no battlefield defeat or military occupation.[7] In analyses of the aftermath of traditional wars, as in the cases of Turkey and Japan, socialization of the defeated state is generally chalked up to the incentives created by the victor(s). Liberals and realists may disagree on

[4] While these transitions were relatively speedy, they did not happen overnight. This is why I am giving approximate dates. A more nuanced account will be developed in the case-study chapters.

[5] Alderson, "Making Sense," 428.

[6] Waltz claims that emulation is a result of competition; those who do not emulate the successful fall by the wayside. The effects of competition are not confined to the military realm; socialization to the system also occurs because refusal to play the game is to risk one's own destruction, though he does not really explain why. *Theory of International Politics*, pp. 74–7, 116–18, 127; *Man, State and the War*, p. 220. See also Thies, "Social Psychological Approach," for an overview of the various socialization mechanisms posited by neorealist approaches. There are similar approaches in sociological realism and economic geography as well, with a generally functionalist understanding of why socialization/emulation/convergence happens. See e.g. North and Thomas, *Rise of the Western World*; McNeill, *Pursuit of Power*. For critiques of such approaches, see Ruggie, "Territoriality and Beyond," 156; Checkel, "Norms, Institutions and National Identity," 86; Wendt, *Social Theory*, pp. 100–2.

[7] See e.g. Wohlforth, "Realism and the End"; Copeland, "Trade Expectations"; Brooks and Wohlforth, "Power, Globalization"; Schweller and Wohlforth, "Power Test," etc. Waltz uses the same logic to explain the socialization of the Bolsheviks as well.

the underlying motivations of victors[8] in such interactions, but they generally agree that socialization is a rational response by defeated states (or elites in those states[9]) to various incentives. Elites are assumed to push for domestic changes either because they have no other choice (neorealism)[10] or because such adaptation is rewarded (liberal institutionalism,[11] but also some veins of classical realism[12] and constructivism[13]). Versions of these cost–benefit types of explanations have been used to explain the cases at hand here: Japan's transformation is often attributed to the American occupation after World War II; Turkey's to Atatürk. What is missing in such accounts is the international normative context that is framing the domestic debates about the country's direction.

In fact, even a cursory comparison of Turkey after World War I, Japan after World War II, and Russia after the Cold War brings forth many other puzzling facts about these transformations that mainstream theories about socialization do not explain. Turkey made its switch to a "Westophilean" strategy *after* it had achieved military victory against the interests of the core Western countries and during a time it was completely free of foreign occupation. Yet the domestic reform package that accompanied this switch displayed such a commitment to Western norms that even the most dyed-in-the-wool colonialist could not have dreamed of implementing it. Japan made its switch *following* military defeat and while it was under occupation,

---

[8] See Fritz, "Prudence in Victory," for a review of the literature on victor behavior in the aftermath of defeat.

[9] E.g. Byman and Pollack, "Let Us Now Praise Great Men."

[10] Alderson, "Making Sense," 421; see also Cortell and Davis, "Understanding the Domestic Impact," Ikenberry and Kupchan, "Socialization and Hegemonic Power," 283.

[11] Ikenberry and Kupchan, "Socialization and Hegemonic Power," 290–2; Ikenberry, *After Victory*; also in general, neoliberal regime theory explains normative compliance as an outcome of a cost–benefit analysis. See e.g. Keohane, *After Hegemony*; Oye, *Cooperation Under Anarchy*; Martin, *Coercive Cooperation*, etc. See also Johnston, "Treating International Institutions," 495, and Checkel, "Why Comply?" 555, for an overview.

[12] See Cortell and Davis, "Understanding the Domestic Impact," 81, and Alderson, "Making Sense," 428, for an overview of the classical realist understanding of state socialization.

[13] The difference between methodologically individualist constructivist approaches and neoliberal understanding of socialization is that constructivists emphasize the internalization of learning.

but *not quite in the way* the occupying power, the United States, wanted. Russia made the switch not after military defeat or occupation, but *completely on its own schedule*, and caught even seasoned observers off-guard.[14] All of these facts point to substantial degrees of agency exercised by these countries in choosing their strategy vis-à-vis "the West," and also indicate that something more complicated than a simple cost–benefit analysis of external material stimuli was going on in each case of strategy formulation.

There are two common features between these three cases of strategy reversal in foreign policy: first, each occurred soon after what was perceived to be a major "defeat"[15] of the previous institutional structure of the country and its legitimating worldview. At the time Turkey made its switch, the Ottoman Empire had been decidedly defeated in World War I and replaced by the Kemalist Republic. The institutions of the Ottoman Empire reflected a worldview which was (old)-worldly, multicultural, hands-off, "advanced organic,"[16] agrarian, nonsecular, segmentary,[17] and anachronistic. The Kemalist regime that rose out of the empire's ashes was obsessed with modernity, staunchly secular, ethnocentric, unitary, hands-on, bureaucratic, and emphasized industrialization above all else. The meteoric rise of the Japanese Empire in early twentieth century had come to a crushing halt at the hands of the Americans during World War II – who made sure afterwards that the militarist regime could never govern the country again. Japan gave up its expansionist militarism and embraced pacifist economic growth instead. Finally, the decade following the collapse of the Soviet Union was marked by Russia's desire to attract foreign investment and implement free-market principles. In all three cases, the ideological worldview espoused by a previous regime was entirely discredited,

---

[14] Deudney and Ikenberry review the relevant literature in "International Sources," 75, fn. 2.

[15] In most situations described by this word, perception precedes any development on the ground that can be objectively measured; i.e. the unclosed gap with the West crystallized in a formal moment perceived by all involved parties as "defeat."

[16] Goldstone convincingly argues that this is a more apt term to describe what are usually called "early modern" empires. Despite being sophisticated in many other ways, these empires depended primarily on organic sources of energy to fuel their economies: crops, animals, men, and timber. Goldstone, "Problem of," 261–2.

[17] See e.g. Durkheim, *Division of Labor*; Gellner, *Plough, Sword*.

and brushed aside for a radically different worldview, one which was in line with the normative demands of the international system.

Second, by the twentieth century, the three countries in question were no longer novices at socializing to system norms or emulating the West – each had followed emulation strategies in the past in order to improve competitiveness, to gain the acceptance of the international society of European states, and to assuage domestic concerns about lagging behind the West. Russia is considered to have taken this step first at the end of the seventeenth century under the leadership of Peter the Great (reign: 1682–1725), followed by his wife Catherine I, and, later, also under the rule of Catherine the Great (1762–92). The reform strategy had been revisited[18] most ostensibly again during the reign of Alexander II (1855–81) who, in 1861, issued the Great Emancipation Statute freeing and elevating 20 million serfs to equal citizen status. Despite a longer history of participating in European affairs and even borrowing military technology, the first Ottoman Sultan to be seriously persuaded of the necessity of comprehensive Westernization was Selim III (1789–1807), but Selim was executed after a rebellion and serious reforms in line with European demands were not implemented until the reign of Mahmud II (1808–39), and continued by his son, Abdülmecid II (1839–61). In 1839, Abdülmecid II issued the *Tanzimat* Declaration (prepared by his father), which recognized the sanctity of life, liberty, and individual honor of his subjects, and decreed that government should be formed according to fundamental principles. As in Russia (1905), these reforms would ultimately culminate in the convening of the first parliament (1876). Meanwhile, on the other side of the Asian continent, Japan faced the necessity of such reforms almost as soon as it came into serious contact with Western powers. This realization ushered in the period known as the Meiji Restoration (1868–1912). In 1868, the Japanese emperor Meiji issued the Charter Oath, recognizing the freedom of each individual to pursue their own calling and urging the abandonment of traditional ways. In 1889, only 13 years after the Ottoman

---

[18] Focusing on "reform" periods is somewhat misleading because even under "traditionalist" rulers, life was not static in any of these empires.

I nevertheless draw the distinction to emphasize periods where reforms were deliberately chosen in order to bring the country more in line with the West.

Empire, Japan adopted its first constitution, and in 1890, held its first national elections.

These facts contribute to a rather curious pattern. Three states, which for one reason or another were not part of the original Westphalian arrangement or the emergent society in Europe in the seventeenth century, became convinced of the necessity of joining it later on: in the case of Russia almost immediately; in the case of the Ottoman Empire somewhat more belatedly; and in the case of Japan, as soon as the decision became unavoidable. Realizing that taking part in this formation as an equal member required changing the traditional ways, various rulers in these countries implemented domestic reforms, some of which were substantive and some of which were for appearances' sake. Domestic politics between the initial realization and the twentieth century was marked therefore by periods of reforms and periods of the inevitable backlashes to these reforms.

In the early twentieth century, each country was taken over by leaders with revisionist agendas. In the Ottoman Empire, this happened just before the defeat and collapse of the empire: the Committee of Union and Progress (CUP), originally a secret society within the ranks of the Young Turk movement, took de facto control of the empire with a coup in 1913 (following the "Constitutional Revolution" of 1908). Between 1913 and 1918, it followed an aggressively revisionist agenda intended to recapture the Ottoman Empire's glory days, and, as a proto-fascist movement, oversaw some of the most brutal actions committed in the name of the empire, including the mass killing of the Armenian population in 1914–15. In Japan, a similar dynamic was repeated in the 1930s, with the military establishing complete control over the government and pursuing an aggressively expansionist foreign policy in Asia, with comparably bleak results for the population there. It needs no recounting that in the early decades of the twentieth century, Russia, too, was taken over by a leadership that was not enamored with the international status quo.

Obviously, there were ideological differences between these three regimes, but these differences should not be over-emphasized. The CUP regime in the Ottoman Empire and the militarist regime in Japan exhibited characteristics that resemble fascism, whereas the Bolsheviks in Russia subscribed to a version of Marxist communism. All three movements, however, were born out of the belief that traditional approaches to foreign policy were not working and that the

lag with the West would grow larger if right measures were not taken.
Ironically, then, none of these movements, now remembered mostly
for their brutality, would have risen if the countries in question could
have been somehow shielded from ideas about progress and modernity
emanating from Europe.[19] The differences do matter, of course: the
fact that the Bolsheviks had a more substantive ideology and a domestic reform plan, and the fact that they took power after Russia's near
defeat in war, and through a popular revolution, made all the difference in terms of the longevity of their regime, in comparison with the
CUP regime in the Ottoman Empire and even the military regime in
Japan. The latter two had risen to power without radically displacing
the existing political structures of their respective countries, and were
neither particularly inspired nor inspiring in terms of their proposed
domestic solutions (as is perhaps the case with all forms of revisionism fed from a traditionalist well).

Nevertheless, the trajectory is the same across the cases even as
its longevity varies: the Ottoman Empire's bout of revisionism was
short and bitter, lasting less than eight years; Japan sustained it for
about twice as long; whereas the Soviet Union held out for an impressive eight decades. Each of these revisionist governments was then
replaced by regimes very receptive to Western norms, ideas, and institutions. Here is the most interesting part, though: in all three cases,
there was a remarkable degree of continuity in terms of the people
involved in the said transitions. Mustafa Kemal Atatürk, who oversaw
Turkey's transformation into a "civilized" state, was a direct progeny
of the Young Turk movement; and "Kemalism" is in many ways a
smooth continuation of the CUP ideology, its main point of difference being the proposed solution to the international status problem.
Shigeru Yoshida, who oversaw Japan's transformation into a pacifist country that puts "economy first," had been an active participant
in the imperialist movement of the war years; in fact, he had been
imprisoned for his involvement just before becoming the prime minister of postwar Japan. There is even more continuity in the Russian
case: party leaders who initiated the transition were the same people
who continued to serve after the transition. It would not be a stretch,
then, to conclude that, in all three cases, leaders who were willing to

---

[19] For a discussion of the perverse effects of progress, see Elias *et al.*, "Toward a
Theory," 359.

fight the great powers of the West one day became the emissaries of Westernization[20] the next day.

To put it another way, none of the aforementioned explanations from mainstream IR as to why these countries reverted (with a vengeance) to emulating the West after revisionist "defeat" provides much mileage. Socialization is not explained by foreign interference or coercion or even persuasion, since there was little in two of the three cases; it is unexplained by leadership change, since in all three cases, the leaders overseeing the transition were simply the younger members of the old guard; and it is not even explained by survival, since the depth of transformation went far beyond what would have been necessary to ensure physical security (not that the physical existence of the state was ever in serious jeopardy in any of the three cases except perhaps Turkey). Detailed case studies in Chapters 3 to 5 will show that in the immediate aftermath of "defeat," leaders in each country chose what was the most status-enhancing strategy given the international norms of the time, despite other avenues being available to them, including some with even greater material yield. Despite the high costs of these status-seeking strategies, leaders were able to get popular support for them because domestic constituencies in these countries are greatly preoccupied by international stature, and especially with the relative standing of their state vis-à-vis "the West." This argument is more in line with the predictions of ideational approaches which hold that states are motivated by considerations of self-esteem, status, and prestige, but what those approaches fail to account for is the backdrop of modernity[21] and the profound impact the diffusion of modern ontology had on the "self-esteem" of certain states.

The aforementioned strategy of willing and deep emulation is only explained by the fact that the countries under investigation here (along with some others) share a unique set of experiences as stigmatized

---

[20] For the moment, I am using this as a blanket category for actions emulating the dominant Western norms and institutions of the time.

[21] Neorealist thinking about socialization *also* fails to account for changes ushered in by modernity, e.g. as manifested in the disparity between the reaction of the Ottoman Empire to the rise of Europe versus how European states viewed the Ottoman Empire at the peak of its power. If material competition is a sufficient explanation for the depth of the transformation that countries such as Turkey, Russia, and Japan underwent after modernity, European states should have exhibited similar responses when they were weak and the Ottoman Empire was powerful.

outsiders which caused them to be especially concerned about international stature. In other words, the insecurities created by the international environment have been built into the national identities of these states. The status-conscious trajectories in the last century can be traced back to that original insecurity, and in fact this was what ultimately drove these states Westward after their respective defeats. The evidence for these claims lies in developments in the nineteenth century.

Modernity, ontological insecurity, and the international system

A handful of political entities that survived from the "pre-modern" era – entities usually lumped together under the category of pre-modern/agrarian/gunpowder empires – experienced a different transition to *modernity* than the Westphalian states that were the locomotives of that transition.[22] They had a different experience because they had to recreate themselves as "modern" states against a backdrop of an emerging international society of states that had already made the transition organically. The material advance of the early-comers was backed by a culture spouting universalizing claims about enlightenment, progress, rationality, and self-interest. As a result, perhaps for the first time in world history, (autonomous) emulation of competitors took on a deeper meaning – in embracing the Western European state models, these agrarian empires were also enveloped in a certain new worldview, one that is specific to and the essence of modernity. By emulating the Westphalian state model and trying to join the European society of states, people[23] in these gunpowder empires also came to accept a continuous worldview in which

---

[22] This is not to imply that successor states to those entities that did not survive the transition intact are exempt from this generalization; they also had a markedly different experience with modernity than Western European states. However, the literature concerned with the political behavior of such cases (as a group) is considerably larger. For starters, see e.g. Ayoob, "Third World"; Clapham, *Third World Politics*; Willetts, *Non-Aligned Movement*; Rodríguez, *Latin American Subaltern*; Chaturvedi, *Mapping Subaltern Studies*, as well as Blaney and Inayatullah's *Problem of Difference* and Mitchell's *Colonising Egypt*.

[23] Originally, this was very much an elite-driven process. More on this issue later.

there are no exceptions; a worldview with a marked emphasis on progress, rationality, and science; a worldview which inevitably generates a universal social hierarchy predicated upon comparisons and measurements.[24] Once the peoples of the old empires started accepting this worldview, it was inevitable that they too would embrace its judgment: *they* found *themselves* as coming up short, not just materially but socially and culturally. "Objective" measures of "progress" could not be ignored. This is what is at the root of the "auto-Orientalism" exhibited by Turkey, Japan, and Russia to this day.

In other words, while emulation, especially as a military strategy, is a relatively frequent phenomenon in world history, it took on a different depth once the processes that constitute *modernity* started rolling. There are two separate issues here: (1) the nature of the modern ontology; (2) the fact that modernity as a shared value system linked previously independent communities – "The figuration of established-outsider arises in the junction and interaction of different groups. It emerges when formerly independent groups become increasingly reciprocally dependent."[25] In modernity, emulation became a vehicle for a totalizing kind of socialization, the like of which had not been witnessed before. Unlike in the agrarian ages, borrowing in modernity could no longer be limited to a certain technique or sector, since inferiority in one sector of life signaled possible inferiority in others.[26] All aspects of life were connected, all governed by laws operating with the same fundamental principles.[27] A remarkable feature of modernity is the assumption that the same universal method of rationality can explain every human dynamic. Modernity is characterized by the

---

[24] See Gellner, *Plough, Sword* and also *Nationalism*. Also see Malesevic and Haugaard, "Introduction"; Haugaard, "Power, Modernity"; and Meyer and Jepperson, "'Actors' of Modern Society."

[25] Olofsson on Elias, in Andersen and Kaspersen, *Classical and Modern Social Theory*, p. 371.

[26] The uniqueness of this universalizing, "scientific," evidentiary (and therefore seemingly indisputable) character of the modern worldview is what Bull misses in the numerous claims he makes about the nature of the nineteenth-century European society of states; for instance, in his foreword to Gong's *Standard of "Civilisation"*, p. 2: "The arrogance of many Europeans, in equating civilization with the particular civilization of Europe, was no less than that of the Chinese." I will have more to say about this distinction in Chapter 2.

[27] Gellner, *Nationalism*, pp. 21–3.

increasing integration of various spheres of social life – all previously thought to have their own separate essences and rules – into one universal ontology.[28] This worldview came to dominate European affairs only in the nineteenth century (and even there was not fully hegemonic until the twentieth), but it had its roots in developments going back several centuries.

A number of simultaneous processes were involved in this gradual transition into modernity. First, the rise of absolutist states with recognized monopolies on state power[29] was a critical turning point.[30] At the same time, the bloodshed of the Thirty Years War had led to a general fear of difference and motivated early-modern thinkers like Hobbes[31] to search for a universal stand-point beyond question,[32] which then led to the emergence of ideas such as natural law, social contract, and rational method, which were used at first to justify absolute sovereignty of monarchs, but later gave rise to an emphasis on individual agency.[33]

The next two centuries in Western Europe are marked by two crucial developments:[34] a transfer of political power to the center and

---

[28] See e.g. Mitchell, *Colonising Egypt*, p. 13; Gellner, *Plough, Sword*; Gellner, *Nationalism*; Elias, *Civilizing Process*; Haugaard, "Power, Modernity." We may also invoke Bauman here, who argues that modernity is characterized by the drive toward order, management, naming, and segregating. See e.g. *Modernity and the Holocaust*; *Modernity and Ambivalence*.

[29] Wight, *Systems of States*, p. 135.

[30] Elias, *Civilizing Process*; Ruggie, "Territoriality and Beyond," 162.

[31] Bauman, *Modernity and Ambivalence*, p. 5; see also Collins, *From Divine Cosmos*, pp. 4, 6, 7, 28, 29, 32.

[32] Blaney and Inayatullah, "Westphalian Deferral," 32. In "Territoriality and Beyond," 157–62, Ruggie has an excellent review of the particular manifestations of this search in a number of social spheres, e.g. on p. 158: "What was true in the visual arts was equally true in politics: political space came to be defined as it appeared from a single fixed viewpoint. The concept of sovereignty, then, was merely the doctrinal counterpart of the application of single-point perspectival forms to the spatial organization of politics."

[33] See e.g. Keene, *Beyond Anarchical Society*; Reus-Smit, *Moral Purpose*. See also Giddens, *Modernity and Self-identity*.

[34] However, we should always keep in mind Ruggie's point that "the reasons for which things were done often had very little to do with what actually ended up being done or what was made possible by those deeds." See "Territoriality and Beyond," 166.

a separation of the economy from the polity.[35] In the pre-modern and early-modern eras the polity and the economy were connected. As wealth was more easily acquired by predation than production, there was an ever-present incentive[36] to reinvest gains in methods of coercion. Kings regarded their kingdoms as their private domains,[37] but their right to levy taxes was constantly challenged by nobles who raised their own armies. The emergence of capitalism changed this dynamic.[38] The surplus generated by capitalism allowed specialists of coercion to be bought off with the tax revenue, shifting power to the economic realm and civil society.[39] The accompanying "civilizing process" gradually converted most warrior nobles to "courtiers and bureaucrats." The centralization of power created networks of interdependence, making individuals more sensitive to the needs of others and putting them in more need of a universal set of manners.[40] In other words, the rise of European "civilization" went hand in hand with the rise of capitalism, and the accompanying march of scientific rationality, as well as the use of such rationality to justify the existence and the power of the state.[41]

One of the key elements in the rise of an autonomous economic sector was a series of political revolutions and reforms in major Western European countries in the eighteenth and early nineteenth centuries.[42] These revolutions gave breathing room to civil society, undercut the power of traditional elites, and in many ways prepared the ground for the last phase for the emergence of the modern sovereign state – characterized by industrialization, rationality, bureaucracy, and efficiency in war-making, manifested especially in the state's ability to

---

[35] Gellner, *Plough, Sword*; Gellner, *Nationalism*. See also Mouzelis, "Nationalism," p. 125; Haugaard, "Power, Modernity," p. 75; Ruggie, "Territoriality and Beyond," 151; Anderson, *Lineages of the Absolutist State*, p. 429; Jones, *European Miracle*, p. 147.

[36] Haugaard, "Power, Modernity," p. 78.

[37] *Ibid.*, p. 79.

[38] All of historical sociology, Marxist or otherwise, converges on this argument.

[39] Haugaard, "Power, Modernity," p. 80.

[40] Elias, *Civilizing Process*.

[41] See Bauman, *Legislators and Interpreters*, where he argues that after the Enlightenment, the state started amassing and administering resources in order to organize society according to some preconceived model.

[42] See Goldstone, "Cultural Orthodoxy."

generate man-power from a new "national" base. All of these later developments in some way flow from the ascendance of a production economy and the accompanying increased integration/differentiation of society[43] (even if the spark of the Industrial Revolution was in some way accidental).[44]

The point of this brief review is that the states that originally remained aloof from these processes were in some ways victims of their own "glorious" pasts.[45] As Goldstone argues, there was nothing unique about the revolutions in Western Europe – the Ottoman Empire and China also had similar revolts around the same time. The difference was in the outcomes. Whereas revolts in Western Europe were interpreted as the failure of existing regimes and as signaling the need for something new, in agrarian empires similar revolts ended up reinforcing the traditional social hierarchies.[46] In other words, while the revolutions in Western Europe gave full steam to the ideas of Enlightenment and social progress that had germinated in the developments of the seventeenth century (i.e. the search for universal rational/natural laws and their applications to social life), in agrarian empires the same processes were originally interpreted as the result of a deviation from traditional methods that had brought success in the past. The success of traditional methods explains why social and economic life in agrarian empires of the European periphery were (temporarily) frozen[47] at around the same time that northwestern Europe started undergoing momentous transformations. This analysis also overlaps with the World-System explanation of why the Ottoman Empire and Russia were originally left outside the growing world-economy – as large agrarian empires, their economies were self-sustaining universes for a longer time than was the case in the smaller states of Europe.[48]

What all of this means is that until the end of the eighteenth century there was no great unbridgeable development gap between the territorial states of northwestern Europe and the agrarian

---

[43] E.g. Durkheim, *Division of Labor*, but also Bauman's entire body of work.
[44] See e.g. Goldstone, "Rise of the West"; Hobson, *Eastern Origins*; Frank, *ReORIENT*.
[45] And in contrast, societies which benefited most from these developments had been facing near destruction not long ago. See Ruggie, "Territoriality and Beyond," 161.
[46] Goldstone, "Cultural Orthodoxy," 130.
[47] *Ibid.*, 131.
[48] Wallerstein, *Modern World-System*, pp. 324–5.

empires outside the European periphery.[49] If that statement sounds controversial, it is only because the nineteenth-century European schemas about the civility, modernity, and social development (or lack thereof) of the various regions of the world are still with us to some degree.[50] Since the nineteenth century, it has become customary to assume that something was culturally wrong with the states left out of the "rise of the West." What is forgotten is that prior to at least the eighteenth century, social and economic life in countries such as the Ottoman Empire, Russia, or China was not so different from other agrarian empires now considered part of "Western Civilization," such as Spain.[51] Wallerstein points out that the development of the absolutist monarchies in the Ottoman Empire and Russia in the sixteenth century shared substantial parallels with developments in Western Europe.[52] Collins documents the indigenous rise of merchant capitalism within Japan,[53] just as other scholars have documented similar processes and trade booms elsewhere in the universe of agrarian empires.[54] I have already pointed to Goldstone's argument about political revolts in agrarian empires occurring around the same time as those in northwestern Europe (1750–1850). These revolts had different outcomes, but were ushered in by similar causes and bottlenecks in the economy.

Broadly speaking, then, prior to the nineteenth century, there were two parallel lines of state development trajectory in the world, which continued to overlap. On the one hand, there were states that were constituted as "advanced organic," agrarian, gunpowder empires, such as the Ottoman Empire, India, Russia, China, and Japan.[55] On the other hand, the smaller territorial states of northwestern Europe, most notably, England, France, Netherlands, perhaps also Sweden,

---

[49] See e.g. Aydın: "The Ottomans followed developments in military technology in Europe very closely and were able to keep pace with the innovations in Europe until the second half of the eighteenth century." *Anti-Westernism in Asia*, p. 17.

[50] See Goldstone, "Problem of"; also see Collins, "Sociological Guilt-Trip"; Wallerstein, "Development of the Concept of Development."

[51] For an antidote to nineteenth-century views of comparative history, start with Braudel, *Mediterranean*.

[52] Wallerstein, *Modern World-System*, p. 313.

[53] Collins, "Asian Route."

[54] Goldstone, "Problem of."

[55] Also Spain – but Spain was an original member of the Westphalian system.

and later Prussia, had avoided imperial constitution as a result of the Thirty Years War and the Westphalian Settlement,[56] but were increasingly interconnected with each other through the formation of a regional society of states (an arrangement formalized by Westphalia and backed by the historical bond of Christendom) and a capitalist economy.[57]

Obviously, even prior to the nineteenth century there were certain key developments within the states of the second group that were not experienced by states in the first, such as the abolition of serfdom, decline of feudalism, and the emergence of early-modern political thought. However, had it not been for the successful revolutions and reforms of the late eighteenth and nineteenth centuries, these developments could have been remembered as divergences that went nowhere, just as in the agrarian empires of their counterparts. Furthermore, empires on the European periphery were not completely oblivious to the beneficial results of various advances in Western Europe, even if they lacked a precise understanding of the causes and were focused mostly on the end results. As noted above, Russia had decided it would be a good idea to copy certain Western institutions as early as the late seventeenth century; the Ottoman Empire had the same idea not too long after, and in fact was borrowing piecemeal military technology long before then. The crucial fact, however, was that all interacting states at that time were ruled by traditional monarchies (leaving aside the issue of religious differences for the moment). This is why, initially, the desire to copy the successful models in Europe was restricted mostly to the military sector.

However, the French Revolution, and subsequently the Industrial Revolution, changed this equation considerably. Prior to the French Revolution, international politics were constrained not by the rule of law but by the principle of dynastic legitimacy and the ensuing homology in the domestic social structures of major states.[58] The French Revolution challenged that order by ushering in the principle of popular sovereignty, articulated in "holistic, messianic

---

[56] Reus-Smit, *Moral Purpose*, p. 88.
[57] Watson, *Evolution of International Society*, p. 272.
[58] Bukovansky, "Altered State," 199. Also see Ruggie, "Territoriality and Beyond," 151–2.

and universalist"[59] form. This development introduced a heteroge-
neous element to what had been a homogeneous system.[60] Mlada
Bukovansky underlines the transformative effect the French Revolution had on the international system: "Revolutionary ideas directly challenged the legitimacy of dynastic, monarchical regimes,
and ... the demonstration effects of the mobilizing power of popular sovereignty and nationalism invited emulation, but emulation
of a technique rooted in popular sovereignty ... would also challenge the legitimacy of dynastic regimes (both from within and from
without)."[61] These developments were further aided by the Industrial
Revolution. Although most scholars disagree with his chronological
ordering, Gellner's general point about the intimate link between
the emergence of industrialization and nationalism[62] in Europe cannot be denied. The geopolitical struggles described by Bukovansky
above gave rise to states with unprecedented infrastructural powers,
which were then used to break down local communities and their
segmentary worldviews.[63]

Along with the advent of mass schooling,[64] the continuous worldview of industria swept over the emerging population of modern
individuals. The modern "individual" constructed by this worldview has no essence and, like atoms, is interchangeable with other
individuals,[65] lives in a world governed by natural laws that can
be discerned through scientific reasoning, and serves the state only
because the state is rational and represents the collective will of
individuals.[66] The twin revolutions in the political and economic
realms at the turn of the eighteenth century dismantled the traditional *gemeinshaft* order for good[67] in the leading states of Europe,
and replaced it with *Gesellschaft* communities integrated through
the principle of nationalism.

---

[59] Bukovansky, "Altered State," 198.
[60] *Ibid.*, 199; Halliday, "International Society as Homogeneity," 435.
[61] Bukovansky, "Altered State," 200.
[62] Gellner, *Nationalism*, p. 32.
[63] Mouzelis, "Nationalism."
[64] See Ramirez and Boli, "Political Construction."
[65] See also Ruggie, "Territoriality and Beyond," 157–8.
[66] Haugaard, "Power, Modernity." Also see Giddens, *Modernity and Self-identity*.
[67] A fact very well recognized by contemporary sociologists such as Tönnies and Durkheim.

The modern international system

The modern international system emerged from these developments. The emphasis on the peace of Westphalia as the origin of the modern states system really does a disservice by obscuring the degree to which modern-day international dynamics, inequalities, and hierarchies were shaped by nineteenth-century events.[68]

Bukovansky argues that it was within that century that European politics truly started resembling a "state of nature."[69] Prior to the nineteenth century, wars had been constrained by the shared norms stemming from the homology in domestic structures: "The balance of power was understood in such a way that compensations in territory, wealth, or prestige, were considered a monarchical right ... Neither contiguity nor national homogeneity were major priorities of eighteenth century monarchs."[70] The French Revolution introduced the idea of fighting in the name of universal principles of liberty, equality, and fraternity,[71] and led to the rise of the belief that any action against a state that did not stand for those principles was legitimate and justified.[72] For a brief while, these developments in France had a destabilizing impact on the European states system, but this destabilization was temporarily resolved after the Napoleonic Wars. Part of the reason for that outcome was the post-revolutionary abandonment of many new ideals in France, which made possible France's reintegration into the society of states. The transition to the new system was managed under the Concert of Europe arrangement, which gave some states time to gradually come around to the new principle of popular sovereignty[73] (completing processes already under way), and bought others time to try to fend off the inevitable.

The effect on the rest of the world, however, of this new, modern European worldview, as politically manifested first in the French Revolution, was much more devastating.[74] E. H. Carr famously analyzed

---

[68] Bukovansky, "Altered State"; Reus-Smit, *Moral Purpose*; Hobson and Sharman, "Enduring Place"; Keene, *Beyond Anarchical Society*; Mann, "Predation and Production."

[69] Bukovansky, "Altered State," 213.

[70] *Ibid.*, 205.   [71] *Ibid.*, 211.   [72] *Ibid.*, 213.

[73] Also see Reus-Smit, *Moral Purpose*, p. 122, for the transformative effect of the nineteenth century on the articulation of state legitimacy in this direction.

[74] Hobson and Sharman, "Enduring Place."

the link between Enlightenment idealism and European imperialism in *The Twenty Years' Crisis, 1919–1939*. As he points out, nineteenth-century European worldviews were increasingly characterized by the belief that self-interest was not only rational but also *moral*.[75] Carr calls this worldview "the harmony of interests" doctrine, and argues that it was first pushed along "by the unparalleled expansion of production, population and prosperity, which marked the hundred years following the publication of *The Wealth of Nations* and the invention of the steam engine."[76] As competition got tougher, this worldview got a second push from Darwinism, which was applied to international politics to justify the ruthless land-grab of the latter part of the nineteenth century:

The path of progress is strewn with the wreck of nations; traces are everywhere to be seen of the hecatombs of inferior races, and of victims who found not the narrow way to greater perfection. Yet these dead peoples are, in very truth, the stepping stones on which mankind has arisen to the higher intellectual and deeper emotional life of to-day.[77]

Not only was this seen as an apt description of how things *were*, but also of how things *should be*. The British in particular believed that their empire was serving a higher purpose. Again as quoted by Carr, Cecil Rhodes wrote: "I contend that we are the first race in the world, and the more of the world we inhabit the better it is for the human race."[78]

Imperialism was not a phenomenon unique to the nineteenth century, but the particular tenor and justifications of nineteenth-century imperialism were unprecedented. As pointed out by Hobson and Sharman, prior to the nineteenth century, a superior Europe-as-West identity had gradually emerged as Europeans, originally held together by the loose ties of Christendom, increasingly came to define themselves negatively[79] against the natives[80] in Africa and the Americas,[81] as well as the infidels of the Ottoman Empire.[82] This would crystallize

---

[75] Carr, *Twenty Years' Crisis*, pp. 43–5.   [76] *Ibid.*, p. 47.
[77] *Ibid*: citing a 1900 international relations book, p. 48.   [78] *Ibid.*, p. 72.
[79] See Mitchell, *Colonising Egypt*, p. 166; Neumann and Welsh, "The Other."
[80] See the discussion of Colombus in Blaney and Inayatullah, *Problem of Difference*, p. 10.
[81] Yet settler states in the Americas were incorporated into the idea of "West" relatively easily. See Watson, *Evolution of International Society*, p. 234.
[82] Hobson and Sharman, "Enduring Place," 85.

into a full-fledged racist ideology in the eighteenth and the nineteenth centuries, affecting even the understandings of what constitutes a "Great Power." Echoing Carr, Hobson and Sharman argue that "the British (and others) engaged in imperialism not simply because 'they could' (as materialists assume). Rather they engaged in it because they *believed they should*."[83] Governing large areas in the "inferior non-European" world was taken as a mark of great power status.

Hobson and Sharman perfectly summarize the new ideas behind the nineteenth-century reconstruction of European state identity.[84] Allow me to quote at length, as it is extremely pertinent to the discussion here:

Particularly important was the construction of the theory of Oriental Despotism ... It prescribed that Western states were progressive and economically successful because they were liberal, while Eastern states were imagined as but tyrannical regimes that stifled economic progress. Moreover, this characterization also enabled Europeans to present or construct the East as a 'despotic threat.' This theory was complemented by the construction of the 'Peter Pan theory of the East'. Here the East was imagined as weak, passive, helpless and inert such that it was deemed axiomatic that it would be fundamentally incapable of self-development or growing up. By contrast the West was imagined as strong, proactive, independent and progressive ... Within this framework, the East was essentialized in terms of a passive and helpless female, the West as a strong and independent male ... Last but not least, social Darwinism and scientific racism were important. This enabled the Europeans to construct a *civilizational league table* in which the "three races" of mankind were classified within three divisions ... – the Whites who resided in the 'advanced' First World of Europe (Division 1); the Yellows who resided in the 'barbaric' Second World (Division 2); and the Blacks who resided in the 'savage' Third World (Division 3).[85]

All of these ideas were clearly manifested in nineteenth-century international law, which was centered on a premise that states had to meet a Standard of Civilization in order to be treated as equal participants in the international system.[86]

Edward Keene points out that, as a seventeenth-century legal thinker, Grotius, who is usually credited with the idea of a European

---

[83] *Ibid.*, 87.
[84] Also see Hobson, *Eastern Origins*, p. 228.
[85] *Ibid.*, p. 88. See also Kingsbury, "Sovereignty and Inequality," p. 69.
[86] See also Gong, *Standard of "Civilisation"*, pp. 6, 14, 24.

society of states, was quite comfortable with the hypothetical idea of equality between European and non-European states.[87] By the nineteenth century, however, the international system was very much divided: "there was an order promoting toleration in Europe, and an order promoting civilization beyond."[88] Focusing only on the former obscures the degree to which international dynamics beyond most of Europe were constituted along hierarchical principles.[89] Keene also argues that, as a result, Europeans thought of sovereignty outside of the Western world very much as divisible:

> While, say, a nineteenth-century British diplomat would have found it inconceivable that he might claim a right to exercise any sovereign prerogatives over the French, his counterpart in the colonial service would have thought it perfectly appropriate to take over some of the sovereign prerogatives that an Indian prince possessed, even ones guaranteed by prior treaties, if that was what it took to facilitate progress or to stamp out corruption and barbarism.[90]

What has to be realized is that the civility various European states accorded each other in the nineteenth century and the utter lack of respect they showed to the peoples elsewhere in the world were consequences of the same modern, "enlightened" worldview. As Michael Mann puts it: "Precisely because Europeans as a whole constituted a moral community, they could not be enslaved."[91] The "freest people" in the world, however, shackled most of mankind in the name of civilization, which was precisely Norbert Elias's point when he observed that civilizing processes go along with de-civilizing processes.

Modernity, stratification, and the production of "Outsiders"

In some ways, then, the growing social inequalities and hierarchy of the nineteenth-century international system can be seen as a

---

[87] Keene, *Beyond Anarchical Society*, p. 109.
[88] *Ibid.*, p. 7. See also Salter, *Barbarians and Civilization*, p. 15: "In the nineteenth century, 'civilization' was taken to represent a mission of homogenization and 'improvement'. Thus, the rhetoric of 'civilization' was quickly appropriated by imperial ideology to mean the 'civilizing mission.'"
[89] *Ibid.*; Hobson and Sharman, "Enduring Place."
[90] Keene, *Beyond Anarchical Society*, p. 7.
[91] Mann, "Predation and Production," p. 65.

natural consequence of the increasing dominance of the "modern" worldview. Two aspects of modernity made such developments possible.[92]

First is the idea that the scientific method can be applied to everything. The scientific method is very much about "objective" measurements and comparisons,[93] which are then used to develop more efficient solutions to problems, leading ultimately to progress. Applied to international politics, the dominance of such a worldview[94] implied that distinctions between states and cultures could only be judged on a universal scale of "scientifically" measured accomplishments.[95] Civilizations that were unfamiliar to Europeans could no longer be understood as simply doing things differently (in ways in which the logic of such difference escaped the Europeans); such difference was interpreted as inferiority. As Mitchell notes:

These differences were not the differences within a self, which would be understood as an always-divided identity; they were the differences between a self and its opposite, the opposite that makes possible such an imaginary, undivided self ... [T]he domination of the West over the non-Western world depended on this manner of creating a "West", a singular Western self-identity.[96]

This conclusion about the superiority of the Western identity seemed to have empirical support in the undeniable material progress of the (north-)West in the nineteenth century.

Second is the rise of nationalism, which on the one hand helped to integrate increasingly atomized individuals and bolster the modern state, yet on the other, gave rise to a marked differentiation between insiders and outsiders,[97] with morality being aligned with the interests, desires, and needs of the former. Furthermore, nineteenth-century conceptions of nationalism were shaped by

---

[92] Gellner, *Nationalism*, pp. 19–39; Bauman, *Modernity and Ambivalence*, Introduction.

[93] See also Mitchell, *Colonising Egypt*, pp. 13, 60.

[94] Mitchell points out that the age of exhibition with its ordering and cataloguing impulse was *"necessarily* the colonial age" p. 13 (italics mine).

[95] See Salter, *Barbarians and Civilization*, p. 16, for a review of nineteenth-century "scientific" theories of societal development.

[96] *Colonising Egypt*, p. 166.

[97] See Chapter 2; as well as Bauman, *Modernity and Ambivalence*, pp. 63–4.

"scientific racism"[98] and were therefore informed by biological conceptions of the "nation" (another side effect of the transferability of modern epistemological principles).

The particular manifestation of nineteenth-century principles in the society of European states as a Standard of Civilization can also be parsed as a common sociological phenomenon, one that often accompanies societal formations. The hierarchical structure of the international system in the nineteenth century resembles very much what Weber called a socially stratified society. According to Weber, in societies where market rules are not in full operation and are, rather, controlled by convention, culture, and rules of conduct, the result is rigid social stratification and monopolistic appropriation (which is an apt description for nineteenth-century imperialism). If a society is stratified by status, social strata and the status groups placed in those strata exhibit features of "closed" social relationships whereby "the participation of certain persons is excluded, limited, or subject to conditions."[99] This is significant because:

A closed social relationship is capable of guaranteeing its monopolized advantages to its members through a) competition freely engaged in within the group; b) regulation or rationing of such advantages; and c) their appropriation by individuals or small groups on a permanent basis, in which case they become more or less inalienable. This last case is a closure within, as well as against outsiders. Such appropriated advantages will be called "rights".[100]

Membership in social strata is determined by lifestyle factors and is usually hereditary. Socially stratified societies are also marked by hierarchies of power, whereby certain high-ranking status groups monopolize economic and political advantages.[101] This monopolization could be legitimized under a rubric of "rights" in the manner described in the passage cited above. As a result, in societies stratified purely according to social status, there is little to no upward mobility. The most familiar example of this type of stratification is the caste system in India.

---

[98] Mann, "Predation and Production," p. 67.
[99] Weber, *Economy and Society*, p. 97.
[100] *Ibid.*, p. 96.
[101] Weber, *Basic Concepts*.

Essentially, the dominant norms of such a society are based on what Raymond Murphy terms "collectivist criteria" of closure. Closure is "the process of mobilizing power in order to enhance or defend a group's share of rewards and resources."[102] Property, credentials, and assessments of individual material capability in general are examples of individualist criteria of exclusion. Collectivist criteria of exclusion are based on group characteristics such as race, culture, religion, and physical traits, and are designed specifically to transfer advantage to members of the in-group. It was no accident that Great Britain, as the first country to enjoy the benefits of the Industrial Revolution, was also the staunchest supporter of the Standard of Civilization. Closure criteria may circumscribe the behavior of group members as well. Keene notes that toward the end of the nineteenth century Germany grew increasingly skeptical about the twin pillars of "toleration" and "civilization," and its revisionist maneuvers as a latecomer to both industrialization and imperialism put its own "civilized" status in question.[103]

Especially pertinent here is Norbert Elias's work on "the Established and Outsiders," which emerged out of Elias's analysis of the social dynamics in Leicester ("The Winston Parva Study").[104] This urban settlement was organized into three districts, Zones 1, 2, and 3. The inhabitants of Zone 1 were white-collar professionals, whereas Zones 2 and 3 were both working class. The entire community believed Zone 1 to be the best area to live. Zone 2 (the "old village") inhabitants, while poor, considered their area respectable and looked down upon Zone 3 dwellers, whom they characterized as dirty and quarrelsome, which was not actually the case for most of Zone 3. The most puzzling part of the study was the fact, observed by Elias, that Zone 3 inhabitants "seemed to accept, with a kind of puzzled resignation, that they belonged to a group of less virtue and respectability."[105] They resented the verdict of the other zones, and were also shamed by it.

Elias explains this curious dynamic by reference to the fact that the "old village" of Zone 2 was indeed older than other zones, and as a result had a network of "old families" who took it upon themselves to

---

[102] Murphy, "Structure of Closure," 548.
[103] Keene, *Beyond Anarchical Society*, p. 123.
[104] Elias and Scotson, *Established and Outsiders*.
[105] *Ibid.*, p. xvi.

protect the respectability of the entire zone. It was this cohesiveness that made it possible for the "old villagers" to exercise exclusionary closure on Zone 3 individuals, barring them from participation in public life. Zone 3 individuals could not retaliate because they lacked the necessary cohesion for such an organization and also because they felt inferior: "to some extent, their own conscience was on the side of the detractors. They themselves agreed with the 'village' people that it was bad not to be able to control one's children or to get drunk and noisy and violent."[106] Even if such criticisms did not apply to them personally, they felt shame because they lived in the same zone with some people who did act that way.

Elias believed that the dynamic exhibited by the subjects of the Winston Parva study was duplicated in most power relations: "In all these cases the more powerful group look upon themselves as the *better people*, as endowed with a kind of group charisma, with a specific virtue shared by all its members and lacked by others. What is more ... the 'superior' people may make the less powerful people themselves feel that they lack virtue – that they are inferior in human terms."[107] A similar process influenced the thinking of the decision-makers, elites, and intelligentsia outside the European society of states of the nineteenth century. They felt shame[108] because they lived in "semi-civilized" or "barbaric" states.

The social impact of the "rise of the West"

While the "rise of the West," which culminated in the great political enlightenment, technological advancement, and material prowess of (north-)Western Europe (and the United States) in the nineteenth century, is an undeniable fact of history, the hierarchical arrangement of the international system at that time was anything but an adulterated reflection of the distribution of capabilities. The European society of states and its Standard of Civilization is best understood as a

---

[106] *Ibid.*, p. 101.   [107] *Ibid.*, p. xvi.

[108] Goffman's point about shame is quite telling: "One assumes that embarrassment is a normal part of normal social life, the individual becoming uneasy not because he is personally maladjusted but rather because he is not ... embarrassment is not an irrational impulse breaking through social prescribed behavior, but part of this orderly behavior itself." Goffman, *Interaction Ritual*, pp. 109, 111.

closed social stratum of actors, who used a collectivist criterion of closure to exclude non-members (and individualist criteria to socially evaluate members). Non-members were denied basic rights such as contractual guarantees. Furthermore, they were stigmatized as being inferior, backward, barbaric, effeminate, childish, despotic, and in need of enlightenment. The fact that non-European states did not have the material capabilities of European states was used as evidence of the scientific validity of these claims. The stigma was then used to further exclude such states from the sovereign protections accorded by society, opening them up to further European exploitation, leading to more relative backwardness, and giving more "objective" credence to the stigma.

What is more important for the purposes of this argument, however, is the fact that such European notions about progress were very much internalized by the elites in the "semi-sovereign" states of the nineteenth century. Even if they did not completely buy into theories of racial inferiority, they accepted the validity of other "objective," "scientific" judgments about their countries and compatriots. This collective psychology is at the root of elite efforts, witnessed all over the semi-periphery in the nineteenth century, to "pass" as Europeans by adopting European fashions, speaking European languages among themselves, and learning European arts. All such behavior could be seen as part of an effort to distance oneself from one's neighborhood.

The elites outside of the Western core accepted the judgment of "civilization" because in their efforts to catch up with the West they had become habituated to the continuous worldview of *modernity*. Every institution they copied in an effort to keep up with the West, starting with military training, brought them closer to the core. Once they accepted the modern worldview, they could not but feel shame (even if at the same time they felt resentment). At some point the words "reform," "modernization," and "Westernization" became synonymous.[109] Moreover, the people most exposed to the ideas of a global social hierarchy were also the people who were in the best position

[109] Even today it is difficult to separate these concepts. At the very least, Europe is still seen as totally and naturally "modern"; whereas in other places, Westerners look for "authentic" experiences untouched by modernity (as if such a thing were possible). Media coverage of non-Western areas almost invariably focuses on un-"modern" aspects of life, which are at best described as cute, quaint, or exotic, and at worst as scary, unsafe, and unpredictable.

to effect domestic change: the intelligentsia, the military (the military was always the first to modernize), and the ruling elite. All of the key institutions of the modern nation state such as nationalism, mass-schooling, and modern bureaucracy took their form around this time; not long afterward they were dutifully emulated outside of Europe by those states that still had the capability to shape their own domestic policies. Bauman's point about East European educated classes being the most avid students of the Enlightenment applies equally to the cases at hand here: "They needed a mighty lever to lift society all the way up to the ideal: only a state wielding absolute power could serve as such a lever, and such a state, both able and willing to serve, was still to be created."[110] The emulation of key institutions of the modern "gardening"[111] state, even in their incomplete forms, at precisely the moment during which the elites in the "backward" countries had internalized the judgment of history, was instrumental in cementing the ontological insecurity created by such backwardness in (proto-) national psyches. As will be demonstrated in Chapter 2, the globalization of the established-outsider dynamic is unique to the modern international system.

I am not implying that elites in the Ottoman Empire or Japan (or even Russia) bought into the European rhetoric of being on a civilizing mission to rescue the rest of humanity from itself. Rather, what I am arguing is that they internalized the idea of linear progress and the idea that European material advancement was somehow connected to European culture and lifestyle.[112] Even those elites who rejected or resented Europe did not reject this dichotomy of backwardness and modernity.[113] They believed, along with their European contemporaries, that there really was a developmental lag between *civilizations.*

---

[110] *Modernity and Ambivalence*, p. 37.   [111] *Ibid.*, p. 20.

[112] Watson observes this dynamic uncritically in "European International Society," p. 31: "the nineteenth century is notable for the creation throughout Asia, Africa, and Oceania of Europeanized or Westernized elites. The Europeans and the Americans offered the instruction, and usually met with an enthusiastic response ... The mastery of Western governmental practice and military technology enabled these elites to run a modern state."

[113] One of the interesting manifestations of this was in the discipline of history. Modernity brought with it the desire to write universal histories (see Fukuyama, *End of History*); so the discipline of history too was a creation of nineteenth-century European ontology. At the same time, history is essential for the nation-construction projects. This is how the ironic

In other words, the problem of relative strength was no longer seen simply as difference in material capability (which is par for the course throughout human history) but had become a moral, social, and cultural issue. It had become an existential dilemma par excellence.

Elites in Russia, the Ottoman Empire, and Japan all entered the twentieth century with the same internalized lesson: their countries were "behind" the West in every aspect and something radical had to be done to change this status quo. That motivation is what gave rise to revisionist governments across the board within the first 30 years of the century. However, the reactionary ideologies of these revisionist governments were themselves very much products of modernity. At the very least, they exhibited the same faith in the power of the "modern" state, a perfectly rational response after the Second Industrial Revolution. Each regime also exhibited an almost feverish commitment to do whatever was necessary, including the sacrifice of millions of lives, to catch up with "the West."

Given the violent lengths these countries went to in the twentieth century to gain equal standing with the West, it really is remarkable that their post-defeat strategies turned out to be so peaceful, at least in terms of foreign policy. Despite appearances, however, the people of these states never stopped seeking status in the international system. There are as many ways of bettering one's status in the international system as there are in domestic societies. It should be evident from the discussion in this chapter that power relations in the modern international system have never been purely about military capability – what they are really about is the subject of the next chapter.

situation of nationalist movements justifying their own *raisons d'être* by historical accounts based in the work of European historians came about. Specific examples of this phenomenon will be discussed in the case-study chapters.

2 | *States as outsiders*

Much could be gained from a better understanding of the dynamics of established-outsider figurations and thus of the problems involved in the changing position of groups in relation to each other, of the rise of groups into the position of monopolistic establishment from which others are excluded, and the decline and fall from such a position to another where they themselves are, in some respects, outsiders.

Norbert Elias, *Established and Outsiders*

Introduction

In this chapter, I advance the argument that social relations between the states throughout the history of the modern international system have often resembled the "established-outsider" figuration outlined by Elias in his seminal work with the same title. I also demonstrate that negative assessments of states in the international system have never been value-neutral objective descriptions of reality, but are best thought of as "stigma" labels in the sociological sense. This, in turn, implies that the integration of the historically outsider states into the modern international system cannot be explained without the larger normative context of international stigmatization.

Stigmatized states are very much driven by that condition. At times when there is the opportunity to give new direction to state policy, such as the immediate aftermath of major defeat, the limited array of social strategies dealing with stigmatization are dominantly featured options in the domestic debates. The specific form those strategies take and which one ultimately gets picked is contingent on the features of the socio-normative hierarchy at a given time, but we may generally predict that strategies which satisfy the social-status cravings of historically stigmatized states will be both immediately preferred and easier to sustain in the long run.

The established-outsider dynamic
in the international system

There are several significant features of an "established-outsider" power dynamic, each presenting a challenge to the established wisdom about power relations in the international system.

First of all, as Elias observed and described it, the "established and outsiders" dynamic is the most generic form of a societal hierarchy, one which, contrary to the predictions of materialist theories,[1] may emerge even in situations where there is great overlap between economic, physical, and even socio-cultural attributes between actors. In Elias's Winston Parva study, for instance, there were "no differences in nationality, in ethnic descent, in 'colour' or 'race' between residents of the two areas; nor did they differ in their type of occupation, their income and educational levels – in a word, in their social class."[2] Nevertheless, there was a marked difference between the social power of the two groups: "one part thought of themselves as vastly superior to those of the Other," and as a corollary, this in-group was able to both monopolize privileges and at the same time make those who were excluded feel that they were socially inferior.

The cause of the power differential is the second salient feature of the established-outsider dynamic. A higher degree of cohesion and organization among some of the members of society is all that is needed for power differentials to emerge. In Winston Parva, "one group was formed by old residents established in the neighbourhood for two or three generations and the other was a group of newcomers."[3] Elias observed that cohesion in the old village was the

---

[1] For instance, according to Waltz, because international competition puts the units' survival at risk, it follows that units cannot afford differentiation – the anarchic structure generates "like units." Waltz does not even consider the possibility that a hierarchy may exist in such a situation; for him, the only way such a system can become hierarchical is through the creation of a formal authority structure, i.e. a world government. *Theory of International Politics*, pp. 89–93. A similar materialist blind spot plagues the otherwise compelling accounts provided by World-System theory. For Wallerstein, the dominance of the European core is entirely reducible to economic dynamics and has nothing to do with cultural or political coherence. See Zolberg, "Review," 260, and Skocpol, "Review," 1085.

[2] Elias and Scotson, *Established and Outsiders*, p. xvii.

[3] *Ibid.*

principal cause of demarcation: "one could see here the limitations of any theory which explains power differentials only in terms of a monopolistic possession of non-human objects, such as weapons or means of production, and disregards figurational aspects of power differentials due purely to differences in the degree of organization of the human beings concerned."[4] In the Winston Parva study, the group of old residents had established among themselves "a common mode of living and a set of norms,"[5] which led them to perceive the newcomers "as failing to observe these norms and restraints,"[6] and as a result, anomic.[7] Furthermore, as noted above, the "newcomers" in general agreed with these assessments and felt humiliated by their association with the "bad" neighborhood. This particular observation of Elias should also raise questions about the early constructivist optimism[8] about the benevolent effect of normative pressures in the international system.

The fact that the dominant group is able to produce feelings of *shame* among the members of the other group is the third notable feature of an "established-outsider" dynamic: the two groups share a common value system, and as such are best thought of as a society. After all, shame does not exist where there are no social bonds[9] – it is as direct evidence of membership in a society as one could find. As Cooley noted, "the thing that moves us to *pride or shame* is not the mere mechanical reflection of ourselves, but an imputed sentiment, the imagined effect of this reflection upon another's mind."[10] Goffman also points out that embarrassment is a sign of abidance by socially prescribed behavior, not a deviance from it.[11] Individuals who are not members of the same society and who do not share the same normative outlook cannot accurately conceive how they will be viewed by the other side.

In his study of stigma, Goffman remarks in passing that there is only one way for a stigmatized individual to escape untouched by

---

[4] *Ibid.*, p. xviii.   [5] *Ibid.*, p. xxii.   [6] *Ibid.*, p. xxiv.
[7] Emile Durkheim described anomie as a state of relative normlessness. See Durkheim, *Suicide.*
[8] E.g. Sikkink, "Transnational Politics," 520.
[9] For an overview of the concept of shame in social theory, see Scheff, "Shame and the Social Bond."
[10] Cooley, *Human Nature*, p. 184
[11] Goffman, *Interaction Ritual*, p. 111.

his social failure: oblivion. Only a person "insulated by his alienation, protected by identity beliefs of his own, [may] feel that he is
a full-fledged normal human being, and that we are the ones who
are not quite human."[12] In effect, only a person who is not part of a
society, and who therefore is aloof from its norms, can fully escape
the shame that comes from being stigmatized as an inferior. For
one to feel inferiority before another, one must have first accepted
and internalized the normative standards that the other is using for
evaluation.

Imagine my grandmother on a tourist trip to Kaokoland in north-
ern Namibia, the territory of the Himba tribe. The Himba have so
far remained insulated from norms that dictate nudity to be sinful,
shameful, or "uncivilized," and the Himba women go about their
daily business topless. My grandmother, having lived her whole life at
the intersection of Western and Muslim cultural norms, is a believer
in the benefits of modernity, an advocate for modesty in dress, and
has little to no awareness of the multiculturalist tolerance trends
of the last decades. My grandmother would strongly disapprove of
the Himba dress code. She would most likely want to convey her
disapproval to the local women, in a misguided attempt to educate
them. However, even if she got over the language barrier somehow,
my grandmother's comments would fall on deaf ears; she could no
more *shame* the Himba women into covering up than they could convince her to shed her blouse. My grandmother's views are irrelevant to
the Himba women, as much as their views are irrelevant to her – they
are not members of the same society, and neither party has to make
any effort to see the world as the other sees it.

In the previous chapter, I argued that prior to the "long nineteenth
century,"[13] autonomous states "outside" Europe had a relationship
with European states that was not unlike the relationship between
my grandmother and the Himba women, with each side being vaguely
aware of each other's existence, but not shamed by the comparison.
Whatever interaction existed would surely (and did) lead to judgment
on each side, but would not have produced shame or pressures to

---

[12] Goffman, *Stigma*, p. 6.
[13] 1789–1917, namely the period in which the modernist ontology discussed
in the previous chapter became hegemonic. See Hobsbawn, *The Age of
Revolution*; *The Age of Capital*; *The Age of Empire*.

assimilate. Interaction between independent states before modernity stopped short of convergence on the same normative standards.[14] There was borrowing, but the act of borrowing was limited to the product borrowed. For instance, impaling prisoners was introduced to the Ottoman repertoire after interactions with Prince Voyvoda Vlad III of Romania (also known as Dracula) in the fifteenth century – but borrowing this technique convinced the Ottomans no more of the superiority of a Christian worldview than borrowing the phalanx formation had convinced the Spartans to worship Persian gods. Cemil Aydın notes that, as late as the eighteenth century, "Ottoman scholars accepted some of the new mathematical and astronomical theories they learned from European books without feeling any need to advocate wholesale importation of the new science."[15] It was not until the articulation of the idea of a modern worldview that the social barriers between states, which had successfully insulated them from the judgments of others, came down. The secular, universal, totalizing claims of modernity gradually washed over alternative visions of socio-political order.[16]

Previously, the surviving agrarian empires of pre-modernity were outside the Westphalian states system, and their insular identity and belief systems shielded them from being stigmatized by Europeans, just as France, for instance, was spared the same fate in its interaction with a more powerful Ottoman Empire in the fifteenth century. Afterwards, they became the first "outsiders" of the Westphalian states system. In other words, these states came to agree with the "established" members of the Westphalian system that they were inferior[17] by internalizing the stigma of this developmental lag. In other words, the "Rise of the West" had the effect of creating an

---

[14] "It was never the case, before Europe unified the globe, that relations between states or rulers that were members of different regional international systems could be conducted on the same moral and legal basis as relations within the system, for this basis was provided in part by principles that *were culturally particular and exclusive.*" Bull and Watson, *Expansion of International Society*, p. 5 (emphasis mine). See also Bull, *Anarchical Society*, p. 14; Naff, "Ottoman Empire," p. 144.

[15] Aydın, *Anti-Westernism in Asia*, p. 17.

[16] As Kingsbury notes, through this process, "Non-European forms of political organization that might have attained widespread legitimacy as alternatives to the European-style sovereign state were subordinated and delegitimized as global models." See "Sovereignty and Inequality," p. 74.

[17] Elias and Scotson, *Established and Outsiders*, pp. xv–xvi.

international society of states where there was none before, yet the evidence for that society is not in participation by non-European actors in international conferences or treaties,[18] but rather in the transformation of the self-images of these actors. The standard English School reading of the expansion of the European society of states glosses over these social dynamics. For instance, Bull states that "while non-European communities in some cases were incorporated in the international system against their will, they have taken their places in international society because they themselves have sought the rights of membership of it and the protection of its rules."[19] While that willingness on the part of the non-European actors is certainly part of the story, what traditional accounts miss is the effect the internalization of a foreign worldview would have on the ontological security[20] of these states. As discussed previously, ontological security first and foremost entails having a consistent sense of self and having that sense affirmed by others. As I will discuss below, the incorporation of the modern worldview created a rupture in the traditionally self-centered worldviews of agrarian empires and forced them to rearticulate their new state identities[21] around the anxiety of "demonstrable" inferiority and the goal of catching up with the West by following its "standards."

In this manner, after the nineteenth century the interactions between non-European states and the Westphalian core came to resemble the established-outsider figuration described by Elias.[22] In other words, from this point onward, the actions of the non-European states which were part of the modern states system are best understood as actions of outsider states dealing with the *stigma* of being developmentally behind.

---

[18] Bull, "Emergence of a Universal International Society," p. 121.
[19] *Ibid.*
[20] See Laing, *Divided Self*, pp. 39–40, and Giddens, *Consequences of Modernity*, p. 92. For a defense of the applicability of this concept to state behavior, see Steele, *Ontological Security*, Introduction, and Mitzen, "Ontological Security," 352–4.
[21] The rearticulation of which was also demanded by the onset of the age of nationalism.
[22] Elias and Scotson, *Established and Outsiders*, pp. xv–xvi.

Stigma in the international system

As Goffman points out, each society has its means of categorizing its members, "and the complement of attributes felt to be ordinary and natural for ... each of these categories."[23] These attributes create anticipations about how various parties are supposed to act; they are, in effect, transformed into "normative expectations."[24] If evidence is presented that the actor in question possesses an attribute (or a number of attributes) which makes him different than what he is expected to be, that agent is "reduced in our minds from a whole and usual person to a tainted, discounted one."[25] An attribute that sets the agent apart in this manner is a stigma. The agents who do not possess a stigma are normals. Bauman adds that "the institution of stigma is eminently fit for the task of immobilizing the stranger in his identity of the excluded Other."[26] I contend that states which fall short of the normative ideals of international society at any given time can be (and have been) stigmatized – in other words, tainted and discounted, both in the minds of others and their own – in the same manner.

Let me anticipate a possible objection here to using the concept of stigmatization to describe relations between states: it may be contended that pointing out negative attributes is a form of truth telling, merely a description of objective reality. This argument may be made in two ways.

First, it may be argued that identity attributes of the states – i.e. the best candidates to qualify as stigma-like labels in international relations – are irrelevant to foreign policy decisions because such decisions are made by states, which are rational actors. For example, in the realist account[27] of international relations, states deduce threat from material capabilities. Such assessments are supposed to be extrapolated from objective measures of empirical facts, such as size of the army, military equipment, natural resources, and wealth.

---

[23] Goffman, *Stigma*, p. 2.   [24] *Ibid.*   [25] *Ibid.*
[26] Baumann, *Modernity and Ambivalence*, p. 68.
[27] The realist literature which shares these basic materialist assumptions is too broad to cite here, but for an overview of the assumptions of the paradigm, see Waltz, *Theory of International Politics*, pp. 74–7; Doyle, *Ways of War and Peace*, Part I; Wendt, *Social Theory*, pp. 96–113, or Keohane, *Neorealism and Its Critics*.

Constructivists argue, however, that seemingly objective assessments of military capabilities are always filtered through an ideational prism.[28] Even great power status is in part socially conferred.[29] For instance, Levy counts the following among the operational indicators of a great power: "possession of a high level of power capabilities ...; *participation in international congresses ...; de facto identification as a Great Power by an international conference or organization; admission to a formal or informal organization of Powers; participation in Great Power guarantees, territorial compensation or partitions; and generally, treatment as a relative equal by other Great Powers.*"[30] All of the italicized operational indicators have something to do with commonly held perceptions of the international community, which is subject to change over time. As Hobson and Sharman point out, "states are not universally imbued with a pre-ordained knowledge of what makes a state a great power."[31] Talleyrand managed to reinstate France as a great power, despite Napoleon's defeat, by arguing that it now had the right kind of government, i.e. monarchy.[32] Austria in 1815 and Britain in 1945 were recognized as great powers because of their democratic experience and cultural status, despite the fact that they lacked raw power.[33] Is it really plausible that it does not matter whether a state is treated thusly or whether it receives the "Sick Man of Europe" attitude the Ottoman Empire got in the nineteenth century (or the diplomatic shunning of the Bolshevik government after the revolution, for that matter)? Social standards masquerading as objective assessments create and perpetuate power hierarchies, and this is why the stigmatization framework is particularly apt for describing relations in the modern international system. Even today, in assessing threat, it matters whether nuclear weapons are held by Israel or Iran, India, or Pakistan.

This brings me to the second objection to thinking about assessments of states as stigma labels. This is the claim, which is closer

[28] See, for instance, Wendt, *Social Theory*, pp. 130–8.
[29] Suzuki, "Seeking 'Legitimate'," 3. Waltz also implicitly concedes this point when he suggests that we can rely on "common sense" to identify the great powers of an era. *Theory of International Politics*, p. 131.
[30] Levy, "Historical Trends," 279.
[31] Hobson and Sharman, "Enduring Place," 87.
[32] Reus-Smit, *Moral Purpose*, pp. 136–7.
[33] Simpson, *Great Powers*, p. 107.

to the liberal school of thought in IR,[34] that even identity-based descriptions are based on objective assessments and, therefore, are not stigmas. In other words, Israel, even with nuclear weapons, is not a threat because it is an objectively democratic, economically developed, rationally managed country, and therefore can be trusted with the responsibility of managing nuclear weapons. The problem with that argument is that even if we were to concede for the sake of argument that labels such as "democratic" or "economically developed" could be objectively affixed to a country's description – which is doubtful at best – whether or not various attributes have a real existence has very little to do with the question of whether they are stigmas or status symbols. By pointing out the stigma-like properties of state assessments, my intention is not to claim that such descriptions are entirely constructed and have no resemblance to "reality." In fact, studies of stigma emphasize just the opposite: the existence of a stigmatizing attribute is often very much observable and rather indisputable.[35] However, a blind person is not blind because of his stigma; but neither is his blindness the cause of his stigma. It is the expectations of the society he lives in that define how such an attribute will be received. Stigmatizing attributes can run the gamut from very "real" physical "abnormalities" to the more obviously socially constructed aspects of identity such as religious affiliation or ethnicity. That the latter kind of attribute is more evidently a product of our collective imaginings than of physically verifiable difference makes it no more or less stigmatizing. Socially constructed attributes of an actor "feel" as "real" as their material counterparts,[36] and both types of attributes have no inherent value in and of themselves – whether they are perceived as normal or discrediting depends on larger social frameworks of value.

In Winston Parva, the newcomers were stigmatized despite the fact that both the newcomers and the members of the old establishment were fellow nationals, members of the same society. As discussed above, members of the old establishment were able to exclude and stigmatize "outsiders" because they had a higher degree of cohesion

---

[34] See e.g. Slaughter, "International Law."
[35] Bauman, *Modernity and Ambivalence*, p. 67.
[36] Even the empiricist Hume recognized this fact. See *A Treatise of Human Nature*, Part II, Section 1.

and organization. Stigmatization not only made the "outsiders" feel inferior, but also cut off their access to certain political, economic, and social privileges in the town. This point bears repeating: far from corresponding to some kind of inherent, objective cause of relative inferiority, stigma labels often are themselves enough to generate inferior conditions, which are then mistaken as a cause.[37]

The same dynamic has plagued the modern international system since its inception. The rise of the West created an objectively mea-surable power differential, but perhaps more significant[38] was the fact that the states in the Westphalian core of the system had cohesion as a group[39] whereas late-joiners to the international society did not. Furthermore, unlike in Winston Parva where the inhabitants were fellow nationals, initially no common culture existed between the late-joiners and the Westphalian core, which made stigmatization easier, if not more likely. Despite the fact that non-Western peoples had their own traditions and cultures, Europeans perceived them as "anomic": at best, they were described as "semi-civilized," but many were labeled as savages or as barbaric. The perception of anomie is the flipside of stigma, and vice versa. All undesirable characteristics of statehood and humanity were projected on the outsider states, just as was the case in Winston Parva, and as a result of their stigmatization, these states also came to see themselves as tainted by such character-istics. This dynamic in turn reinforced the power differential which had emerged as a consequence of the rise of the West, as described in Chapter 1.

The causal processes I have been hinting at until this point are structurally generated and not driven by any one particular actor. For a stigmatizing "established-outsider" dynamic to emerge in a social system, there does not have to be a deliberate master plan of oppression formulated with an eye on the monopolization of resources (although sometimes there are those as well). In fact, simple un-reflectiveness is often sufficient, and even if a politically correct awareness about

---

[37] Goffman, *Stigma*, p. 6; Elias and Scotson, *Established and Outsiders*, p. xxvi.
[38] It is telling that the nineteenth-century Standard of Civilization had no explicit references to measurements of material strength.
[39] This is essentially what is meant when it is argued in the English School literature that the European society of states was a *Gemeinschaft* society. See e.g. Buzan, "From International System," 333.

stigma labels were to emerge among some members of the in-group, the dynamics would persist as long as power relations remained constant. This is because social exclusion is a nearly inevitable side effect of one's own quest for autonomy and meaning.[40] What is unique about the modern international system is the fact that these dynamics have been elevated to the global level and that social hierarchies are now universal.

In social hierarchies, the resources being monopolized are not really the ends themselves; often the resources are more meaningful as evidence of one's worth – just desserts, special identity, autonomy, and independence. What I have in mind here is Hegel's discussion of the master–slave relationship.[41] As Hegel pointed out, the self's inability to secure certainty of its independent existence through satisfaction of material desires[42] leads it to a struggle for recognition.[43] Satisfying material desires is insufficient evidence of one's autonomy because "consumption does not so much master objects as destroy them."[44] By consuming an object, we show that we are more powerful than the object, though we do get a brief confirmation of our independent existence. But as soon as the moment of consumption is over, we need to consume more, which reminds us of our own corporeality. Therefore, material objects are not enough to give the conscious self the validation it seeks: "If an external object is to provide more than fleeting self-certainty, it must somehow both be negated in its independence and yet continue to exist ... And the only sort of thing which can 'abdicat[e]' its own claims to independence in this way is ... another self-consciousness."[45] In seeking recognition, we want more than to exist as a physical being: we want our value, our awareness of ourselves, and to be affirmed by another.

In other words, the search for recognition is an extension of our desire for "positive freedom" (or vice versa).[46] As Berlin explained it, "the 'positive' sense of the word 'liberty' derives from the wish on the part of the individual to be his own master."[47] This is separate from the notion of "negative freedom," which entails simply the freedom

---

[40] See also Mitchell, *Colonising Egypt*, p. 167.
[41] Hegel, *Phenomenology of the Spirit*.
[42] *Ibid.*, pp. 104–10.   [43] *Ibid.*
[44] Markell, *Bound by Recognition*, p. 104.   [45] *Ibid.*
[46] See also Wendt, "Why a World State is Inevitable," 511.
[47] Berlin, "Two Concepts of Liberty," p. 131.

from interference by others.[48] Positive freedom requires not only that one is free from interference but also that one is a "somebody," a "doer,"[49] someone who can impose his will on the world, and who is sovereign in all senses of the word. The difference between negative and positive understandings of freedom matters more than it appears at first glance, and I will return to this distinction below.

Because each actor's goal is to confirm his own sovereignty (or to achieve positive freedom for himself), the quest for recognition is mutually exclusive. Thus the quest for recognition takes the form of a "life-and-death struggle,"[50] which either ends with one party dead or when one party surrenders. The defeated party confirms the sovereignty of the victor by recognizing him as the master; he becomes the slave.

Hegel argued that the master–slave relationship is ultimately unstable because the master is recognized by someone who is not quite an agent himself: "What now really confronts him is not an independent consciousness, but a dependent one. He is, therefore, not certain of being-for-self as the truth of himself."[51] Such recognition is unfulfilling because it comes from someone who is not recognized as an equal or quite as human.[52] Patchen Markell points out that the problem for Hegel lies in the *asymmetry* of the recognition relationship,[53] an argument used by recent Hegelian scholarship to recast Hegel both as a champion of the norm of equal recognition in societies and as a forecaster of a future where such an equilibrium will be attained among diverse groups.[54] According to Markell, however, Hegel had a much more radical point than calling for equal recognition:

[Hegel] suggests that the very desire that animates the struggle for recognition is impossible to fulfill, that the "good" to which it is devoted is not really what we ought to be after; consequently, the asymmetry and thus the inadequacy of the relation of master and slave lies in the fact that only

---

[48] The notion of "negative freedom" has a corollary in the discussions of "thin recognition." See Wendt, "Why a World State Is Inevitable," 511.

[49] Berlin, "Two Concepts of Liberty," pp. 131–2.

[50] Hegel, *Phenomenology of the Spirit*, p. 114; see also Kojève, *Introduction*, pp. 7–15.

[51] Hegel, *Phenomenology of the Spirit*, p. 117.

[52] See also Kojève, *Introduction*, p. 19.

[53] Markell, *Bound by Recognition*, p. 106.

[54] *Ibid.*, p. 92.

one of the two parties has acknowledged this, admitted the impossibility of satisfying its own claims, and conceded its own dependence.[55]

Markell argues that despite the inherent instability of the master–slave relationship, such dynamics can persist for a very long time (or indefinitely) because while we can never fully achieve the kind of recognition we essentially seek, the master status in the master–slave dynamic creates a very viable approximation of the self-as-it-would-be-if-it-really-were-positively-free image one desires:

The master–slave relation thus accommodates the contradiction between dependence and independence by spreading it out over social space, making one person bear the disproportionate weight of the fact of human dependence on the material world ... These roles give substance to the social identities of "master" and "slave" and lend relative stability to the intersubjective world, making it possible for the master to experience his own status – like the slave's – as a reflection of who he always already is, rather than as the political (and therefore fragile) effect of an ongoing practice of subordination.[56]

In other words, in social figurations where one is recognized as less than the other, the ongoing interaction continuously creates and recreates the identities of the parties involved, which are then perceived as reflecting inherent, innate, and fixed characteristics. The slave becomes a natural slave;[57] the master is the master because he deserves to be. More importantly, *both* parties recognize these roles as such.[58]

The same dynamic is observed by Elias in the Winston Parva study: "Just as established groups, as a matter of course, regard their superior power as a sign of their higher human value, so outsider groups, as long as the power differential is great and submission inescapable, emotionally experience their power inferiority as a sign of human inferiority."[59] Obviously, this is a more satisfying dynamic for the established group – i.e. "the master" – than it is for the outsiders,

---

[55] *Ibid.*, p. 108.   [56] *Ibid.*, p. 112.

[57] Even a thinker as astute as Aristotle was fooled by this dynamic. Aristotle, *Politics*, Book I.

[58] Kojève, *Introduction*, p. 18.

[59] Elias and Scotson, *Established and Outsiders*, p. xxvi.

because through this exclusion the members of the established group get an approximation of fully realized self-sovereignty, of positive liberty, in the form of the superior group image. To be fully sovereign as a human being, as a consciousness, is to be the master of one's destiny – it requires the ability to make and impose one's own rules on the world, to stand up against and defeat the vagaries of nature and one's own appetite.[60] From Plato[61] to Rousseau,[62] positive freedom, as fully realized agency, has been associated with rationality for this reason. As Plato recognized early on, it is very difficult to realize this ideal of positive freedom[63].

However, once a relationship dynamic is created, one can feel as if one has achieved it (or gone a long way in achieving it) in *comparison*:[64] "By refusing to risk his life in a fight for pure prestige, [the Slave] does not rise above the animals. Hence he considers himself as such, and as such is he considered by the Master ... While the Slave still remains an 'immediate,' natural, 'bestial' being, the Master – as a result of his fight – is already human, 'mediated.'"[65] Yet, at the end of the day, being a master in the master–slave dynamic does not guarantee sovereignty over things or oneself. Humanity is not attained fully; the master in this dynamic still struggles to control his animalistic side. One cannot become positively free in the truest sense by asymmetric recognition alone; such recognition does not mediate against one's inner desires, nor does it fully solve one's relation to external nature (although it does mediate against it in the form of the slave's servitude, expressed through natural work). So the master recognizes something is missing from his dominant position – in Kojève's words, he is at an "existential impasse."[66] Unfortunately, there is not much the master can do to transcend this impasse.

It is easier to distinguish oneself from the slave than it is to truly overcome one's own animalistic side, easier to project all bestial qualities onto the slave than it is to eradicate them from one's own

[60] Berlin, "Two Concepts of Liberty," p. 132.
[61] See e.g. Plato, *The Republic*, Book IX.
[62] See e.g. Rousseau, *Social Contract*, Book I.
[63] Plato, *The Republic*, Book IV–VII (and he did not believe such mastery against external nature was possible).
[64] Plato is not immune to such trappings either. Plato, *The Republic*, Book IX.
[65] Kojève, *Introduction*, p. 18.
[66] *Ibid.*, p. 19.

consciousness or to bring them under the control of one's reason. Notice Elias's observation that the outsiders are characterized as anomic, untrustworthy, undisciplined, lawless, dirty,[67] and having loose morals.[68] In other words, outsiders are perceived as being dominated by the animalistic side of human nature – they are supposed to be the ones who are ruled by appetite instead of reason, i.e. they are the ones who are not masters of their own destiny. In comparison, the existential impasse of the established, of the masters, becomes tolerable. By projecting all (or most) undesirable attributes as stigma properties onto the excluded outsider, the established group[69] can create an image of relative sovereignty and simulate possessing a fuller, superior humanity.[70]

Why the emergence of the modern state projected stigmatization onto the international system

The importance of the group dynamic in Elias's analysis should not be underestimated. In the Hegelian abstract construct, one self-consciousness meets another – the dynamic is set between two individuals.[71] However, it is telling that the master–slave figuration is most frequently employed in the analysis of communal relations, e.g. group rights. The master–slave relation usually takes group form because group cohesion allows for ordinary individuals to simulate sovereignty without actually risking their lives. Average, or even weak, individuals get to enjoy recognition as "masters" by sharing in the group's charisma.

---

[67] Elias and Scotson, *Established and Outsiders*, p. 124.
[68] *Ibid.*, p. 125.
[69] Or "the normals" of Goffman.
[70] This is essentially the point Mitchell is making in his discussion of colonialism:

> As with the example of the colonial city, by establishing a boundary that rigorously excludes the Oriental, the other, from the self, such a self acquires its apparent cleanliness, its purity, its uncorrupted and undivided identity. Identity now appears no longer self-divided, no longer contingent, no longer something arranged out of differences; it appears instead as something self-formed, and original. (*Colonising Egypt*, p. 167)

[71] Hegel, *Phenomenology of the Spirit*, pp. 104–10. However, it is worth noting that Hegel did not intend his analysis to be reductive to the individual unit.

Berlin also observed that the quest for positive freedom, for self-sovereignty, tended to become associated with group efforts: "Presently, the two selves [i.e. the rational and the animalistic] may be represented by something wider than the individual ... as a social 'whole' of which the individual is an element or aspect: a tribe, a race, a church, a state, the great society of the living and the dead and the yet unborn."[72] Although Berlin does not point directly to this link, I think a strong case could be made that this fact (or at least its dominance) is a side effect of modernity.[73] On balance, modernity has helped humanity along in its struggle for negative liberty, but has made it much more difficult for individuals to attain positive liberty. There may very well be a trade-off involved between the two understandings of freedom.[74]

The modern view sees the state as Hobbes's Leviathan, "the mortal god"[75] with no stake in social conflicts, or as the very embodiment of rationality or pure objectivity in Hegelian terms. While it is appealing to think of the modern state as a site of reconciliation, to do so is "to treat the state like a deus ex machina that appears from outside the social, which – by virtue of its sovereign elevation above the conflicts of social life – can serve as a mediating institution."[76] Markell suggests instead that it is more realistic to think of the state "as one of the central objects of identification onto which persons displace, and through which they pursue, the desire for independent and masterful agency."[77] Furthermore, by designating social issues as "nonpolitical," political emancipation "disguises their status as forms of power and makes them more difficult to address politically."[78] The modern state promises political emancipation through the equal recognition of citizenship for all, but such recognition entails the

---

[72] Berlin, "Two Concepts of Liberty," p. 132.

[73] Berlin indirectly recognizes this in the introduction to the essay: "there has, perhaps, been no time in modern history when so large a number of human beings, both in the East and West, have had their notions, and indeed their lives, so deeply altered, and in some cases violently upset, by fanatically held social and political doctrines." Berlin, "Two Concepts of Liberty," pp. 118–19.

[74] See also Bauman, *Modernity and Ambivalence*, p. 69.

[75] Hobbes, *Leviathan*, Introduction.

[76] Markell, *Bound by Recognition*, p. 125.

[77] *Ibid.*   [78] *Ibid.*, p. 128.

danger of entrenching existing social inequalities. Something similar is at work internationally – the notion of sovereign equality makes it very difficult to speak of social hierarchies in the international system as power relations, let alone combat them. Such depoliticization is not accidental, at either the domestic or the international level: it legitimates the hold on power certain groups have, and allows them to simulate self-sovereignty by comparison to others in what is supposed to be a framework of equal recognition.

There is another way that equal recognition undermines the quest for positive freedom. The modern man living under the rational Westphalian state is also the faceless, atomized individual, the calculator, and the rational consumer.[79] While he gets equal recognition from the state as accorded to the fellow members in his society, he gets that recognition not for his essence or even his accomplishments, but rather because he is a part of a large group – the nation or "the people." It is the nation as the general will that justifies the existence of the modern state.[80] Within the nation, the "individual" is one of many, a generic citizen; the distinctions between the "individual" and others are completely leveled and discarded as irrelevant (at least in theory).[81] Bauman calls this the state administered universal identity: "individuals have their self manipulated in order to erase differences between individuals, according to a planned, managed and rational set of state actions … The notion of the 'social' makes governmental interventions into the area of the personal appear both natural and rational."[82] In this manner, the "individual" is created by the modern nation state and therefore is perpetually bound to the state in his quest for recognition.[83]

---

[79] Edmund Burke recognized and bemoaned this fact even before Marx: "the age of chivalry is gone. That of sophisters, economists, and calculators has succeeded; and the glory of Europe is extinguished forever … All the pleasing illusions which made power gentle and obedience liberal … are to be dissolved by this new conquering empire of light and reason." From *Reflections on the Revolution in France* (1790).

[80] "Each of us places his person and all his power in common under the supreme direction of the general will … This public person … at present takes the name *republic* or *body politic*, which is called *state* by its members." Rousseau, *Social Contract*, Book I, chapter 6.

[81] "… as one we receive each member as an indivisible part of the whole." *Ibid.*

[82] Best, "Review," 312.

[83] Bauman, *Modernity and Ambivalence*, p. 64: "National states promote 'nativism' and construe its subjects as 'natives'. They laud and enforce the

There is also the fact that the road to equal recognition by the state and political emancipation ran through the modern realization that human nature is often and inevitably dominated by base instincts. Hobbes, who, in many ways, was the first thinker to explicitly reduce humanity to the desire to survive, was also perhaps the first to advocate a state that stood equidistant to citizens.[84] In other words, the notion of equality requires, in some ways, the reduction of the society to its lowest common denominator. Whereas positive freedom and self-sovereignty requires overcoming one's baser side, negative freedom, through equal recognition and protection, requires acknowledging it. As a result, while the emergence of nationalism and the nation state equalized the distribution of recognition within sovereign borders to a degree not seen before in history, these developments simultaneously brought about the loss of other types of "recognition" which were more conducive to achieving positive freedom.

This is why the very changes welcomed by Hegel as the march of reason were bemoaned by other observers of modernity – from Burke[85] to Tönnies,[86] from Tocqueville[87] to Nietzsche[88] – who did not share Hegel's belief that the state could act as a substitute for, let alone improve upon, the individual quest for positive freedom.[89] It is incredibly difficult to find *deep* meaning in life or to be *positively* free as the generic man. Tocqueville, who among the authors mentioned above was the most observant and also the most tolerant of what was lost in the transition to the modern age of democracy, was very much aware

ethnic, religious, linguistic, cultural homogeneity. They are engaged in incessant propaganda of shared attitudes. They preach the sense of common mission, common fate, common destiny."

[84] Hobbes, *Leviathan*, chapter XVIII.

[85] "On this scheme of things, a king is but a man, a queen is but a woman; a woman is but an animal, and animal not of the highest order." Burke, *Reflections on the Revolution in France*, Paragraph 129.

[86] Tönnies, *Gemeinschaft and Gesellschaft*, pp. 34, 44, 87, 216.

[87] "... if the equality of conditions gives some resources to all the members of the community, it also prevents any of them from having resources of great extent, which necessarily circumscribes their desires within somewhat narrow limits. Thus, among democratic nations, ambition is ardent and continual, but its aim is not habitually lofty; and life is generally spent in eagerly coveting small objects that are within reach." Tocqueville, *Democracy in America*, vol. II.3, chapter 19.

[88] Nietzsche, *Genealogy of Morals*, First Essay.

[89] Of course, these commentators also disagreed among themselves as to what, if anything, could, or should, be done to combat these changes.

of this fact. He was willing to tolerate the loss of grand ambition, heroism, and genius because he believed this transformation was, on the one hand, unavoidable and, on the other, not without benefits: "if you hold it expedient to divert the moral and intellectual activity of man to the production of comfort and the promotion of general well-being; ... if your object is not to stimulate the virtues of heroism, but the habits of peace; ... if such be your desire, then equalize the conditions of men and establish democratic institutions."[90] In modern political thought, therefore, the exploration of the possibility of attaining positive, substantive freedom is either completely ignored or concluded to be within the purview of the state. Thinkers who are still hopeful about the individual attaining full sovereignty, such as Rousseau[91] and Hegel,[92] end up arguing that such an outcome is possible only through the state. This is no accident – the trade-off that accompanies equal recognition of the mass age is that modern man is much smaller and less powerful than the best of his predecessors.[93] Even Plato believed that how the city was run would have an effect[94] on the chances of an individual to attain a just soul,[95] and he believed this despite his attribution of such chances *mostly* to individual nature, as in the accident of birth. Modern thinkers, having conceded a man's equality with other men, were even more bound to see the state as the stage of positive freedom.

To put it another way, with the emergence of the "last man" of egalitarian modernity, the hope of attaining positive, substantive freedom has to either become a group endeavor or be abandoned.[96] This hope is placed either in the nation (the general will) as Rousseau saw it, or in

---

[90] Tocqueville, *Democracy in America*, vol. II.
[91] "... the acquisition in the civil state of moral liberty ... alone makes man truly the master of himself. For to be driven by appetite alone is slavery, and obedience to the law one has prescribed for oneself is liberty." Rousseau, *Social Contract*, Book I, chapter 8.
[92] "... self-consciousness, by virtue of its disposition, has its *substantial freedom* in the state as its essence, its end, and the product of activity." Hegel, *Philosophy of Right*, Section 3, §257.
[93] Nietzsche, who is not satisfied with the solution offered by the state, called for the "last man" to be replaced by the *Ubermensch*.
[94] Plato, *The Republic*, Book I.
[95] Plato's definition of a just soul is where reason rules over appetite with the help of the spirit. Plato, *The Republic*, Book V.
[96] Lebow makes a similar argument in *Cultural Theory* about the link between modernity, the emergence of the individual, and the search for self-esteem on the international plane. See e.g. pp. 17–25.

the modern state as Hegel saw it. Equal recognition, which guarantees
negative freedom for all citizens, is insufficient, thin recognition. The
original desire for recognition that sets consciousness on a life-and-
death struggle seeks an affirmation of the individual's sovereignty,
autonomy, and self-mastery. The desire for recognition is a craving
for positive freedom, and a society or state which guarantees only
negative freedom, a theoretical, abstract equality, does not quench
the desire for substantive mastery. In fact, abstract egalitarianism and
universalism make it very difficult, if not impossible, for individuals
to attain positive freedom by themselves without the state: whatever
they do, they cannot truly impose their will on the world – the state
has the legitimate monopoly on authoritative force.[97]

Hence, a modern state that is not explicitly directed toward the
attainment of positive freedom for its society will be unstable, because
the guarantee of negative equality is not enough – human beings want
more than that. They need meaning in their lives; they need a substantive purpose. A state that does not *promise* to fulfill that purpose
for its citizens is not a *modern* state, perhaps not a state at all: it is
neither "actual" nor "rational." This is why the modern state makes
"progress" its business.[98] To say that the state exists to serve its citizens is really to say that the state exists to help men satisfy their urges
for positive freedom: through education, resources, social engineer-
ing, etc.

However, as noted above, the state is not the objective, apolitical
deus ex machina it is imagined to be. Its quest for equal recognition
for all of its citizens often ends up privileging the self-image of
the majority. Markell explains this problem with reference to the
nineteenth-century emancipation of German Jews through their
inclusion as equal citizens:

On the one hand, Jewishness (otherness) must be eradicated, in this case
through a peaceful act of inclusion; on the other hand, in order for the
consequent recognition of the sovereignty of the state to be more than

---

[97] Weber, "Politics as a Vocation."
[98] Even John Stuart Mill, who was more skeptical of state power than most,
recognized that the modern state has something to do with this end – in his
view, the state can promote progress and civilization by staying out of its
citizens' affairs, and by keeping them out of each other's social life. See Mill,
On Liberty.

momentary and ephemeral, the institutions of the state must maintain a vigilant surveillance of the Jews to be sure that they are conforming to the terms of their emancipation – and such a surveillance requires that Jews be recognizable.[99]

Each state has its "others," the presence of which perpetuates the dynamic described by Markell above, which means that the project of sovereignty remains an ongoing affair. Yet the state has to be legitimated despite its continuous failure to deliver upon its promise to secure sovereignty. An interim solution to the problem of legitimation, therefore, is to move the simulation of mastery to the international domain. However, just as it is difficult for one individual to achieve real sovereignty, and much easier for him to create a relationship dynamic with another individual to have the image of sovereignty mirrored back to him, such is also the case for states and nations. Therefore, it is no coincidence that in the nineteenth century the master–slave hierarchy was increasingly projected outside state borders in Europe – the group struggle for recognition, for positive freedom, is the essence of the age of nationalism. It is easier (and more realistic) for states to recreate the "master–slave" figuration within the international system, and to be recognized as masters of their own destiny *relatively speaking* than being objectively so.

In fact, the idea of nationhood (or its more generic version, a society which has achieved statehood) is very readily collapsible onto the master–slave figuration, because the idea that some people deserve recognition, whereas others do not, is built into the concept.[100] As Bernard Yack points out:

If we raise people's status by making them formally equal members of a community, then we are bound to make them somewhat more uncomfortable than they used to be with the individuals who stand outside of that community ... A touchy *amour propre* toward foreigners seems an

---

[99] Markell, *Bound by Recognition*, p. 146. See also Bauman, *Modernity and Ambivalence*, where he points out that the closer German Jews came to assimilation, the more their Jewishness came into prominence.

[100] In fact, as Bauman argues, the nation state "is designed primarily to deal with the problem of strangers not enemies." *Modernity and Ambivalence*, p. 63. Similar notions are to be found also in Simmel, e.g. in "The Stranger."

inevitable accompaniment of the way in which nationalism satisfies " ... desire for status."[101]

Yack makes these remarks in his review of Liah Greenfeld's book *Nationalism: Five Roads to Modernity*, in which Greenfeld argues that while Anglo-American nationalism is compatible with liberalism because it respects individuality, ethnic nationalisms – starting with Germany and Russia – followed a dangerous path because they were marked with *ressentiment* against their more advanced neighbors to the West. Yack rejects Greenfeld's Anglo-American exceptionalism and argues that it is more fruitful to think of *ressentiment* as a feature of all nationalist formations, civil or ethnic.

Indeed, in making *ressentiment* a feature exclusively of only "backward," "ethnic" nationalisms, Greenfeld misreads Nietzsche. When Nietzsche wrote about *ressentiment* and "slave morality," he had in mind exactly the kind of societies that Greenfeld praises, i.e. liberal, egalitarian, and individualistic. Egalitarianism for Nietzsche is born out of *ressentiment*. The democratic man, "the last man," is the product of *ressentiment*. Modernity is dominated by slave morality. The "slave" in Nietzsche's argument is unable to achieve greatness on his own, and he resents those who can. He is not free in the positive sense, so he rejects positive freedom:

While all noble morality grows out of a triumphant affirmation of one's own self, slave morality from the start says "No" to what is "outside," "other," to "a not itself." And this "No" is its creative act. This transformation of the glance which confers value – this necessary projection towards what is outer instead of back onto itself – that is inherent in *ressentiment*. In order to arise, slave morality always requires first an opposing world, a world outside itself.[102]

In other words, the very act of creating an "Other" against which one defines oneself implies *ressentiment*. It is not only those at the losing end of comparison who are in thrall to this state, but anyone who is deriving self-knowledge from the comparative act. The positively free man does not need the negative category of the "Other" to know himself.[103]

---

[101] Yack, "Review," 178.
[102] Nietzsche, *Genealogy of Morals*, First Essay.
[103] In other words, the "master" in the Hegelian dialectic and the "noble man" of Nietzsche are not the same person. Nietzsche's nobleman does not need the recognition of the "other" to achieve self-sovereignty.

The mediocre man, on the other hand, unable to achieve positive freedom, compensates for his lack of sovereignty by substituting his own "weak" morality for what is "good." The mediocre man feels "good" in his righteousness – his power comes from the fact that the world recognizes his normative framework, and not from any objective achievement of positive freedom. This new morality, according to Nietzsche, allows for the mediocre man to feel superior without being truly superior. Bauman quotes Sander Gilman who "wrote of the 'conservative curse' which hangs over the liberal project: 'The more you are like me, the more I know the true value of my power, which you wish to share, and the more I am aware that you are but a shoddy counterfeit, an outsider.'"[104] It is the relative superiority of "good" over "evil" which allows the mediocre man to get recognized *as if* he were "noble":

It's not a matter of fear. Rather it's the fact that we have nothing more to fear from man, that the maggot "man" is in the foreground swarming around, that the "tame man," the hopelessly mediocre and unpleasant man, has already learned to feel that he is the goal, the pinnacle, the meaning of history, "the higher man," – yes indeed, that he even has a certain right to feel that about himself, insofar as he feels separate from the excess of failed, sick, tired, spent people, who are nowadays beginning to make Europe stink, so that he feels at least relatively successful, at least still capable of life, of at least saying "Yes" to life.[105]

In other words, the normative standards of modernity allow for average members of modern societies to feel as if they are the pinnacles of history, as masters of their own destiny in comparison to those who do not live up to those standards.

By discussing Nietzsche in this manner, my goal is not to insinuate that the West suffers from a "slave morality" whereas the East is full of noble, great men who are being oppressed. Rather, I have invoked Nietzsche because of his observation that there is a dark side to the rhetoric of equal citizenship that pervades modern society. This is not to deny that there is an empowering aspect to the liberal values of equal recognition: "The message amounts to a standing invitation to all and

---

[104] Bauman, *Modernity and Ambivalence*, p. 71; Gilman, *Jewish Self-Hatred*, p. 2.
[105] Nietzsche, *Genealogy of Morals*, First Essay.

everybody to take their fate in their own hands and make it as good as they can."[106] However, too often we focus on this promise and ignore what happens in practice, which is the manifestation of an inner contradiction in liberalism/egalitarianism/thin recognition: "to deform the problem of 'de-estrangement' ... as the question of decency and industry of the stranger's effort at assimilation-through-acculturation, is to reaffirm the inferiority, undesirability and out-of-placeness of the stranger's form of life."[107] In other words, equal recognition within the modern state itself can be used to create a social hierarchy, by allowing mediocre members of society to feel a sense of smugness, a sense of superiority in comparison to the stigmatized foreigners outside and strangers nearby.[108] The privileges offered by the modern state end up serving a function beyond whatever substantive value they offer to the citizen; they become the foundation for another comparative rubric that enables the citizen to simulate mastery, *relatively* speaking. This is more so the case for the members of the titular nation (if there is one) which controls the state, because their affiliation with the state is the most direct and unproblematic. They easily derive ontological security benefits from the recognition of the state, domestically and internationally. Inter-societal routines help the members of society to maintain identity coherence vis-à-vis others.[109]

However, it is not only the members of the titular nation, the class which dominates the state or the "normals" in the domestic society, who derive identity affirmation from their state's international standing. In fact, often the state's simulated mastery of the world vis-à-vis other states and groups in international society is the only cushion of legitimacy it can offer the lowest members of its citizenry. The right of citizenship, beyond whatever degree of negative freedom it offers the individual, becomes a normative good in the service of satisfying the individual's craving for positive freedom, for the simulation of positive recognition, precisely because it is not offered to others. Such others (non-citizens) can then be seen as something less than human,

[106] Bauman, *Modernity and Ambivalence*, p. 69.
[107] Bauman, *Modernity and Ambivalence*, p. 71
[108] This is not to say that the entirety of the modern project of ordering and comparing is a sham masking *ressentiment*. However, it is also undeniable but a rather neglected aspect of modernity that the seemingly objective tool of scientific method has been used in this rather subjective manner.
[109] Mitzen, "Ontological Security," 352.

less than people, making one feel more sovereign in comparison, however lowly one's standing may be in domestic society.

To sum up thus far, modern statehood creates its own paradox. The universal citizenship and equal recognition the state offers all members of the nation promises negative freedom for all, but makes the attainment of positive freedom through individual effort increasingly difficult.[110] By guaranteeing that no citizen of the state will be legally recognized as superior to another citizen, it closes one ancient avenue[111] for the expression (or simulation) of positive freedom: mastery over one's environment, including members of one's society. By distributing formal recognition equally, the modern state in a way demands that if one is to rise, all are to rise with him, and if all cannot rise, neither can the individual. This makes sovereign recognition much more of a group issue than it was in the past. And in separating the "nation" from foreigners, and in positing that the members of the nation uniquely deserve recognition, the modern state offers a quick fix for a group that demands positive recognition as masters of their own destiny.[112]

The modern state is supposed to achieve positive freedom for all of its citizens. But the goal of positive freedom for all is incredibly difficult to attain in absolute terms, and in any case it is a goal with a long-term horizon. Simulating its attainment in relative terms is easier and immediately available, because the modern state already has an irrational discriminating mechanism against foreigners, who are, by definition, less deserving of recognition. In exercising this mechanism, the modern state actually embodies a principle that contradicts its rationality, but while doing so creates the impression that it is closer to achieving positive freedom, which is the very embodiment of rationality. In this way, the modern state, the very thing that made positive recognition primarily a group endeavor, *comes to be seen as* the embodiment of humanity, rationality, and sovereignty, of positive freedom, *precisely when it is not*.

---

[110] See e.g. Tocqueville, *Democracy in America*, vol. II.2, chapter 8.

[111] Other avenues remain: for instance, economic success or political engagement. Nevertheless, this is a loss, and the fact that it was a loss was observed by many nineteenth-century political thinkers, as was discussed above.

[112] This is not unlike Hegel's argument that conflict among states can unite subjectivity and objectivity. Hegel, "German Constitution," pp. 15–20.

However, while the citizen–foreigner distinction goes some way in satisfying demands for positive recognition, it is not enough by itself because the mastery can be simulated only if the "slave" is also a party to the recognition dynamic. In other words, a world where each party defines the other simply as a foreigner does not satisfy the group ideal for positive freedom. For such demands to be met at a satisfactory level, the foreigner also has to recognize himself as somehow less deserving of recognition, as something less than human.

This is achieved in an international context the same way as it was in Winston Parva: "One group can effectively stigmatize another only as long as it is well established in positions of power from which the stigmatized group is excluded. As long as that is the case, the stigma of collective disgrace attached to the outsiders can be made to stick."[113] At a certain level of abstraction, there is not much of a difference between the dynamics sustained by the "old village" in Winston Parva and those perpetuated by the European society of states in the international system in the nineteenth century. The developments ushering in modernity also gave birth to the concept of "civilization" or the "civilized world." In other words, the group dynamic necessary for the simulation of mastery was thus carried onto the international stage.

Established-outsider dynamic on the international stage

The established-outsider dynamic did not disappear when the nineteenth-century Standard of Civilization was abandoned in the twentieth century. In one form or another, it has persisted. However, it is worth noting that the trend, at least formally, is from exclusivity toward increasing inclusivity and pluralism.

This can be explained by reference to two factors. First, modernity is an ontology based in rationality, and as such there is an inherent pull toward an objective, universal language of modern norms.[114] In other words, normative criteria for the evaluation of actors come to be expressed in increasingly individualist, rationalist, merit-based terms.[115] This is true in both domestic and international society.

---

[113] Elias and Scotson, *Established and Outsiders*, p. xx.
[114] The World Polity school in sociology offers the most comprehensive studies of this trend.
[115] Once again, Hegel may be cited for support – but this is a trend noted by all observers of modernity.

However, sociologists have long observed that "the long run tendency for collectivist criteria of exclusion to be replaced by individualist criteria represents a modification of the legal and political foundation of exploitation rather than its elimination."[116] This relates directly to the second underlying cause of this trend.

As noted above, the more asymmetrical the recognition relationship, the less satisfying it is for the dominant group. If the "slave" is merely a "thing," the slave's recognition does not offer much to the "master." This is why it is sometimes argued that only relationships of equal recognition can be stable in the long run;[117] but another way to think about it is that the dominant groups have some incentive to grant recognition to inferior groups if they can, at the same time, maintain their position of power. I have pointed out above that formal recognition of equality has a tendency to create precisely that dynamic: equal citizenship or the principle of sovereign equality leaves entrenched social hierarchies in place while de-politicizing them. Therefore, it is not surprising that the normative trend internationally has been in the same direction as it was domestically: formal equality is granted because it is always accompanied by the relegation of social struggles out of the political sphere.[118] This is not to discount entirely the substantive gains that accompany the granting of such rights as sovereign equality – formal rights, for whatever reason they are established, have an empowering effect as well. My point simply is that the story does not end with formal recognition.

This trend toward inclusivity was becoming evident by the end of the nineteenth century, during which time the Standard of Civilization became increasingly secularized and de-Europeanized.[119] Japan and the South American states embraced the Standard of Civilization, and civilized states came to be defined as "those entities that accorded basic rights to their citizens and aliens, boasted an organized bureaucracy, adhered to international law and possessed capacity to enter into diplomatic relations."[120] The developments during World War I,

---

[116] Murphy, "Weberian Closure," 25.
[117] See e.g. Wendt, "Why a World State is Inevitable."
[118] As Kingsbury notes in "Sovereignty and Inequality," p. 84, "it is all too evident that the high twentieth-century commitment to virtually universal formal equality of states in the sovereignty model has not resolved many of the underlying problems."
[119] Simpson, *Great Powers*, pp. 256–7.
[120] *Ibid.*, p. 256. See also Gong, *Standard of "Civilisation"*, pp. 14, 24.

however, threw the civilized status of Germany and Russia into question, raising doubts about using Christianity as implicit shorthand for civilization.[121] In the meantime, the break-up of agrarian empires in Eastern Europe forced the Western powers to articulate a more inclusive framework for deciding which groups were entitled to self-determination.[122]

The interwar period: the West vs. Zealots and Herodians

Arnold Toynbee's[123] works about Greece and Turkey are quite illuminating in terms of the prevailing mindset of this period vis-à-vis outsider states that had recently joined the international society. In *The Western Question in Greece and Turkey* (1923), Toynbee argues that the Turks are unfairly stigmatized, whereas the Greeks are unfairly spoiled:

When you have made a spoilt-child of the Greek, it is no good rounding on him as an impostor; and when you have used the Turk as a whipping boy, you do not heal the stripes that you have inflicted by congratulating him on his fortitude ... In both cases, the evil that we have done them exceeds, and will probably outlive, the good.[124]

On the one hand, Toynbee is critical of his Western counterparts' prejudicial attitudes toward non-Western states, observing that "the non-Western societies are oppressed by our chilly shadow, while we are resentful when they assert their individuality. This is partly what arouses our animus against the Turks and the Russians."[125] Yet at

---

[121] Simpson, *Great Powers*, p. 237:

    At first, Christianity was the test of "good breeding". Wheaton's *Elements of International Law*, published in 1836 and translated into Chinese in 1864, characterised international law as Christian, civilised and European and marked out the standard to which Asian empires had to aspire if they were to be admitted to the international legal community. Later civilisation became the key term.

[122] Wallerstein, "World-System after the Cold War," 2.

[123] Both Fukuyama and Huntington count Toynbee among the few who shaped early-twentieth-century thought about world affairs (along with Spengler, Pareto, and Sorokin).

[124] Toynbee, *Western Question*, p. 348.

[125] *Ibid.*, p. 362.

the same time, even Toynbee cannot avoid a degree of paternalism toward the subjects of his study.

Toynbee provides compelling evidence for the argument I am advancing here: that the Western core of the international society in effect stigmatized outsider states. In fact, just four years after he lauded the Turks for having authentic souls and characters in comparison to the Greeks who were trying to pass themselves off according to the expectations in Europe,[126] Toynbee wrote a book devoted solely to Turkey, where he praised Turkish efforts for adapting to Western civilization: "Indeed, it is no exaggeration to say that everything in contemporary Turkey which has life in itself or interest for a foreign observer can be traced back to some Western stimulus and will be found to be a reaction against Western influence when not an emanation from it."[127] He concluded by remarking that Turkey is a forerunner of changes to come in the rest of the world because the issues facing Turkey are confronted by all Eastern peoples: "Everywhere these peoples stand at the parting of the ways, with the choice of entering the camp of the Zealots or the camp of the Herodians. They can no longer remain neutral; for the West, in its restless activity, will not let them alone."[128] What Toynbee recognized here was the fact that by the end of World War I, the future for Eastern peoples had been reduced to two options: embrace the Western normative standards, or reject them entirely; the same options available to a stigmatized individual in domestic society (attempt to survive among normals or retire to one's own community). Rejection is not at all the same thing as aloofness.

Furthermore, by the interwar years, it had become rather commonplace to assume that there was one and only one trajectory for civilization. Or rather, the main change from nineteenth-century assumptions, which espoused the same general idea, was that non-Christian or non-European peoples[129] could, theoretically, join the

---

[126] It could be argued that the Greeks at this time were engaged in a different form of stigma-response; in order not to be treated as outsiders, they were passing as the idealized heirs of Plato and Aristotle. Toynbee describes the disappointment of Westerners in finding out that the reality on the ground did not match the image.

[127] Toynbee, *Turkey*, p. 3. [128] *Ibid.*, p. 300.

[129] For instance, Gong notes that "the 1928 fourth edition of International Law still records that some non-European countries were 'certainly civilized states ... however, their civilization had not yet reached that condition

civilized world,[130] though this had to be done by progressing through certain fixed stages. This notion is clearly expressed in the League of Nations mandate system,[131] which had replaced the categories of the Standard of Civilization with more progressive, temporal language.[132] In the discussions about the mandate system from this period, there is an almost evangelical tone that replicated (rather than replaced) the imperialist attitudes of the nineteenth century. In fact, a number of commentators compare the League to the British Empire, and found hope for its success in that fact. Here is but one example from 1930:

In the last ten years, and largely as a result of the World War and the part played by the British Empire in the World War, we have found this solution

> which was necessary to enable their Governments and their population in every respect to understand, and carry out, the rules of International Law.'" *Standard of "Civilisation"*, p. 83.

[130] To contemporary eyes, the change seems minor. However, when we recall that it was only in 1860 that Asa Gray wrote the following in his review of Darwin's *Evolution of the Species*, the modification of the early twentieth century seems almost revolutionary:

> The prospect of the future, accordingly, is on the whole pleasant and encouraging. It is only the backward glance, the gaze up the long vista of the past, that reveals anything alarming. Here the lines converge as they recede into the geological ages, and point to conclusions which, upon the theory, are inevitable, but by no means welcome. *The very first step backwards makes the Negro and the Hottentot our blood-relations; – not that reason or Scripture objects to that, though pride may.* (italic added)

[131] See, for instance, Article 22 of the Covenant of the League of Nations:

> Certain communities formerly belonging to the Turkish empire have reached a *stage of development where their existence as independent nations can be provisionally recognized* subject to the rendering of administrative advice and assistance by a Mandatory until such time as they are able to stand alone. The wishes of these communities must be a principal consideration in the selection of the Mandatory.
>
> Other peoples, especially those of Central Africa, are at such a stage that the Mandatory must be responsible for the administration of the territory under conditions which will guarantee freedom of conscience and religion, subject only to the maintenance of public order and morals, the prohibition of abuses such as the slave trade, the arms traffic and the liquor traffic, and the prevention of the establishment of fortifications or military and naval bases and of military training of the natives for other than police purposes and the defense of territory, and will also secure equal opportunities for the trade and commerce of other Members of the League. (Italics added)

[132] Watson perhaps overstates this fact in *Evolution of International Society*, p. 284.

which was absent in the eighteenth century. We found it, and if we are wise people we shall go into the future with this talisman of what is called Dominion status, and we shall keep one-fourth of the human race together in perpetual peace and friendship, pursuing ideals of liberty and progress, and helping in building up a new world. Is not that something? Oppressed by the weight of these ideas, men's characters and minds develop slowly. Growth is arrested and social conditions become static. Hence the fact that Asia, the home of civilisation, is also a place where civilisation has scarcely advanced for thousands of years, and has now begun to move only in response to an impulse received from Europe.[133]

As exemplified by this passage, the dichotomies of this period hardly need restating: East was static, despotic, and had not moved for thousands of years, whereas the West was dynamic, progressive, modern, and the pinnacle of civilization. The only way out of backwardness was to emulate the West, to advance through the same stages the West had already gone through. The East was only now coming to this profound realization, thanks to the impetus from the West. The Soviet model was hardly an alternative to this recipe: "Leninism, which posed itself as the radical opponent of Wilsonianism, was in fact its avatar ... The construction of socialism was economic development of the Third World clothed in more radical verbiage."[134] Both the right-wing and left-wing ideologies of this time were teleological, and therefore hierarchical.

After World War II: modernity and economic development

By the time World War II had come and gone, the emphasis of international norms had shifted[135] to the economic sector.[136] This was a culmination of certain trends that had their roots in nineteenth-century social thought.[137] In a 1966 article, authors Nettl and Robertson observe that

---

[133] Smuts, "British Empire," 144.

[134] Wallerstein, "World-System after the Cold War," 2.

[135] Gong notes that "the holocausts of the Second World War and the threat of nuclear destruction further changed the meaning of 'civilized' and 'uncivilized.'" *Standard of "Civilisation"*, p. 87.

[136] See e.g. Mitchell, *Rule of Experts*, p. 4.

[137] In more ways than one: Watson argues that even though the post-World War II international society was dominated by the United States and Russia, two actors "outside the original Europe," "they and their allies agreed that the

even though analyses of change were anchored in the notion of progress since the earliest periods of industrialization in the West, it was "not until Marx that an attempt was made to create a formal synthesis between industrialization and social change in one coherent process."[138] Before Marx, the emphasis in analyses of economic change was very much on the prominent role and autonomy of the individual: "There was in fact very little specific social analysis – and even less general recognition – of any conception of industrializing societies."[139] Nineteenth-century thought brought an impressive array of thinkers – from Hegel to Marx to Durkheim to Weber – who mounted serious challenges to reductionist analyses of society. It was probably no accident that the individualist analyses of social change tended to emanate from England, where the state had played a less explicit role in capitalist development, whereas the emphasis on structural analysis had a definite German accent.[140] In later industrializing countries such as Prussia, the role the state would have to play in attaining "positive freedom" had become rather obvious by the nineteenth century.[141]

However, among the nineteenth-century thinkers who challenged individualist notions of progress, Marx stood alone in placing economics and materialism front and center in his analysis of social history. Furthermore, the second half of the nineteenth century was also marked by the increasing fragmentation of social sciences. As a result, initially Marx's materialist explanation for all social phenomena did not make many inroads outside of his ideological following.[142] Therefore, it was not until the Great Depression that economics

---

rules and practices of the previous period should remain provisionally in force with minor changes." *Evolution of International Society*, p. 289.
[138] Nettl and Robertson, "Industrialization, Development and Modernization," 275.
[139] *Ibid.*
[140] See Lebow's discussion of Heeren, Clausewitz, Ranke, and Treitschke and their views on the state in *Cultural Theory*, p. 10.
[141] There was an economic angle to this as well. As Stavrianos notes, the Second Industrial Revolution all but eliminated small family businesses. The capital investment needed for most modern plants was so huge that it was beyond the means of most individual investors – this is why the state became the primary vehicle for industrialization in most of the globe from this point onward. British capitalists were spared this necessity to some degree thanks to the cartels operating on accrued capital from the First Industrial Revolution and the profits generated overseas. See Stavrianos, *Global Rift*, p. 258.
[142] Nettl and Robertson, "Industrialization, Development and Modernization," 276.

grabbed the mantle of dominance among the social sciences, and "by the time of World War II, the primacy of economics was firmly established both in terms of policy formation and in the great influx of economists into positions of power and influence."[143] This influence became critical after the end of World War II, when every problem facing those countries ravaged by war and the newly independent colonies seemed to have an economic answer. The dominance of the economic field was also reflected in the newly created United Nations, which defined its agenda mostly around the new problem of "underdevelopment." As Nettl and Robertson observe:

Thus, far from regarding the post-war aspirations for economic development as a natural consequence of a given situation, they can be seen as the consequence of externally generated inducements of a rather special kind, which were framed and channeled in particular directions for reasons which did not necessarily have very much to do with the felt needs or value systems of the deprived societies. (A clear distinction has here to be drawn between the autonomously generated idea or value of independence – and its obverse, imperialism – and the induced one of underdevelopment or *atimia*). This leads directly to the notion of the existence of an international system of stratification, with its own and currently somewhat indeterminate value system ... [144]

In other words, while the focus of normative standards shifted to economics, social stratification remained a fact of the system. In the passage above, Nettl and Robertson draw our attention to the fact that "underdevelopment" is a socially generated category that did not exist prior to World War II. As we saw above, before World War II, the same "underdeveloped" countries were described as being at lower stages of the civilization trajectory. Before that, in the nineteenth century, the same countries were considered frozen in time as "barbaric" or as "semi-civilized" entities.

The dominance of economics in stigma standards post-World War II had the consequences predicted above. On the one hand, because the focus on economic development implied a more "objective" metric, post-World War II restructuring of international society turned out to be more inclusive – even prior enemies such as Germany

---

[143] *Ibid.*   [144] *Ibid.*, 277.

and Japan, and illiberal states such as Spain and Argentina, were retained in the fold despite initial protestations by some circles during the San Francisco negotiations.[145] As Ian Clark points out, the postwar order was intended as "a form of social and economic 'protection' for the bloc of Western states that found itself exposed to the vagaries and inconveniences of the increasingly open political 'market' of the global state system."[146] Furthermore, the economic emphasis on "development" helped make the decolonization process relatively painless,[147] as it gave "'national liberation movements' ... hope for the future."[148]

On the other hand, however, the new objective, economic rubric carried strong echoes of the older value systems.[149] While discussions of "civilization" were now mostly passé, the "modernization theory" behind the concept of "development" and "underdevelopment" also held that there were certain stages a country had to progress through.[150] The emphasis on development instead of civilization did give lower-ranking (outsider) countries something more concrete to work with in theory, but like the idea of civilization, the concept of modern development was also abstracted entirely from the Western experience. Francis Fukuyama remarks that modernization theory can be thought of as the last product of the nineteenth-century universal history tradition because it posited that "industrial development followed a coherent pattern of growth, and would in time produce certain uniform social and political structures across different countries and cultures."[151] The implication was that "only the West's political development represents a valid model."[152] Even Samuel Huntington, hardly the poster child for sensitivity about social stratification, observed that modernization theory was an old tale in new disguise: "These categories were, of course, the latest manifestation

---

[145] Simpson, *Great Powers*, pp. 264–8.
[146] Clark, "Another 'Double Movement'," p. 238.
[147] As Blaney and Inayatullah rightly point out, "it is important to remember that modernization theory develops as a postcolonial theory – in part a response to the emergence of newly independent states." *Problem of Difference*, p. 96.
[148] Simpson, *Great Powers*, p. 268.
[149] See also Dallmayr, *Beyond Orientalism*, pp. 149–50.
[150] See e.g. Huntington, "Political Modernization"; Tipps, "Modernization Theory."
[151] Fukuyama, *End of History*, p. 68.   [152] *Ibid.*

of a Great Dichotomy between more primitive and more advanced societies which has been a common feature of Western social thought for the past one hundred years."[153] The modernization framework of developmental stages is best described as a stigma theory because these views were underlined by the assumption that "development" was an individual state problem and not a systemic issue.

In fact, despite the dominant emphasis on economics, the concepts of modernity/backwardness and/or development/underdevelopment were used as catch-all categories for all sorts of shortcomings attributed to "outsider" states. Backward/agricultural societies were supposed to be marked by differential stratification, simple occupation roles, ascriptive norm patterns, and limited mobility; whereas modern/industrial societies were characterized by egalitarianism, complex occupations, universal norms, and high social mobility.[154] The view from the Soviet Bloc was no different. Wallerstein points out that Stalin's stages of development could easily be substituted for Rostow's and that "Stalinist bureaucrats and Western experts competed for which one could be the most efficacious Saint-Simonian."[155] As Huntington notes, the common belief among modernization theorists was that "the essential difference between modern and traditional society ... lies in the greater control which modern man has over his natural and social environment,"[156] and the Marxist model shared the same belief. Therefore, it is not hard to see how postwar international norms once again reproduced the simulation of sovereignty by attributing to the "outsider" states a lack of control over the natural environments that they had to overcome. In comparison, the "established" states seemed positively in control of their own fates.

After the Cold War: governance

Most scholars date the next normative shift in the international system to the end of the Cold War, but it can be argued that the developments of the 1970s and 1980s also had something to do with the displacement of economics from the limelight. By the 1970s, it was

[153] Huntington, "The Change," 285.
[154] *Ibid.*, 286. Huntington is discussing the modernization theories of Parsons, Shils, and Sutton here.
[155] Wallerstein, "Development of the Concept of Development," 111.
[156] Huntington, "The Change," 286.

becoming obvious that "development" for the "Third World" could not follow the prescribed stages of progress. As a result, both the Dependency School and Wallerstein's World-System theory challenged modernization theory. However, both of these approaches still emphasized economic factors above all else. In the meantime, the economic dominance of the "established" countries was challenged through efforts such as the call for a "New International Economic Order."[157] While ultimately unsuccessful, these calls did indicate a growing skepticism of the dominant international stigma theory of developmental stages.

The oil crises and the subsequent collapse of the economies of many "developing" countries in the 1980s also contributed to the general malaise about economic solutions to international inequality. However, in the 1980s, this disillusionment was tempered (or delayed) by the heavily promoted prescription from the "core" that the North–South problem was one rooted in economic approach and not in any structural power disparity. The forced neoliberal lessons[158] from the relative success of East Asian economies were also aided, at least temporarily, by the collapse of the Soviet Union. "The End of History" as proclaimed by Francis Fukuyama was supposed to mean that state-centered approaches to development were discredited once and for all.

Democratic governance[159] became the normative buzzword of the 1990s. The shift described above from "developmental" stages to neoliberal economic approaches as the proposed solution to economic disparity helped along a normative return to socio-political/cultural litmus tests. Some observers contended that, as a result, "the East–West divide with its two superpowers has been replaced by a division between North and South,"[160] but the obituary for the East–West divide was also premature. It is much more reasonable to argue that the bifurcated division of previous periods has been replaced by one single, global social hierarchy, in which the Western core dominates according to all normative metrics.

---

[157] See e.g. Bhagwati, *New International Economic Order*; Cox, "Ideologies and the NIEO."
[158] Clark, "Another 'Double Movement'."
[159] Simpson, *Great Powers*, p. 281.
[160] Castles, "Nation and Empire," 203.

Ian Clark argues that the period after the Cold War did not usher in any new substantive principles and that it is better understood "as an important stage in the advancement of this 'double movement' towards a more overtly normative style of international society, as defined by the core states within it."[161] He sees the legitimizing principles of the post-Cold War order as a "revised" Standard of Civilization.[162] These legitimizing principles were: "principles of multilateralism and a commitment to a global economy; a collectivization of security; and adherence to a set of liberal rights values."[163] Thus construed, this new Standard of Civilization helped integrate the former communist countries of Eastern Europe to the core of international society.

Clark is not the only author to recognize that international hierarchies persist in the post-Cold War system in new guises. Goldgeier and McFaul argue that the new international order can be analyzed as the "tale of two worlds." In their story, the core is secure, wealthy, and democratic, whereas the periphery is dependent, unpredictable,[164] and conflict-prone.[165] Wallerstein also observes[166] similar trends and predicts further polarization between the core and the periphery.[167] Blaney and Inayatullah argue that "the landscape of world politics" in the post-Cold War era is best understood "in terms of a binary that recycles the content of modernization theory into a new, international form: between a zone of peace, democracy and a separate zone of anarchy, turmoil, authoritarianism, and (optimistically) development."[168] This binary perpetuates the same social divisions of the past, with "the cultural conceptions of Western liberals … constructed as normal or natural in relation to today's 'barbarians.'"[169]

---

[161] Clark, "Another 'Double Movement'," p. 238.
[162] See also Kingsbury, "Sovereignty and Inequality," p. 90.
[163] Clark, "Another 'Double Movement'," p. 238.
[164] Goldgeier and McFaul, "Tale of Two Worlds," 469.
[165] Iver Neumann criticizes a book by Holm and Sorensen in the same vein for distinguishing between "zones of peace" versus "zones of conflict": "There is a teleological quality to this categorization that betrays the main idea that, although premodern, modern, and postmodern states can coexist, these are also developmental stages." See "Review," 351.
[166] Wallerstein, "World-System after the Cold War," 5.
[167] Also see Hurrell and Woods, *Inequality*, p. 1.
[168] Blaney and Inayatullah, *Problem of Difference*, p. 116, citing Singer and Wildavsky, *Real World Order*, pp. 1–3, and Russett, *Controlling the Sword*, p. 120.
[169] *Ibid.*, p. 117.

To sum up, a specific normative framework marks each major period in the history of the international system. These normative frameworks point to several things. First of all, they are indicators of an asymmetric power dynamic between countries similar to that observed by Elias in Winston Parva; namely countries that we may call "the established" (the core) and countries that we may call "the outsiders" (the semi-periphery and the periphery). The normative frameworks always represent values that are abstracted from the existing attributes of "the established," but at the same time represent an idealization of those qualities. In other words, by holding the outsiders to an ideal standard and thereby guaranteeing that they will fall short, the established feel secure in their approximation of the desirable attributes. For instance, irregularities in election processes in the periphery are perceived to be a much more serious problem compared to similar incidents in Western democracies. A similar distortion happens in regard to security issues – the current perception in the West is that peripheral regions are more vulnerable to terrorist violence.[170] Terrorist attacks of any scale outside the core set off a frenzy of canceled tourist reservations for many months ahead, whereas hardly anyone thinks twice of passing through New York City or London weeks after major terrorist incidents.[171]

The same stigmatizing result is also achieved by projecting all unwanted, but somewhat desirable or intriguing, characteristics on the outsider states. Such an attitude was especially evident in the nineteenth-century standards of civilization. The East was supposed to be static, despotic, and uncivilized, but also decadent and libidinous. However, a version of this attitude has made a comeback along with the rise of multicultural trends in the West. The Western tourist of the present day holds locals outside the core responsible for satisfying her in her search for "authenticity" and comes away disappointed any time she encounters "imitations" of Western comforts, as if not being Eastern/Southern enough was a moral failing on the part of the locals. At any given point in time, then, there are international

---

[170] See Bankoff, "Regions of Risk."

[171] In fact, in most public recounts of major terrorist attacks since 9/11, attacks in places such as Jordan and Indonesia are left off the list, as if the terrorist attacks there were not as extraordinary as events in London or Madrid.

anti-norms, which once affixed to the description of a country, display the properties of stigma labels. In the next section, I will discuss how the presence of such stigma labels associated with outsider status affect the behavior of states.

How stigma labels shape behavior

Possessing attributes that could be stigmatized has several consequences for any actor. First, normals perceive the stigmatized actor as something less than human. Because he is perceived as such, he is subjected to "varieties of discrimination," which "reduce his life-chances."[172] Second, as Goffman argues, in such situations, the discriminating behavior is often backed by a "stigma-theory," which is an ideology constructed by the normals "to explain … inferiority and account for the danger [the stigmatized agent] represents, sometimes rationalizing an animosity based on other differences."[173] As discussed above, other imperfections are imputed to the individual with stigma, and sometimes such imperfections may have the characteristic of "desirable but undesired attributes."[174] If the stigmatized person becomes defensive about his stigma, his response is usually understood as a "direct expression of his defect" and "hence a justification of the way we treat him."[175] In other words, the stigmatized individual is caught in a bind. To challenge the stigma only reinforces his association with it; on the other hand, to not challenge it amounts to embracing that association.

This situation creates an existential dilemma for the stigmatized actor because he himself is not free of the standards being used to judge him. As a member of the society that stigmatizes him, he is

intimately alive to what others see as his failing, inevitably causing him, if only for moments, to agree that he does indeed fall short of what he really ought to be … Shame becomes a central possibility, arising from the individual's perception of one of his own attributes as being a defiling thing to possess, and one he can readily see himself as not possessing.[176]

---

[172] Goffman, *Stigma*, p. 5.   [173] *Ibid.*   [174] *Ibid.*
[175] *Ibid.*, p. 6.   [176] *Ibid.*, p. 7.

To put it another way, an actor who has internalized the normative standards of the society he is a member of cannot escape stigmatization even if he isolates himself or rejects those standards as unfair. Once he has internalized these standards, the subsequent choices of isolation or rejection are as much a response to the stigma as embracing the stigma would be.

Therefore, once internalization has occurred – in individuals this usually happens through childhood socialization – the stigma becomes the driving force of the agent's behavior. As Goffman points out, the central feature of the stigmatized agent's situation in life is a question of "acceptance": "Those who have dealings with him fail to accord him the respect and regard which the uncontaminated aspects of his social identity have led them to anticipate extending, and have led him to anticipate receiving; he echoes this denial by finding that some of his own attributes warrant it."[177] In other words, the stigmatized agent deals with two kinds of "acceptance" issues: one that he requires from the wider society and the other that he requires from himself. The two are intimately related, however; without equal recognition from the wider society he may not be able to accept himself, and without accepting himself, he may be forced to live the dissonant life of the "discreditable."[178]

Once a stigma is internalized, there is no escape from it; all subsequent actions are a product of this original condition. A stigmatized state, much like the stigmatized individual, faces additional social constraints, such as a decrease in social stature and an uncertain ontological environment. Its subsequent strategies are, therefore, best understood as mechanisms for coping with such social constraints.

The two most realistic choices for a stigmatized actor are either to attempt normalcy or to embrace one's stigma. Within each choice, there are also two alternatives. Normalcy can be attempted by fixing one's discrediting characteristics – Goffman's example for this is the person who has plastic surgery to eradicate a physical disfiguration or someone who devotes private effort to excel in areas ordinarily closed to one with such a shortcoming.[179] Or one may attempt normalcy by "passing." With individuals the choice between overt corrections or passing is usually determined by the quality of the stigmatizing

---

[177] *Ibid.*, p. 8.   [178] *Ibid.*   [179] *Ibid.*, p. 10.

attribute – if it is immediately noticeable, passing may not be an available strategy. This implies that stigma categories that have less of a correspondence to physical reality are more conducive to the "passing" strategy. The obvious example is racial categories which are perceived to be dichotomous descriptions of one physical dimension – say skin color – but are in reality catch-all labels for a cluster of variables ranging from skin color to socio-economics. Such a cluster of variables creates a lot of fuzziness around the demarcation and opens up the "passing" option for many individuals who possess attributes from both sides of the divide.

The analogy to states is not as tortured as one would imagine. Obviously, states do not have the option of leaving their neighborhood and creating a new identity elsewhere. Therefore, the first option of trying to overcome stigma labels by taking direct, corrective action is the dominant strategy for states. Nevertheless, there are historical examples of behavior similar to "passing" on the international level. For instance, in the example of Greece at the turn of the twentieth century, as discussed by Toynbee (see above, pp. 84–5), we see shades of "passing," a strategy that was replicated by many East European states later in that century. In the case of countries, "passing" is usually accomplished by sweeping under the rug certain historical periods of dissimilarity with the core and constructing a national identity that is centered on a period of common lineage. So the Greeks, for instance, treated the 500-year-old Ottoman "interruption" as irrelevant to their national identity formation (except as an "Other"), thereby forging a link with Europe through the Ancient Greek heritage. The East European countries had a similar approach to their communist past after the fall of the Iron Curtain. One may call this the ugly duckling approach to "passing" – the potentially stigmatizing attributes are treated not so much as something to be fixed, but rather as external inauthentic impositions that can easily be shed. Underneath it all, the ugly duckling is actually one of the beautiful swans, inherently entitled to swim in the best pond at the country club.

Leaving the "passing" issue aside, which is not really an option for countries that cannot mount a plausible claim to a common heritage with the core, the more viable option for a country which wants to overcome its stigmatization is "correction." However, as Goffman warns us, this is only a half-way solution even when it is successful: "Where such repair is possible, what often results is not the

acquisition of fully normal status, but a transformation of self from
someone with a particular blemish into someone with a record of having corrected a particular blemish."[180] This is an obstacle to autonomy
in several ways: the taint of once having the discreditable attribute
remains (hinting at the possibility that one can easily fall back); a
sense of inauthenticity (externally imposed and internally felt) persists, which threatens ontological security; and resources which may
otherwise be utilized are directed to the ultimately fruitless goal of
correcting the "stigma." As Bauman notes, "the stranger cannot cease
to be a stranger. The best he can be is a former stranger, 'a friend on
approval' and permanently on trial, a person vigilantly watched and
constantly under pressure to be someone else than he is."[181]

On the flip side, there is also the possibility that a state can embrace
its stigma. Goffman outlines two such approaches: on the one hand,
"the person with a shameful differentness can break with what is
called reality, and obstinately attempt to employ an unconventional
interpretation of the character of his social identity."[182] On the other,
"he may also see the trials he has suffered as a blessing in disguise."[183]
The Soviet Union embraced the mantle of "Easternness" as a way of
claiming a leadership position outside the core – this would be the
former strategy, shared by present-day Iran. In other words, when
states employ this strategy, they claim to reject the dominant norms of
the international system and substitute their own version of "reality."
The latter strategy of seeing past stigma as a "blessing" is employed at
times by countries such as present-day Turkey and Japan, who often
claim to be a "bridge" between the East and the West.

Goffman argues that the precise timing of when one acquires a
stigma (or learns of the existence of one's stigmatizing attribute)
is crucial in shaping the subsequent response of the actor. In other
words, there is a difference between the responses of those who are
raised with the awareness of their disadvantageous situation and those
who learn later in life that they are stigmatized. Goffman further
distinguishes among those in the latter group: some learn late in life
that they have always been discreditable, which involves "a radical

[180] *Ibid.*, pp. 9–10.
[181] Bauman, *Modernity and Ambivalence*, p. 72.
[182] Goffman, *Stigma*, p. 10.
[183] *Ibid.*, p. 11.

reorganization of [the] view of [the] past"[184] and others become stigmatized as a result of joining a new community and when they "must learn a second way of being that is felt by those around them to be the real and valid one."[185] The main difference in response has to do with whether the actor's identity is built around the fact of stigma, or if stigma is later attached to an already formed (or semi-formed) identity.[186] Actors in the latter group display a more tenuous identification with others who share the stigma, and are more likely to try to manage their stigma instead.[187]

The timing of the stigmatization makes a difference in the international system as well. Countries with colonial pasts mostly articulated their national identities after the stigmatization of the nineteenth and early twentieth centuries. Countries that were not colonized, however, are more similar to individuals who acquire stigma after adulthood. Awareness of stigma comes after the country has cultivated an institutional character, a world-vision, and a certain habitus of its own. This is what sets countries like Turkey, Japan, and Russia apart from the rest of the "East."

States, habitus, and stigma

I have been arguing thus far that state identities, just like individual identities, can very much be tainted by stigmas. Stigmatization shapes the long-term state strategies in the international system, just as the presence of a stigmatizing attribute ends up framing a person's long-term attitude toward survival in society. Yet states are not people,[188] and they do not have a "psychological make-up," so what precisely is the mechanism through which a stigma label may affect state behavior?

It is possible to circumvent this question by arguing that once the state response to social constraints has been formulated we can treat states as individual persons as far as their international actions are concerned. This point applies to strategies and motivations of a social nature as much as it applies to strategies based on material capability.

---

[184] *Ibid.*, p. 34.   [185] *Ibid.*, p. 35.
[186] Obviously, identity formation is an ongoing process.
[187] Goffman, *Stigma*, pp. 92–5.
[188] In "State as a Person," Wendt considers the possibility that states may be thought to have a collective consciousness similar to other superorganisms such as beehives. He finds the argument difficult to square with physicalism,

The argument will work just as well if we simply treat states "as if" they are persons. Realists treat states as unitary actors who care only about their physical security, and therefore do not extend the "as if" treatment to social relations. However, the physical security assumption is no less problematic than assumptions regarding more "social" aspects of state behavior: "Physical security assumes that states have something like 'bodies' that can die."[189] In other words, any IR theory that treats states as unitary actors inevitably requires heuristic leaps. Therefore, there is no reason why the personification of statehood should stop with an application of Hobbesian state-of-nature theory about self-help.

There is another way of conceptualizing how stigma may affect state identity, and that is through the concept of *habitus*. I discussed above how perceptions of normality and stigma may affect a group's charisma and self-image. Such understandings become incorporated into the habitus of the group's members. An individual's habitus is "an active residue or sediment of his past that functions within his present, shaping his perception, thought, and action and thereby molding social practice in a regular way. It consists in dispositions, schemas, forms of know-how and competence, all of which function below the level of consciousness."[190] The habitus of an individual does not fix the individual's response to a particular situation in a functionalist way, but does affect the boundaries of an individual's perception of the situation: "social agents are like players in a game" and "habituses predispose agents to act in particular ways without reducing them to cultural dopes or inhibiting their strategic capacities."[191] Furthermore, for Bourdieu and other sociologists who have worked on the concept,

---

but points out that we often do refer "to states 'as if' they have emotions and therefore conscious," 313. One way of conceiving the consciousness of the state would be as state subjectivity and memory, constituted by narratives. If states had collective consciousness, it would follow that they feel various human emotions associated with the act of recognition, such as humiliation and loss of self-esteem. For an extended discussion of this issue, see also Ringmar, "On the Ontological Status"; Hall, "Getting Emotional"; Wight "State Agency"; Neumann, "Beware of Organicism"; Jackson, "Hegel's House."

[189] Mitzen, "Ontological Security," 351.

[190] Crossley, "The Phenomenological Habitus," 83, quoting Bourdieu, *Distinction*, p. 466.

[191] *Ibid.*, 84.

no habitus can ever be an isolated, individual creation: "Since the history of the individual is never anything other than a certain speci-fication of the collective history of his class or group, *each individual system of dispositions* may be seen as a *structural variant* of all other group or class habitus, expressing the difference between the trajecto-ries and positions inside or outside the class."[192] Elias also associates habitus with the larger group: in his seminal work, *The Germans*, he builds an entire explanatory framework around this concept. In that work, it becomes clear that, for Elias, the "national" group is espe-cially instrumental in shaping individual habituses:[193] "The fortunes of a nation become crystallized in institutions which are responsible for ensuring that the most different people of a society acquire the same characteristics, possess the same national habitus."[194] For Elias, common language is an obvious example of such an institution.

There is an implication even from this first example[195] that *the state* must be instrumental in shaping the "national habitus." In fact, Elias goes on to immediately bemoan the fact that "it is not yet common practice today to link the current social and national habitus of a nation to its so-called 'history', and especially to the state formation process it has experienced."[196] To argue that it should be otherwise is not to push for an essentialist or functionalist understanding of his-tory, but to realize that certain group-understandings (independent of their veracity even at the time they were formed) can get reproduced (almost) *ad infinitum* and inform present-day behavior. This is espe-cially the case in modernity, in the nation-state era.[197]

Obviously, not every reaction to past events leaves indelible marks on the national habitus: generally speaking, significant events influ-encing state formation have a greater impact on shaping the national

---

[192] Bourdieu, *Outline of a Theory*, p. 86.
[193] Elias's use of this term pre-dates Bourdieu, but the two approaches are not contradictory. Elias seems to use this term to imply a "second nature" or "embodied social learning." Dunning and Mennell, "Preface," p. ix.
[194] Elias, *The Germans*, p. 18.
[195] Elias does not point out this link explicitly in reference to this example, but it is well documented that a common language, at least in the way we understand the term today, very much presumes a common state. See Connor, "Illusions of Homogeneity."
[196] Elias, *The Germans*, p. 19.
[197] The same argument is captured by the concept of ontological security discussed earlier.

habitus than later developments. State formation, or modern state formation, is what makes the conceptualization of the nation possible in the first place. Therefore, state formation may be thought of as a rough equivalent to childhood socialization. In his discussion of the Germans, Elias points to four peculiarities of state formation which to him seem to be of particular significance in understanding the German habitus: (1) the "middle" position of the Germanic-speaking peoples between people who spoke Latin derivations and people who spoke Slavonic languages; (2) the difficulty of living in the shadow of a greater past; (3) discontinuities in the German state formation; (4) the fact that the unification of Germany was achieved through military and not peaceful means (which consolidated the elevated status of the military and bureaucratic nobility over the bourgeois middle class).

It is not the purpose of this book to analyze the national habituses of Turkey, Japan, or Russia, but the arguments I have presented thus far can easily be read into the framework Elias provides. In other words, there are two commonalities between the national habituses of these three former empires: (1) the experience of stigmatization as a result of comparative "backwardness" from the onset of modern state formation; and (2) the difficulty of living in the shadow of a greater past.[198] Of course, there are also differences: Japan's geography, for instance, sets it apart from both Turkey and Russia. Russia's Christian heritage sets it apart from Turkey and Japan. The Ottoman Empire's trauma as a result of being "double-crossed" by Christian *millets* sets Turkey apart from both Russia and Japan (which have specific traumas of their own). Yet as far as state identity from a systemic perspective is concerned, the two similarities I have pointed out have been the most determinative.

Explaining strategy selection

While the concept of national habitus goes a long way to explain a shared sense of stigmatization shaping the worldview of the decision-makers and the population, analyses of strategy selection are

---

[198] Elias argues that "it is a proven fact that the members of states and other social units which have lost their claim to a position of highest rank ... often require a long time, even centuries, to come to terms with this changed situation and consequent lowering of their self-esteem." *The Germans*, p. 19.

complicated by the fact that state identity is always contested at the domestic level.

Domestic contestation over state interests can be explained in reference to three fields of struggle: political, economic (material), and social (cultural).[199] Economic and social fields generate their own form of capital and classes, and politics is the sphere where the interests that have their sources in these other fields clash. At times, the economic struggle will dominate the domestic field of politics, and in those cases the state will play off classes against war factions in other states. At other times, the divisions in society will be over social capital, and the identity of the state may even be at stake. During those times, the state elite will play off social strata (or status groups)[200] within domestic society against classes or war factions and other states.[201]

I cannot offer a universal theory of domestic contestation versus state autonomy within the scope of this book. What I can do instead is to point out that there may be certain contexts in which the international strategy of the state will be contested primarily within the domestic socio-cultural sphere as opposed to the economic sphere. In those contexts, the societal divisions over understandings of state identity will be more determinative of the outcome than economic bases. I propose that major defeat of the state in the international system and/or state breakdown create exactly the type of context where the struggles within the social sphere to define the state's identity would be elevated to special prominence in the political sphere. In a general sense, state identity is always contested at the domestic level. There are always groups within any society who are not satisfied with the way state goals or normative ideals are defined. However, certain cataclysmic events such as military defeat and/or state breakdown create particularly acute dynamics of contestation because they sap the legitimacy of the traditional order.

---

[199] I am simplifying Bourdieu's distinction here by following disciplinary convention: he distinguished between social, cultural, and symbolic fields.

[200] Social status groups and economic classes often overlap, but they are not one and the same. High levels of education, for instance, give individuals access to social capital which may be exchanged with economic capital.

[201] Even this dichotomy is false because both of these struggles are ongoing and ever-present. Nevertheless, for purposes of social analysis we may bracket one off while we focus on the other.

A state's ability to compete and command respect in the international system depends on how closely its domestic norms align with the normative ideal of the system at a given period. Stigmatization is obviously an obstacle to respect and equal treatment. If that is the case, it would follow that the prestige of the state in the international system depends at least in part on how well the state negotiates the social constraints of the system. The sovereignty project of the state in some sense depends on satisfying the expectations stemming from the national status. Therefore, we can conclude that whichever group emerges from the period of readjustment following military defeat will sustain its legitimacy to the degree that it delivers on this promise, which in turn is predicated on the social norms of the international system.[202]

I argued above that there are two broad strategies available to a state dealing with international stigmatization: attempting normalcy (either by passing or by correction) or embracing the stigma (by reinterpreting normative reality in general or the value of the stigma in particular as a "blessing in disguise"). To put it in the other terminology I have been employing thus far, such a state can attempt to join the "established" or accept that it will remain an outsider in the system.

We may deduce from the above discussion that several factors influence an agent's response to stigmatization: the past of the stigmatized actor (habitus), the imagination of the actor, the present-day ability of the actor, and the larger normative framework. Let's take each in turn.

The habitus has a bearing on the issue because those who have had power in the past are more likely to resent the loss of it. It is possible to read Nietzsche as arguing that the man of *ressentiment* is someone who is physically weak but nevertheless lusts for political supremacy because he feels entitled to it.[203] The *slave* revolt in morality does not originate with the *slaves*; it originates with *priests* who had a supreme position in society (and continue to feel entitled to it) but were defeated by the brute force of the *nobles*. The attitude of the *slave* is different than that of the *priests*: "not at all used to positing values himself, he also attached no more value to himself than his masters attached

---

[202] See also Wendt, *Social Theory*, pp. 235–7.
[203] Reginster, "Nietzsche on Ressentiment."

to him."[204] The slave is thus resigned to a worthless (or, we may say, stigmatized) way of life. Unlike the slave, who benefits from a value system organized around the feeling of *ressentiment* but is not creative enough to invent it, the priestly originator of *ressentiment* values is someone who is used to exercising power, but has now lost that power to someone who is physically stronger.

Among states, countries (and titular nations within those countries) which are used to being masters of their own domain are more likely to suffer doubly from defeat. First, they suffer like everybody else from the immediate threat to physical security which inevitably accompanies the loss of empire and military defeat. Yet, the real suffering is in the other, more social aspects of corporate identity. Especially jeopardized is the state's ontological security. The transition from being a threat to being a loser, by definition, impinges on the desire to have a stable social identity in the system. Relationship routines are damaged or broken. This threat to ontological security does not sit well with the national interest in "collective self-esteem." We can assume, therefore, that the more powerful and/or prestigious the state before defeat and imperial collapse, the longer it will take to readjust to the new international environment.

The past matters in another way – if enough common historical affinity exists between the defeated and the victors, the stigmatized and the normals, defeat may become the opportunity to reclaim that common ground to reconstruct a new identity narrative. As discussed earlier, one strategy available to (some) new regimes is to "pass" by claiming stigmatization to be an aberration caused by the previous regime and not something attached to the nation itself. "Passing" is not that different than "correction"; or rather the difference is a matter of degree not substance. Both strategies involve emulation of the normative standards as opposed to a rejection of them. In domestic society, actors who pass are those whose different or discreditable attributes are not immediately known – in other words, they are those people who look and behave in ways *similar* enough to the normals. States which are similar enough to the established – in geography, religion, race, etc. – have also tried strategies similar to passing.

Such affinity works another way, however. If, for some reason (generally stemming from the condition of the normative hierarchy),

[204] Nietzsche, *Beyond Good and Evil*, p. 261.

passing is not attempted or fails to achieve the desired outcome, such frustrated actors are more likely to attempt *ressentiment* or simple rejection strategies. Just as Moses was initially a member of the Pharaoh's household, states which have a higher affinity to the core (the outsiders among the insiders) are more likely to take up the plight of the stigmatized as a cause. By doing so, they benefit from the very stratification that they purport to fight – the same normative order which ranks them lower than the established also makes them a leader among the stigmatized outsiders.

Therefore, the flexibility of the larger normative framework in terms of the promise of upward mobility also makes a difference in strategy selection. As long as we are on the subject of *ressentiment*, we may also invoke Scheler's description of the *arriviste*, who "vigorously pursues the goods and stations in life which are associated with the values possessed by the noble, but he does not pursue these goods for their intrinsic worth."[205] Instead, the *arriviste* is concerned with "being more highly esteemed than others."[206] The *arriviste* is a social climber: "He must unceasingly construct a sense of his worth through comparisons with others. Feelings of self-satisfaction are accumulated through looking down upon those he has surpassed, but these feelings are impermanent."[207] According to Scheler, what separates the man of *ressentiment* from the *arriviste* is a sense of impotence. The strategy of the *arriviste* is built on the belief that one can rise through the ranks by taking corrective action. If there is no upward mobility in the hierarchy, or if for whatever reason the closure criteria is defined in such a way that the actor has no hope of gaining entry, the *arriviste* strategy becomes unsustainable.

The imagination of the actor also matters to some degree if the choice is between living with the way things are versus rejecting the reality of the situation. To put it in state-centric terms, it matters whether an alternative value system is available through which the defeat can be recast as something other than defeat, a moral victory even. This is what *ressentiment* value systems achieve – weakness, i.e. stigma, becomes a blessing. While *ressentiment* values, as Nietzsche warned us, are not real, substantive values, but rather inversions or negations

[205] Morelli, "Ressentiment and Rationality."
[206] *Ibid.*   [207] *Ibid.*

of existing value demands, it still makes a difference whether they can be articulated as a coherent ideology (as in, say, present forms of Islamic fundamentalism). A child who stomps off the playground in anger will have few followers, if any, and only for a short time, if at all; a child who convinces himself and others that the playground itself is dirty and undesirable can maintain that stance for much longer.

The present-day resources of the actor also matter, but to a limited degree. Both passing and correction – i.e. the *arriviste* strategies – require some material resources, and so does leading a *priestly* charge of *ressentiment* against the established. We can speculate that resources make a difference at the extreme ends: without resources, no strategy can be attempted, and one is relegated to the *slave* position in the typology; with great resources one can maintain a strategy of rejection even without ideological justification. The greater the material performance of the state, the less is the need to emulate the dominant norm or to avoid stigmatization because domestic legitimacy can also be attained to some degree by delivering concrete material results. In the middle, once chosen, both the *arriviste* and the *priestly* strategies are equally sustainable (keeping all other factors constant) because they tend to generate their own resources: the former gives access to privileges and rights (to the degree it is successful), the latter elevates one's position among the stigmatized and the excluded.

To sum up, the two broad strategies available to outsider states are: embrace the international normative order and deal with the problem of stigma by casting it as an endogenous problem, or reject the international normative order and deal with the problem of stigma as an exogenous challenge. Passing and correction are strategies which are variations of the first option. *Ressentiment* and rejection are variations of the latter. If any middle ground exists, it is in what we may call, for lack of a better term, the *arriviste priesthood* option: the strategy of the actor who seeks esteem by not challenging the established normative order but acting as a gatekeeper and disseminator for it. In any outsider country, groups favoring each of these options are always present, but after cataclysmic events which throw state identity into question, such groups come to dominate national debates. Depending on the larger international context and current conditions of the country (as outlined above), which one of these responses is going to be more attractive to the domestic population varies. In the following chapters, I will demonstrate how this dynamic played out in the specific cases of Turkey after World War I, Japan after World War II, and Russia after the Cold War.

PART II

An imperial message

The Emperor – so they say – has sent a message, directly from his death bed, to you alone, his pathetic subject, a tiny shadow which has taken refuge at the furthest distance from the imperial sun ... The messenger started off at once, a powerful, tireless man. Sticking one arm out and then another, he makes his way through the crowd. If he runs into resistance, he points to his breast where there is a sign of the sun. So he moves forwards easily, unlike anyone else. But the crowd is so huge; its dwelling places are infinite. If there were an open field, how he would fly along, and soon you would hear the marvellous pounding of his fist on your door. But instead of that, how futile are all his efforts. He is still forcing his way through the private rooms of the innermost palace. Never will he win his way through. And if he did manage that, nothing would have been achieved. He would have to fight his way down the steps, and, if he managed to do that, nothing would have been achieved. He would have to stride through the courtyards, and after the courtyards through the second palace encircling the first, and, then again, through stairs and courtyards, and then, once again, a palace, and so on for thousands of years. And if he finally burst through the outermost door – but that can never, never happen – the royal capital city, the centre of the world, is still there in front of him, piled high and full of sediment. No one pushes his way through here, certainly not someone with a message from a dead man. But you sit at your window and dream of that message when evening comes.

Franz Kafka
From *An Imperial Message* (1919)

3 | *"The barbarians": Turkey (1918–1938)*

I had thus learned a second fact of great importance: this was that the planet the little prince came from was scarcely any larger than a house! But that did not really surprise me much. I knew very well that in addition to the great planets – such as the Earth, Jupiter, Mars, Venus – to which we have given names, there are also hundreds of others, some of which are so small that one has a hard time seeing them through the telescope. When an astronomer discovers one of these he does not give it a name, but only a number. He might call it, for example, "Asteroid 325." I have serious reason to believe that the planet from which the little prince came is the asteroid known as B-612. This asteroid has only once been seen through the telescope. That was by a Turkish astronomer, in 1909.

On making his discovery, the astronomer had presented it to the International Astronomical Congress, in a great demonstration. But he was in Turkish costume, and so nobody would believe what he said. Grown-ups are like that …

Fortunately, however, for the reputation of Asteroid B-612, a Turkish dictator made a law that his subjects, under pain of death, should change to European costume. So in 1920 the astronomer gave his demonstration all over again, dressed with impressive style and elegance. And this time everybody accepted his report.

Antoine de Saint-Exupéry, The Little Prince, Chapter 4

Introduction

In 1909, the same year a Turkish astronomer discovered the home planet of one of the most charming characters in literature, Lord Robert Cecil wrote in his notes: "A fanatically ignorant people, a barbarous nation; they want the capitulations lifted … Turks will always be Turks. They will never become Europeans. Their only redeeming

---

quality is their military skill."[1] The question of whether Turkey will ever become European is still up for debate, but his assessment of Turks' military skill was verified in the next decade. The Ottoman Empire was defeated in World War I and most of its territories occupied soon after; yet the Turkish forces under Mustafa Kemal's leadership were able to force out occupying armies in three years – foiling best laid plans – and sit down to negotiate a treaty with the great powers in 1922 on their own terms. By 1938, Lord Robert Cecil must have been surprised by how European-friendly the state forged by this treaty would turn out to be. In 1922, it would have been almost impossible to predict such an outcome.

Coming off such an unexpected victory against the West, it was anybody's guess what the Turks would do. In 1922, Greek Prime Minister Venizelos warned the British "there was nothing that could stop Mustafa Kemal ... from turning against the Allies. He would by that time have his head swelled more than ever. In such circumstances he would probably be a match for the French in Syria, and throw them into the sea. He would undoubtedly then go for Constantinople, and close the Dardanelles."[2] He asked whether the British believed that "having so reconstituted the Turkish Empire, MK [sic] would hesitate to pursue actively the problem of the reconquest of the Arab countries, and engage in every kind of hostile action against [the British Empire] in the East?"[3] He was not wrong: the British Empire had two causes for real concern about the direction the new leadership in Turkey would take.

First was the possibility that Turks would use their hold on the seat of the Caliph, the leader of the Muslim World, to foment revolt in the Eastern colonies of the British Empire. This worry was constantly expressed in British reports during the Independence War. For instance, in 1922, a British officer reported:

I have been convinced during this visit that there is a great Mohammedan movement on foot now directed against the British in India and

---

[1] Uğurlu, *Türkiye'nin Parçalanması*, p. 128.
[2] Record by Sir E. Crowe of a conversation with M. Venizelos, May 25, 1922, p. 270 in Şimşir, *İngiliz belgelerinde*.
[3] Record by Sir E. Crowe of a conversation with M. Venizelos, May 25, 1922. *Ibid.*

Mesopotamia, up until now the Nationalist Turks ... Kemal up until now has refrained from attacking England by means of the great weapon of Islam but ... Kemal at dinner informs me that if now this time he does not get peace, he will use this weapon and it will have far and wide reaching results, great wars and bloodshed.[4]

This worry, which was also shared by France, is reflected in numerous discussions[5] and it was corroborated to some degree by the pressure Britain was getting from its Asian colonies to reach a settlement with Ankara.[6]

The other worry stemmed from the close relationship the Turks had established with the Bolshevik regime in Moscow. Throughout the Independence War, British intelligence reported the financial assistance Ankara was getting from the Bolsheviks, and Mustafa Kemal's impassioned speeches did nothing to quell the worry that Ankara was on its way to becoming a satellite of Moscow:

Mustafa Kemal's response [to Aralov] was chiefly remarkable for his emphatic affirmation of the unity of the Turkish army with the Russian army which he stated formed one line of defence on the East from North to South; Turkey had come to realize that the forces at work against her were identical with those which were seeking to destroy Russia, and all Eastern nations were in the same position as Turkey, i.e. menaced by the same enemy; Turkish relations with the East were not designed to deceive the West, for the world could be divided to-day into two distinct parts, East and West, and the long line of defence on the East could only be maintained by complete solidarity of Eastern peoples.[7]

[4] Memorandum by Major General Sir Charles Townsend, July 27, 1922. *Ibid.*, p. 384.
[5] A few examples: Debates in the House of Commons and Speech of the PM Mr. Lloyd George in British Near Eastern Policy (August 4, 1922); British Secretary's Notes of Conference between the French President of the Council and the British Secretary of State for Foreign Affairs at the Quai d'Orsay (September 20, 1922); Letter of Sir H. Rumbold to the Marquess Curzon of Kedleston (May 22, 1922). *Ibid.*
[6] For example, President of the Central Khilafet Committee in India: "By their support of Greek military adventures British government had broken faith with India and the Muslim world ... If England goes to war with Turkey now ... she never will be able to regain prestige in Asia" (September 19, 1922), in Şimşir, *Homage*, p. 21.
[7] A report by the British Secret Intelligence Service, Constantinople Branch (April 21, 1922). Şimşir, *İngiliz Belgelerinde.*

For almost a decade, even after the war was over, the Turkish leadership in Ankara seemed poised to go over to the Bolshevik camp any day.[8]

The Turks themselves were divided on which course was the best one to follow. They had been debating the road to salvation for more than 100 years: Neo-Ottomanism, Pan-Turanism, Pan-Islamism, British assistance, Westernization, American mandate, theocracy, communism, and other ideologies had been proposed at one time or another. After the Independence War, three main camps had emerged: those who proposed complete Westernization, those who proposed Bolshevism, and those who proposed Islamism. The fears of the Western powers were not unfounded. The fate of new Turkey hung in the balance.

The rest, as they say, is history. By the time of Atatürk's death in 1938, Turkey had become an ally of Britain and had moved away from Moscow. Both the Sultanate and the Caliphate had been abolished. Turkey never tried to stir trouble in the East but, on the contrary, pushed a strong peace agenda through the Sadabad and the Balkan Pacts she spearheaded into existence. As the former French Prime Minister M. E. Herriot noted in 1933: "Seemingly relegated to Asia, Turkey, with her desire for order, peace and progress, moves into Europe now."[9] In the 1930s, Turkey was so active in regional order pacts, and so thoroughly committed to a process of Europeanization domestically, that it seemed impossible to believe that the country was still ruled by the same people who had been a thorn in Europe's side slightly more than a decade before.

From the unexpected foreign policy choices such as Turkey's insistence on being formally invited to the League of Nations in 1932 to the wide-sweeping scale of domestic reforms such as the decision to abolish the Caliphate in 1924, Turkey's actions in the interwar period cannot be understood without an understanding of the established-outsider dynamic in the international system. Turkey's actions in this period were driven by the overwhelming aim of joining the community of "civilized nations" – a community that she had not been

---

[8] Extracts from a speech by Sir Charles Townsend, MP, in the House of Commons (May 30, 1922): "If Turkey should be driven into an alliance with Russia and Germany, there is no one here who will doubt what that means to our Indian Empire, to Iraq, and every where else." *Ibid.*

[9] Uğurlu, *Yabancı Gözüyle*, p. 158.

able to penetrate when the country was an empire – and of escaping the stigmatization of backwardness, barbarity, and Easternness. As Mustafa Kemal asked rhetorically of a French reporter: "Which nation with a desire to enter civilization has not turned towards the West?"[10] Modern Turkey had won its independence in the battle, but independence would not guarantee autonomy if Turkey remained an outsider. This lesson was very much in the Turkish leaders' minds as they navigated the international system in the interwar period and as they clashed with other groups in Turkey who favored alternative courses of action.

Chapter 3 explores these choices and their consequences in three main sections. The first section gives a brief account of the historical background of the Turkish case: the late Ottoman period and the burdens the nineteenth-century international society placed on the Ottomans are examined. The second section constructs a narrative of the unexpected choices the Republic of Turkey made after independence in 1923 until Mustafa Kemal's death in 1938 (and the beginning of World War II in 1939). The third section analyzes these choices through the framework of stigmatization offered in Chapter 2.

The stigmatization of the Ottoman Empire

I, who am the sultan of sultans, the sovereign of sovereigns, the dispenser of crowns to the monarchs on the face of the earth, shadow of God on earth, the sultan and sovereign lord of the Mediterranean and the Black Sea, of Rumelia and Anatolia, of Karamania and the land of Rum, of Zulkadria, Diyarbakir, of Kurdistan, of Azerbaijan, Persia, Damascus, Cairo, Aleppo, of the Mecca and Medina, of Jerusalem, of all Arabia, of the Yemen and many other lands, which my noble forefathers and my glorious ancestors – may God light up their tombs – conquered by the force of their arms and which my august majesty has made subject to my flaming sword and victorious blade, I, Sultan Süleyman Han, to thee, who art Francis, king of the land of France. (Opening of a letter sent by Ottoman Sultan to King of France, 1525)

The Sublime Porte promises a firm protection to the Christian Religion and to its Churches; it further permits the Ministers of the Imperial Court of

---

[10] Interview with French Reporter Maurice Pernot (October 29, 1923), in Atatürk, *Atatürk'ün Bütün Eserleri*, p.23. Also see Yılmaz, *İngiliz Basını*.

Russia to make in every circumstance various representations to the Porte in favor of the below-mentioned Church erected at Constantinople, no less than of those who serve it, and promises to receive those remonstrances with attention, as made by a respected person of a neighboring and sincerely friendly power. (Article 7, The Treaty of Kuchuk Kainardji, 1774)

The first capitulation privileges granted by the Ottoman Empire were to Francis, King of France, who is the addressee of the letter cited above. The original capitulations were designed to give France an edge over her European rivals by exclusively profiting from trade within the Ottoman Empire. As is evident from the opening paragraph of the letter Suleiman the Magnificent wrote to King Francis, the Ottoman leaders of the sixteenth century had no worries about their standing vis-à-vis Europe.[11] It is interesting to compare that letter and others from that period with late-eighteenth- or nineteenth-century documents. For instance, the language of the Treaty of Kuchuk Kainardji (Küçük Kaynarcı) of 1774 provides a stark contrast. This treaty ended a six-year war with Russia but was the basis of future conflicts. It was interpreted by St. Petersburg to give Russia the right to act as the sole guardian of the Orthodox Christians in the Ottoman Empire. The Crimean War of 1853 was provoked by Istanbul's refusal to recognize this claim.[12]

It is not hard to see why Russia would use this treaty to make such an advantageous claim. Article 7 is written in rather odd language: it calls Russia a friendly power, and makes it sound as if the Sublime Porte was looking for a consultant to advise it on affairs of the Church. The power that Russia claimed Article 7 granted is so out of keeping with what was usually achieved through military battle that some historians regard the treaty as an example of "Russian skill and Turkish imbecility."[13] Other observers, such as Metternich, had a more limited reading of the rights conferred to Russia under the treaty (privileges having been granted to other powers previously).[14] Nevertheless, the Western powers controlled almost the entirety of commercial transactions within the empire, thanks to the privileges of capitulations, and frequently interfered in domestic affairs on behalf of the non-Muslim groups.

---

[11] See also Bull, *Anarchical Society*, p. 14; Naff, "Ottoman Empire," pp. 143–4.
[12] Davison, *Essays in Ottoman and Turkish History*, p. 30.
[13] *Ibid.*, p. 29.   [14] *Ibid.*

It would be tempting to chalk this entire situation up to the changing power dynamics that resulted from the weakening material capacity of the Ottomans. The Ottomans had lost control over important trade routes and had fallen behind Europe in terms of military advancement. However, to attribute the developments of the eighteenth and nineteenth centuries simply to material strength would miss an important point: the degree to which the Ottomans, in addition to their losses on the battlefield, were weakened by the burdens imposed on them by the new stigmas they encountered (and internalized) as a consequence of their increasing participation in the European international order.[15]

For instance, judging from the historical record of the Ottoman *millet* system up to the nineteenth century,[16] it was not entirely clear why the Christian groups in the Ottoman Empire needed special protection.[17] Intervention in domestic affairs on their behalf was usually justified by reference to the fact that the Ottoman Empire was ruled by an absolutist regime[18] and that there was no constitutional protection of individual rights within its borders.[19] Ironically, every step the Ottoman rulers took to neutralize this criticism brought them ever closer to internalizing the normative order of the European society.

In 1839, the Sublime Porte issued the *Tanzimat* Declaration, which was intended as a binding contract between the Palace and its subjects. With this declaration, the Sultan accepted limits on his authority, recognized the sanctity of life, property, and individual honor, and declared that government would be formed not by his will but in accordance with "fundamental principles" embodied in written laws.[20] Since it was unclear what these "fundamental principles" were, the Ottoman High Council issued a verdict saying they would

[15] Cemil Aydın's *Anti-Westernism in Asia* makes this point most convincingly.
[16] Leaving aside the human toll of the original conquests, most brutal acts by the empire against the Christian *millets* took place in the nineteenth century.
[17] Or more protection than the other subjects of the Sultan. See Göçek, *Rise of the Bourgeoisie*; Göçek, *Social Constructions of Nationalism*; Braude and Lewis, *Christians and Jews*; Shaw, "Financial and Administrative Organization"; Shaw, *Between Old and New*; Davison, "Turkish Attitudes."
[18] See the discussion of the theory of "Oriental Despotism" in Hobson and Sharman, "Enduring Place," 88.
[19] Davison, *Essays in Ottoman and Turkish History*; Berkes, *Türkiye'de Çağdaşlaşma*.
[20] Berkes, *Türkiye'de Çağdaşlaşma*, p. 188.

have to be derived from the *Sher'ia* rules. This decision put the rights of non-Muslim subjects in question. Could the laws derived from the *Sher'ia* principles of Islam really protect their rights? At the end, *Tanzimat* worsened the situation that it sought to prevent; starting with Britain, the Western powers became the entitled inspectors of how the *Tanzimat* Declaration was going to be implemented.[21]

In response to Western pressures, the Porte issued another declaration in 1856 (*Islahat Fermanı*). This declaration recognized all Ottoman subjects as citizens. Muslim and Christian subjects were to be treated equally, and have common courts. Christians would have representation in local councils and serve in the army[22] and freedom of speech was recognized. As specially requested by the British ambassador, there would be no punishment for converting. European merchants were invited to participate in increased commerce. Fuat Pasha, the foreign minister, defended the declaration to detractors by saying that the interventions of Western powers would now be prevented.[23]

Yet the 1856 declaration satisfied no one. The local Christian leaders were unhappy because the *millet* system had taken a huge blow, and their authority had been severely limited. Dr Stephan, a high-ranking Greek, complained to the Sultan: "Are the sectarian inequalities in Europe, in France, England, Prussia any less?" He went on to question why there was a need to give so many special privileges to the Christian *millets* in the Ottoman Empire.[24] The Christian public was unhappy about the military service provision. The British ambassador was not pleased with the declaration because he did not believe it went far enough in protecting missionary activities. The French ambassador was not happy because it was not guaranteed that French methods in education and the French Civil Code would be used after the reforms. The Austrian ambassador brought advice from Metternich, who told the Ottoman leaders that there was no need for Turks to become Europeans and they should formulate their own laws without paying heed to what Europe thought.[25]

---

[21] Engelhardt and Ali, *Türkiye ve Tanzimat*, pp. 130–3; Berkes, *Türkiye'de Çağdaşlaşma*, p. 189.

[22] The previous arrangement was that Christians had their own *millet*, with separate representation. They did not serve in the army, and paid taxes in lieu of military service.

[23] Berkes, *Türkiye'de Çağdaşlaşma*, p. 191.

[24] *Ibid.*   [25] *Ibid.*

Taking Metternich's advice was not on the cards. This was partly because the Ottoman Empire, by this time, had become "the Sick Man of Europe." However, this was not just a simple description of the poor material conditions of the empire as it is often assumed to be. To the contrary, such subjective judgments themselves, accompanied by double standards and lifestyle intrusions, were contributing to the loss of material capability by weakening the domestic administrative system. French observer Ubicini wrote in his *Lettres sur la Turquie* that the rights granted to non-Muslims in the Ottoman Empire were creating a stark contrast to the situation of Jews in Britain. The reality was that the European society of states was very much acting like the established "old village" of Winston Parva.

The underlying issue in nineteenth-century developments was that the rulers of the Ottoman Empire were under the illusion that they would be left alone in their domestic affairs and that the sovereign rights of the empire would be recognized only if they met civilization standards,[26] as Russia supposedly had a century before. Meeting civilization standards, they believed, would leave them free to address the problems of the economy and military shortcomings without interference. In reality, this illusion drove them to accept the nineteenth-century Standard of Civilization that would never treat a Muslim power as an equal, and simultaneously undermine, by their own hands, the already weak hold the Ottoman government had over its territories. The Ottoman Empire did not lose all of its sovereign power in battlefields; that power was chipped away by her own gradual acceptance of and aspirations to the Standard of Civilization by which the European powers ostensibly operated. The more the Ottoman Empire aspired to meet European standards, the weaker it became. Indeed, the more the Ottoman Empire participated in the international system, the more she internalized the norms of modernity, the more "ashamed" the leaders became of their own people and institutions, dedicating limited resources to emulation efforts which were doomed to fail.

The internalization of Western judgment about the Ottoman Empire happened gradually. The initial exposure to the West was through the non-Muslim minorities, especially the Greeks, who often

---

[26] Aydın, *Anti-Westernism in Asia*, p. 19.

were employed in translator positions and made up a good portion of the empire's intellectual elite. For instance, the first example of the "declinist"[27] analyses of Ottoman history (which dominates Turkish historical accounts to this day – more on this below) can be found in Dimitri Kantemir's 1716 tome *The History of the Rise and Fall of the Ottoman Empire*. Toynbee also points to this link: "By the later decades of the seventeenth century, however, the general attitude of Oriental Christendom towards the West had undergone a profound change – partly, perhaps, because the bitter memories of Western oppression had gradually been effaced by time, and partly because at this moment the West itself rather suddenly ceased to fight wars of religion."[28] In this way, the Ottoman Greeks became the locomotives of Westernization in the Ottoman Empire and the influence of their newly acquired worldview increased after the Ottoman defeat in the Russo-Turkish War of 1768–74, which had led to the aforementioned Treaty of Kuchuk Kainardji. Toynbee notes:

It had been bitter for the Osmanlis to be beaten by the peoples of the West ... It was far more humiliating to be beaten by an Oriental Christian people and to be compelled to grant to that people privileges which would place it in the same rank as the Western Powers ... The shock produced by the Treaty of Kuchuk Kainarja [sic] was so great that it inspired Ottoman statesmen to attempt reforms on Western lines; but these first Ottoman reformers started from the military end like Peter the Great, and not from the commercial end as their own Oriental Christian subjects had started in Peter's generation, now a century past.[29]

Toynbee criticizes the Turks' military emulation as being shortsighted and faults the Turks for not realizing that "the military efficiency of the West was a symptom, and not the cause of the West's general superiority."[30] Yet in any other age, not only would this be the appropriate response to military competition, it would also be a sufficient response.[31] As discussed in Chapters 1 and 2, the onset of modernity had changed the equation, but one can hardly blame the Turks (or the Russians for that matter) for not realizing at first that military emulation

---

[27] Beinin, *Workers and Peasants*, pp. 18–19.
[28] Toynbee, *Turkey*, p. 34.   [29] *Ibid.*, p. 36.   [30] *Ibid.*, p. 37.
[31] As Aydın notes, "the development of the image of a universal West was not a simple product of 'previously ignorant' Ottoman, Chinese or Japanese intellectuals 'discovering' the superiority of European civilization." *Anti-Westernism in Asia*, p. 15.

would not be enough. Not that it mattered in the end: once the Ottoman Empire took Westernization to be a state project, internalization of the modernist ontology at all levels and sectors became a question of when, not if.

The declinist historical tradition referred to above is a perfect example of this process. According to this tradition, still taught in Turkish high schools, the Ottoman Empire went through five distinct historical phases: Foundation (1299–1453); Rise (1453–1566); Stagnation (1566–1699); Decline (1699–1774); and Collapse (1774–1922). This tradition has come under attack in recent decades from historians[32] for overlooking very complicated processes after the onset of the supposed "stagnation" phase – the last three centuries of the Ottoman Empire follow an uneven trajectory, with some periods of progress and peace, and some periods of regression and turmoil.[33] For instance, despite its depiction in the West as *the* example of Oriental despotism par excellence, the Ottoman Empire in the seventeenth and eighteenth centuries was also marked by the kind of increased bureaucratization which was the harbinger of the modern state in Western Europe.[34] Ironically, this development was later interpreted, even by Turks themselves, as one of the causes of Ottoman decay.[35] Two things were influential in turning this account into the official history of the empire: the trauma of loss of empire and the internalization of the Western view of all things Ottoman. The former explains why this account was favored by the republican regime after the official collapse, the latter explains why we find the view in wide circulation before the collapse.

In other words, while the account of Ottoman backwardness became the official history after 1923, there was plenty of internalization of Western standards before that date,[36] first among the non-Muslim elite, then among the educated elite among the Muslim population,[37] most notably the newly Westernized military cadets.[38] As Aydın notes,

[32] E.g. İnalcık, Karpat, Hodgson as quoted and discussed in Armağan, *Osmanlının Kayıp Atlası*, chapter 1.
[33] See also the discussion in Chapter 1.
[34] Darling, "Finance Scribes"; Faroqhi, "Crisis and Change."
[35] Armağan, *Osmanlının Kayıp Atlası*, p. 75.
[36] Aydın argues that the main shift happened in the two decades after the Vienna Congress. *Anti-Westernism in Asia*, pp. 16–17.
[37] E.g. works of Mustafa Sami Efendi, Sadik Rifat Pasha, as discussed by Aydın, *Anti-Westernism in Asia*, pp. 18–21.
[38] *Ibid.*, p. 72. Also see Tunaya, *Türkiye'nin Siyasi Hayatında*.

"parallel to their recognition of a superior universal civilization in Europe, members of the Ottoman elite agreed that they themselves were less modern and less civilized than the Europeans and hence needed rapid reforms in order to develop in the same direction."[39] Throughout the nineteenth century, there was a growing worry among the elites that the Ottoman Empire was really "the Sick Man of Europe." Toynbee's remarks about the applicability[40] of this term to Turkey are quite interesting:

> The picture of the Turk as "the Sick Man" has had a curious history. It substituted itself in the imagination of the West for the older picture, in which the Westerner was the sinner and Turk was the Scourge of God ... The phrase ... was coined by the Czar Nicholas I in 1853, during a conversation with the British Ambassador in St. Petersburg. "We have on our hands a sick man – a very sick man ... He may suddenly die upon our hands ..." From that day to this, the imminent decease of the supposed invalid has perpetually been awaited by his neighbours – by some of them with pleasurable expectancy, by others with anxiety, but by all with a dogmatic faith which seems capable of surviving any number of disillusionments. It was awaited in 1876 and in 1912 and, most confidently of all, in 1914; and now, when the Turk has given incontrovertible evidence of outward health and vigour by imposing the peace-settlement of Lausanne upon the victorious Allied Powers, his imminent dissolution through some hidden internal disease is prophesied with all the old assurance ... This persistence of the "Sick Man" theory indicates how powerfully the Western attitude towards Turkey is governed by *a priori* notions and how little it is based upon objective facts.[41]

Toynbee was quite right in observing that the term was an exaggeration at best, but he was underestimating the damage done by this label. A great deal of Ottoman sickness was actually caused by the belief that it was sick – like a patient who is hospitalized for a curable ailment but catches some deadly virus in the ward. In fact, Ottoman efforts at liberalization, which were intended to keep the empire together, only seemed to speed up its dismantling. By the end of the nineteenth century, the Ottoman Empire had lost almost all of its territories in Europe. This created a backlash against the

---

[39] *Anti-Westernism in Asia*, p. 24.
[40] See also Stavrianos, *Ottoman Empire*.
[41] Toynbee, *Turkey*, pp. 9–10.

liberalization reforms and strengthened various reactionary ideological currents among the Muslim elite such as pan-Turkism and pan-Islamism.

The 1856 declaration had two major consequences: it increased the speed of nationalization processes among the Christian groups – who were also the main beneficiaries of increased European commerce[42] – and created a backlash among the now disgruntled Muslim subjects who were shut out of any benefits this new European-style administrative system was supposed to provide.[43] It did earn the Ottoman Empire a half-hearted recognition as a European power in the Paris Peace Conference. However, this recognition did not bring any real change in practical treatment.

In 1876, the Ottoman Empire adopted a constitutional monarchy regime and assembled its first Parliament. The parliamentary regime was suspended after only two years following the blunders of the humiliating Turko-Russian War of 1877–8. The constitution was restored following the Young Turk revolution in 1908. In the interim period, the model for the Ottomans favoring Westernization had become Japan.[44] It was believed that Japan had been successful because the Japanese had been able to Westernize selectively.[45] The Ottoman intelligentsia and ruling class by then had jumped on various ideological bandwagons that were quite different in tone than the conciliatory measures of the early nineteenth century. The Sultan chose to emphasize pan-Islamism and stress his position as the Caliph in order to retain Muslim subjects such as the Albanians and the Kurds within the empire. The military elite and the Young Turks increasingly favored a revisionist strategy.[46] Here we may turn to Goffman for

---

[42] In contrast, Tsarist Russia – not a paragon of individual rights by any stretch – as a European power, had the right to shut its borders to the influence of Western trade.

[43] The Ottoman Muslims in general, and the Turks in particular, had a strong belief that they had earned, by their past victories, the right to be *Hakime-i Milliye* (the Ruling Millet). See Akçam, *Türkiye'yi Yeniden Düşünmek*, p. 191; see also Lewis, *The Emergence of Modern Turkey*, p. 127; Bozkurt, *Azınlık Imtiyazları*, pp. 60–1.

[44] For an extended discussion of this development, see Worringer, "'Sick Man of Europe'."

[45] Berkes, *Türkiye'de Çağdaşlaşma*, p. 370.

[46] "While the despot of Turkey and the despot of Russia tremble and hide ... it has come to pass in the Far East among this admirable people that, like the Turks, have been treated ... as barbarians ... [that] the Japanese tended

insight: "Instead of cowering, the stigmatized individual may attempt to approach mixed contacts with hostile bravado, but this can induce from others its own set of troublesome reciprocations."[47] The important point is that both the conciliatory and the revisionist measures were formulated as a response to the Ottoman Empire's characterization (and self-characterization) as a tyrannical, backward, semi-civilized state.

As the break-up of the empire continued, the Ottoman intelligentsia who may otherwise have tempered the excesses of the Sultan became radicalized themselves: "Concluding that their liberal experiment had been a failure, the [Committee of Union and Progress] leaders turned to Pan-Turkism, a xenophobic and chauvinistic brand of nationalism that sought to create a new empire based on Islam and Turkish ethnicity."[48] In 1908, the Parliament reopened, and the Committee of Union and Progress (CUP) took the helm of government. However troubling the Pan-Turkism of the CUP regime may seem in light of the subsequent events, such as the mass killing of Armenians, it has to be acknowledged that this ideology came of age at the end of the nineteenth century and as a result was very much shaped by the dynamics described in Chapter 1.

The strategy of the CUP can be seen as a last-ditch effort to overcome the general insecurity caused by Ottoman stigmatization and the simultaneous unraveling of the empire. As difficult as it is to understand in hindsight, the leaders of the CUP firmly believed, at this late date, that the dissolution of the empire could be stopped if only the right measures were implemented domestically. In foreign relations, the Young Turks became embroiled in some destructive wars,[49] not the least of which was World War I. The Ottoman Empire's desire

---

to develop in all the Far East their material and moral influences, 'to make themselves the guardians, otherwise the masters, of the yellow world.' ... They whose civilization, achieved in half a century, has become superior to European civilization which has fallen into decay; they who do not have to reproach massacres, who do not have to gag any mouths out of which a liberal word came, who do not have to exile or suppress patriots. ... Indeed, for our part, it is this 'yellow' civilization that we wish to see universalized." *Mechveret Supplement Français*, French organ of the CUP, 1905, as quoted in Worringer, "'Sick Man of Europe'," 207.

[47] Goffman, *Stigma*, p. 18.
[48] Melson, "Paradigms of Genocide," 157.
[49] See the Balkan Wars.

to recapture lost territories in the West was partly motivated by its desire to hold on to its remaining territories in the East. The empire's status among her Muslim subjects hinged on her potential to stand as an equal to Europe.[50] The Young Turks, and other Ottoman leaders, still believed in 1913 that the empire was salvageable.[51] Unfortunately for them, along with her allies Germany and Austria-Hungary, the Ottoman Empire was defeated in 1918. The Armistice of Mudros was signed on October 30, 1918. Soon afterwards, most of the remaining territories of the empire were under occupation. The Ottoman Empire had failed miserably in her quest to regain equal footing with Europe.

Turkey's renewed quest for normalcy

When they took Belgrade from us, the enemy delegates also asked for the town of Niş. The Ottoman delegate stood up. "Why ask for so little?" he said, "We'll be happy to give you Constantinople!" For our fathers, this is how close Niş was to Istanbul. We thought that the Turkish nation could not survive if we left Vardar, Tripoli, Crete and Medina.[52]

The War of Independence (1918–1922)

Understanding the developments of the interim period between the Mudros Armistice (1918) and the abolition of the Sultanate (1922)

---

[50] For example, see the letter from Earl Kitchener, British High Commissioner in Egypt, to Edward Grey, British Minister of Foreign Affairs (November 3, 1913):

Turkish collapse appears complete. From now on, they cannot maintain their old position either in Europe or elsewhere. A Mussulman in Cairo told me that if the Turks cannot stay in Europe by force they will no longer have the right to rule over Islam. The population, while disliking the Turks, is very upset about the defeat of a Muslim power, (In Şimşir, *İngiliz Belgelerinde*)

[51] Letter from Gerald Lowther, British Ambassador in Istanbul, to Edward Grey, British Minister of Foreign Affairs (January 6, 1913): "Turks still cannot face the bitter reality. They still think they can negotiate," in *ibid*. Letter from Edward Grey, British Minister of Foreign Affairs, to Gerald Lowther, British Ambassador in Istanbul (January 11, 1913): "I've met with the Ottoman Ambassador Rashid Pasha. I told the Turks that if they want to save Istanbul they should give up Edirne, and they would lose everything if there is a war. All my words were in vain. Rashid Pasha notified that the Ottoman delegation was going to leave the conference," in *ibid*.

[52] Atay, *Zeytindağı*, p. 10.

is essential to contextualizing the foreign policy choices open to the Republic of Turkey in the interwar period. During the four years of the Independence War,[53] the Western powers were the deadly enemies of the Turks, whereas the Bolsheviks and Muslims of Asia provided monetary and moral support.

After Mudros, the remaining territories (Asia Minor) of the Ottoman Empire, namely those territories that had not been officially partitioned, came under occupation. The ostensible justification was Article 18 of the Armistice, which provided that the Triple Entente and its allies could occupy parts of Turkey to provide for the security of local non-Muslims. Having already moved into Arabia and the Levant, the British stationed their ships in Istanbul; Greek forces took control of Western Anatolia; Italians were in the Mediterranean region; and the French moved into the southeast.

In 1918, Turkish leadership and the intelligentsia in Istanbul were divided on what would be the best course to retain some semblance of independence after defeat. One group favored appealing to principles of self-determination, as outlined by the US President Woodrow Wilson. It was unclear, however, how effective this approach would be, considering that Wilson had not recognized Turkey as a nation that was entitled to self-determination.[54] Another group favored asking for a mandate status from one of the Western powers, the United States being the popular choice. Yet another group believed that the only salvation lay in the Turkish hold over the Caliphate seat. Some believed that the British would help and protect what was left of the Ottoman Empire because they would have use for a friendly Caliph, who would help control the large Muslim populations under British

---

[53] This is how this period is referred to in Turkish history (*Kurtuluş Savaşı* – the term may also be translated as War of Liberation or Salvation). Because the alternatives from Western accounts (Greco-Turkish War, Turkish–Armenian War, etc.) give an incomplete picture and, furthermore, obscure the role of Western powers in this war, I see no reason not to defer to the Turkish terminology.

[54] "Although the US maintained a policy of careful neutrality towards Turkey, President Wilson's exhortations to his countrymen to be neutral in thought as well as in deed in the war, apparently were not meant to apply to the Turks ... When Woodrow Wilson was considering the appointments shortly after his election in 1912, Colonel House suggested Henry Morgenthau as Ambassador to Turkey; Wilson replied, 'There ain't going to be no Turkey,' to which House rejoined, 'Then let him go look for it.'" Evans, *United States Policy*, p. 29.

colonial rule. In other words, the Sublime Porte had given up any remaining hope of countering European power, and was now looking to prolong its own existence under any conditions.

The Ottoman Army was disbanded by the Armistice. In the meantime, local resistance movements started popping up around Anatolia. Through some clever maneuvering, Mustafa Kemal,[55] who had resigned from his post in the Ottoman Army, managed to take control of the umbrella council of resistance movements, and brought all the militia in the various battlefronts under his leadership in the last quarter of 1919. It was also around this time that he first met with the Bolsheviks, and got some guarantee of support from them by implying that an independent Turkey might be friendly to communism.[56] The Treaty of Kars, declaring mutual friendship, was signed in 1921, in effect shutting down the Eastern Front.

The British pressured the Istanbul government of the Sultan to delegitimize the resistance movements of Anatolia. Mustafa Kemal and all those who joined him were declared traitors by the Istanbul government. In response, Mustafa Kemal argued that the Sultan was a prisoner of Western powers, and that a legitimate government could only be formed in unoccupied areas. He called all of his supporters to Ankara. When the Ottoman Parliament issued a decree in support of Kemal, the British forces took official control of Istanbul, dissolved the Parliament and arrested any representative who had not yet fled the city (March 1920). This was a strategic mistake on the part of the British. Soon after, on April 23, the nationalists opened their own assembly in Ankara, and Mustafa Kemal was able to claim that, since the Ottoman Parliament had been closed unconstitutionally, the Ankara Assembly was the true representative of Turkish people. He further grounded the Ankara government's legitimacy by appealing to the Islamic world for support. He argued that the Anatolian resistance movement was trying to save the Caliph from Western hands.[57]

Because the Ottoman Empire had mostly depleted her resources during the protracted wars of the early twentieth century,[58] the Anatolian resistance could not count on any local funds in its

---

[55] Having previously made a name for himself as a great soldier in the quashing of the infamous March 31st rebellion, when the fundamentalist mobs tried to sack the Sultan, and also in the famous Battle of Gallipoli during World War I.

[56] Perinçek, *Atatürk'ün Sovyetlerle.*   [57] Aydemir, *Tek Adam.*

[58] Italian invasion of Tripoli; the two Balkan Wars; World War I.

battles against the occupying armies. The military expenditures were financed partly by the Bolsheviks[59] and friendly Asian Muslim groups.[60] Throughout the war, Mustafa Kemal continued to reaffirm the Ankara government's trust in and friendship with the Bolshevik cause: "Both armies are fighting to end the intrusion of capitalist Europe into Asia. Therefore, the two armies are united in cause and purpose. One of them has ensured the victory of the red banner of revolution, and the other has protected the dignity of the red Turkish flag."[61] During the Independence War, the British regarded this alliance as a marriage of convenience.[62] They were more concerned with how their support of Greece versus Turkey was being perceived in India.[63]

The Turks were able to organize an army strong enough to convince the French and the Italians to withdraw without much fighting. Since the Eastern Front was closed after the Treaty of Kars, the Ankara government was able to concentrate all of its forces in the Western Front, and defeat the Greek forces after several battles in

[59] A report by the British Secret Intelligence Service, Constantinople Branch (April 21, 1922):

   The Financial Position of the Angora Government: ... In drawing up the new budget, the Finance Department of the Angora Government had made a special effort to make it appear moderate and the total expenditure was estimated at 25 million liras Turkish. This amount, it was estimated, would be covered by gold to the value of 2 millions which had been promised by the Ukrainian Government. Taxes were expected to produce ten million Turkish liras, and the balance of five millions was to be covered by special war contributions including the contribution imposed upon every village and district. Şimşir, *İngiliz Belgelerinde.*

[60] M. M. H. J. Chotani, President of Central Khilafet Committee, Bombay, sent 50,000 pounds to Angora through Netherland Bank (February 18, 1922); Mr. A. H. S. Khatri, Hon. Gen. Sec. Cent. Khilafet Committee Bombay, wrote that 90,000 pounds were already sent, and another 10,000 were on the way (September 14, 1922). Şimşir, *Homage.*

[61] Bolluk, *Kurtuluş Savaşı'nın*, p. 113.

[62] See the memorandum by the Secretary of State for Foreign Affairs respecting intervention between Greece and Turkey in Şimşir, *İngiliz Belgelerinde.*
   It was after the war had been concluded, and both the Ankara and the Bolshevik governments had shown their staying power, that the British grew more concerned about the durability of this alliance.

[63] See for example debates in the House of Commons and speech of the Prime Minister Mr. Lloyd George on British Near Eastern Policy (April 8, 1922) in Şimşir, *İngiliz Belgelerinde.*

1921 and 1922.[64] Greece withdrew all of her soldiers from Anatolia in the course of weeks, and the British remained the only occupying power with her continued presence in Constantinople. The two sides sat down in Mudanya to negotiate an armistice. In the meantime, Greece continued withdrawing and left Eastern Thrace under Turkish control. Mustafa Kemal indicated to the Western powers that Turks were willing to fight until all territories with a Turkish majority were under their control.[65] An armistice was signed in October 1922.

The last of the Ottomans and the birth of modern Turkey (1922–1923)

"İsmet," Lord Curzon said, "You remind me very much of a music box. You play the same old melody every single day, until you make us all ill: Sovereignty, Sovereignty, Sovereignty ..." (From the memoirs of Joseph C. Grew, American observer at Lausanne)

The Ankara government had most of its terms accepted at the Mudanya Armistice and had recaptured control of most of the Anatolian territories occupied after World War I. By contrast, the Istanbul government had shown no willingness to fight the occupation and had sabotaged most resistance efforts. The Istanbul government had therefore lost all legitimacy. The Parliament in Ankara abolished the Sultanate on November 1, 1922, and declared Turkey a republic. The last Sultan, Mehmed Vahdeddin, and all the remaining members of the Ottoman dynasty left Istanbul on a British military ship. The office of the Caliphate was separated from the Sultan and was retained for the time being. The British forces remained in Constantinople until the Lausanne Treaty recognizing the new borders of modern Turkey was signed in 1923.

[64] In the meantime, the Istanbul government signed the Treaty of Sevres. The treaty left Turks only the middle part of Anatolia that had not come under any occupation. The Ankara government refused to recognize the treaty, claiming that the Istanbul government was no longer authorized to sign treaties and that the Turkish Parliament would have to ratify the treaty for it to be binding.

[65] As enumerated in the National Pact, which was contained in the last decree of the Ottoman Parliament. The current borders of Turkey coincide with the National Pact, minus Mosul and Western Thrace, plus Antioch.

The conference for the peace treaty was convened in Lausanne on November 20, 1922. Mustafa Kemal had sent his second-in-command, İsmet Pasha, as the chief negotiator. The Western powers were in for a surprise: İsmet Pasha made it clear from the start that Turkey would accept nothing less than equal treatment. This was not what the Western powers had in mind. For instance, French newspapers cautioned prior to the conference that while the capitulations should be lifted eventually, the Turkish courts were not yet up to par with their European counterparts and that no decisions should be taken in haste.[66] The British delegation seemed confident that it was going control the negotiations throughout the conference.[67]

İsmet Pasha was aware of the fact that, despite the recent military victories, the Western powers respected neither the new Ankara government nor Turkey. Therefore, he started the conference with a significant symbolic gesture. After Lord Curzon, the head of the British delegation, had made a speech welcoming all the delegates, İsmet Pasha stood up, and gave a long-winded speech himself.[68] In the early days of the conference, İsmet Pasha made it known that Turkey would no longer put up with capitulations, nor would she accept any foreign interference in domestic affairs: "Turkey is a nation that wants autonomy … Foreign populations and their property, foreign rights are guaranteed under the public laws of Turkey."[69] Ironically, it was the Japanese delegate, Hayachi, who most vehemently opposed Turkish demands for the lifting of capitulations. Hayachi told İsmet Pasha that Japan, too, had suffered from capitulations, and so he sympathized with Turkish demands. However, not even in Japan had the capitulations been lifted before the implementation of necessary administrative and legal reforms.[70] İsmet Pasha was not persuaded by this argument; he said that there was no possibility of Turkey agreeing to keep the capitulations when they were not being utilized "*even* in Greece or

---

[66] Karacan, *Lozan*, p. 59.   [67] *Ibid.*, p. 50.

[68] Joseph C. Grew reports that this made a very bad impression, but as the conference went on, he would grow to respect İsmet Pasha to the degree that he personally pushed for a unilateral agreement between the United States and the Ankara government. See Grew, *Turbulent Era*; Grew, *Lozan Günlüğü*.

[69] Karacan, *Lozan*, p. 131.

[70] Goffman, *Stigma*, p. 107: "The stigmatized individual exhibits a tendency to stratify his 'own' according to the degree to which their stigma is apparent and obtrusive. He can then take up in regard to those who are evidently more stigmatized than himself the attitudes normals take to him."

the Balkan countries."[71] He further argued that Turkey saw no justice in an international system that would spare former Ottoman territories such as Greece from capitulations and would implement them in Turkey. He said, "We came to this conference because it was guaranteed we would be treated as equals. However, we are constantly faced with demands that would impugn our independence. No sovereign nation, *not even Greece*, has faced these sorts of demands! The Turkish nation, before anybody, is entitled and has the right to be treated as other sovereign nations."[72] It was the constant refrain of the Turkish delegation during the conference that the Turkish laws were up to European standards and that there was no need for intervention in Turkish domestic affairs. The conference had reached an impasse. An editorial in *The Times* argued on December 29, 1922: "Either the Turks will accept the reasonable demands before them and secure the necessary support for the development of their country, or they will relegate Turkey into the position of a completely isolated country in an Asian desert." Despite these gloomy predictions, the Turkish delegation would not accept anything less than full sovereign equality.[73] The conference proceedings were suspended in February 1923.

Even after the proceedings were resumed in April, there were some glitches. The British wanted to keep the High Commission of Health in Istanbul operational, arguing that for the last 70 years it had kept contagious diseases out of Europe. İsmet countered that the right place for this commission was either Arabia or India; that Turkey had established a perfect medical system during the war and that Turkish medical schools were on a par with their European counterparts.[74] When the treaty was signed on October 2, 1923, Turkey had forced

---

[71] Karacan, *Lozan*, pp. 133–4; italics added.

[72] *Ibid.*, p. 198; italics added.

[73] From Joseph C. Grew's memoirs, February 5, 1923:

Child, Bristol and I were almost immediately in Lord Curzon's chambers ... Curzon suddenly appeared; he rushed into the room like an angry bull, gave us a sideways glance, and started pacing around, shaking his fists into the air. He was sweating profusely while he looked us up and down. He started yelling: "We sat here for four fatal hours and İsmet responded to everything we said with the same tired refrain: Independence and Sovereignty. We did everything we could. Even Bombard shook his fist and told İsmet that what he was doing amounted to war provocation."

[74] Karacan, *Lozan*, p. 231. Also, here we see an example of the identification of Asia/East with disease.

Western powers to agree to most of her demands.[75] An American reporter with a penchant for hyperbole observed that the West had never bowed so low before the East.[76]

A sovereign Turkey: now what? (1923–1938)

It was not clear from the outset what direction the Ankara government would take after sovereign recognition. One possibility the Western powers feared was that it would try to influence the Asian Muslims by using the power of the Caliphate. Another distasteful possibility for the West was that it would adopt communism, as had been implied and promised during the Independence War. The first of these fears was soon put to rest.

Turkey's relations with the "East": 1923–1938

As noted in the previous section, the Ankara government enjoyed widespread support from the Muslim world throughout the years of the Independence War. Once the final battle had been won, Ankara was flooded with telegrams[77] of congratulations and visits from representatives of Muslim communities around the world.[78] The correspondence during and in the immediate aftermath of the Independence

---

[75] Article 28: Each of the High Contracting Parties hereby accepts, in so far as it is concerned, the complete abolition of the Capitulations in Turkey in every respect.

[76] Atay, *Çankaya*, p. 338. On the same page, Atay also reports that on seeing the Turkish Army enter Istanbul, Lt. Armstrong said: "I hear my spirit rebelling. Turks think they are in Suleiman the Magnificent's times. It hurt my pride to see the British Empire's honor soiled in the mud before all of Asia."

[77] A few examples: Letter from the President of the Khilafat Committee (September 10, 1922) – "Following resolution passed meeting of Delhi citizens tender hearty congratulations to Kemalists on their decisive victory in Asia Minor"; Letter from the President of the Khilafat Committee (November 10, 1922) – "Convey to Ghazi Mustafa Kemal and mujahidin on behalf of Sind Moslems heartiest congratulations on their brilliant victory ..."; Letter from Indian Community of Johannesburg (September 14, 1922) – "Indians both Muslims and Hindus in South Africa congratulate you, your colleagues and your brave noble invincible army for having saved the honour of Islam by the valour of your selfless and Islamic spirit in having vindicated the cause of righteousness ..."; for more letters from communities in Bombay, Shahjanpur, Surat, Balliasub, Ballia, and others, see Şimşir, *Homage*, pp. 13–21.

[78] "Debates in the HoC and Speech of the PM Mr. Lloyd George in British Near Eastern Policy (4/8/1922): Lt. Comm. Kenworthy: ... In Angora, which

War is marked by two themes: that Turks were fighting in the name of Islam, and that Turks were fighting against colonial intrusion. Both were considered righteous causes.[79]

However, relations started cooling off when Muslim representatives in Ankara became aware of the Turkish discussions to abolish the Caliphate. Perhaps because the Ankara government needed the support of Muslim communities during the negotiations in Lausanne, the office of the Caliph was spared when the office of the Sultanate was abolished in 1922 and Turkey proclaimed a republic in 1923. Ankara continued to attract and inspire representatives of Eastern communities.[80] In the first couple of years after the military victory, there were even those who came to declare their official loyalty to the Ankara government[81] or proposed that Mustafa Kemal should become the new Caliph.[82]

Nevertheless, the Turkish Parliament, with Kemal's prodding, voted to end the office of the Caliphate on March 3, 1924. The reasons for

> is now the capital of the Turkish nationalists, there is a representative of every Moslem community in the world ..." Mustafa Kemal is interviewed by the owner of Islamic News, Indian Reporter Abdulkayyum Malik (26/8/ 1923): "Us Turks are grateful for the services of our Indian brethren who have helped us through the darkest of times." Şimşir, *İngiliz Belgelerinde*, p. 329.

[79] And not just by Muslims either:

> Report of the British Consul at Sarajevo to Sir C.A. Young (Belgrade) 25/9/1922: ... on Sept 12th the following passage occurred in the 'Hrvatska Sloga,' an organ of the Croatian Peasant Party. "In Kemal the World sees the protagonist of a nation struggling for existence. The sufferings of the Turks find sympathy in the hearts of all the Oppressed. We greet Kemal's victory with joy, not only because many Croatians are Muslims, but because it is the triumph of truth over evil, of law over lawlessness, of the national spirit over imperialism and oppression"

> In Şimşir, *İngiliz Belgelerinde*. See also "Extract from the 'Jugoslawski List' (pro-Government Organ in Yugoslavia) of September 15th, 1922," in Uğurlu, *Yabancı Gözüyle*.

[80] *The Westminster Gazette*, July 9, 1923, in Yılmaz, *İngiliz*, p. 69.

[81] "Extract from the minutes of Kemal's meeting with Upmal, representative from Moscow (1/1/1921): Mustafa Kemal: The Yemenis ... came here as the subjects of the Ottoman Empire and declared their trust in the Ankara government. I told them that we did not want their servitude. I instructed them to organize around a popular sovereignty movement and maybe after that we could discuss a federation. Yes, there is a nationalist government in Baghdad. They, too, came to me for assistance. Because we do not have enough resources to support them at the moment, I dispatched a small battalion to Mosul for motivational support ..." in Şimşir, *Homage*.

[82] Atay, *Çankaya*, p. 377.

this controversial move[83] will be discussed later in more detail. Let us note at this point that in British newspapers this decision was considered a strategic mistake on the part of Turkey. Both *The Times* and *The Economist* were under the impression that this was going to hurt Turkey's relations with the Sunni Muslim community and also with Muslim states that had been admirers of the new Ankara government, such as Egypt, Afghanistan, and Iraq.[84] In the end, while relations with the Muslim communities under British control almost disappeared, Turkey managed to establish friendly relations with sovereign Muslim states.[85]

Afghanistan had gained her independence from Britain in 1919, and was one of the first states, along with the Soviet Union, to recognize the Ankara government with a friendship treaty. The treaty acknowledged the awakening of Eastern nations against imperialism.[86] Iran also quickly established diplomatic relations with Turkey. During the 1920s, their mutual friendship was reaffirmed with several treaties. In 1935, Turkey, Iran, and Iraq came together to sign a tripartite treaty, and were later joined by Afghanistan. Two years later, the Sadabad Pact[87] was signed. The parties recognized each other's sovereignty and promised to consult others in matters of common concern and to take any disputes to the League of Nations.

[83] "General Review of the British Secret Intelligence Service Information During the Period April–August, 1922: … it is noteworthy that a number of delegates from Moslem countries, who assembled at Angora earlier in the year to discuss a scheme to convoke a Pan-Islamic conference, refused to participate in such a conference on discovering that one of its objectives was to discuss changes in the Khalifat." Şimşir, *Homage*, p. 71, 74.
[84] *The Times*, March 5, 1924; *The Economist*, March 8, 1924, in Yılmaz, *İngiliz.*
[85] After Mustafa Kemal's death in 1938, he was deeply praised throughout the Muslim world, e.g.:

Press interview with Jinnah, President, All India Muslim League: He was the greatest Mussalman in the modern Islamic world and I am sure that the entire Mussalman world will deeply mourn his passing away. It is impossible to express adequately in a press interview one's appreciation of his remarkable and varied services, as the builder and the maker of Modern Turkey and an example to the rest of the world, especially to the Mussalman states in the Far East. The remarkable way in which he rescued and built up his people against all odds, has no parallel in the history of the world. (Şimşir, *Homage*, 204)

[86] Dilan, *Türkiye'nin*, p. 73.
[87] The pact became moot after Iran was invaded in World War II.

Turkey's relations with the Balkans[88] took a similarly peaceful turn soon after 1923. Turkey signed a friendship treaty with Albania in 1923 and with Bulgaria and Yugoslavia in 1925. Friendly relations with Greece were also established.[89] The first Balkan Conference was convened on October 5, 1930, with Albania, Bulgaria, Romania, Turkey, Yugoslavia, and Greece in attendance. The attendees issued a joint declaration recommending the formation of a Balkan Pact. War between the members of the Balkan Pact would be prohibited; economic, social, cultural, and political cooperation would be encouraged. The second Balkan Conference took place in October 1931, and Turkey took an active role in trying to maintain the status quo in the Balkans.[90] In the next two conferences, Turkey and Greece cooperated to curb the revisionist aims of Bulgaria. In 1933, Turkey and Greece signed the Pacte d'Entente Cordiale. The sides agreed to respect each other's borders, to consult each other in international disputes, and to protect each other's interests in international conferences (by possibly sending a common representative). Turkey signed cooperation treaties with Romania and Yugoslavia in 1933 as well. These three treaties formed the basis of the Balkan Pact, from which Albania and Bulgaria were excluded. The Balkan Entente was formed in 1934 and operated successfully[91] until 1936. After 1937, the actions of Germany and Italy in Eastern Europe brought about the dissolution of the pact, despite Turkey's efforts. The pact had its last meeting in 1940.

Ankara–Moscow relations: 1923–1938

As noted in the previous sections, when the Republic of Turkey was proclaimed in 1923, relations between Moscow and Ankara were as close as they had ever been. The two sides remained relatively friendly in the interwar period. Tevfik Rüştü Aras, Minister of Foreign Affairs from 1925 to 1938, wrote in his memoirs: "The friendship between Turkey and the USSR came out of the interwar period even stronger

---

[88] Though the Balkans are not really East, at this time in history they were not really West either. Toynbee considered the Balkan states to be part of the "Near East."

[89] Discussions of a Turkish–Greek "EU" in the late 1920s. See Clark, *Twice a Stranger*, p. 201.

[90] Dilan, *Türkiye'nin*, p. 89.

[91] Acting together during Italy's invasion of Ethiopia and also during the Montreux Conference over the status of the Straits.

for the trials imposed by the unexpected, chaotic developments of the international system."[92] While this friendship was a significant contributing factor to Turkish independence in 1923, it is hard to believe that Moscow would agree with Aras's optimistic assessment; this was a "friendship" that gave the Bolsheviks much less than they bargained for. In fact, throughout the interwar years, the ties between the two states gradually decayed and completely snapped after World War II.

As previously discussed, during the Independence War, members of the Ankara government frequently hinted that they were going to adopt socialism once they were fully sovereign.[93] They even promised to use the seat of the Caliph[94] to help the Bolshevik designs in foreign relations. When Mustafa Kemal sent Tevfik Rüştü Aras to Moscow on a diplomatic mission, he told Aras: "If the world does not recognize us, we will unite with the communists, and find our place in the new world order. But under no conditions will we ever accept foreign

---

[92] Aras, *Atatürk'ün*, p. 33.
[93] "From the editorial of Hakime-i Milliye, the official organ of the Ankara Government (8 March 1921): ... We will adopt most principles of socialism without giving up our national administration. For example, we will gradually nationalize factories. We will increase public ownership for the benefit of the people. In other words, we will become state socialists ...";
"Mustafa Kemal: ... faced with the ominous possibility of losing our country to British colonialism, if the practical application of Bolshevik principles offer salvation, we might need to adopt those principles regardless of how difficult it might be to implement them ..."; "Letter from Mustafa Kemal to Ttcherin: ... It is my sincere belief and that of my compatriots that once the Western proletariat on the one hand, and the enslaved Asian and African peoples, on the other hand, figure out how the international capital exploits them for maximum profit and tricks them into killing and enslaving each other, and once they know in their hearts that colonization policies amount to murder, that day will be the last day of the hegemony of the bourgeoisie." Perinçek, *Atatürk'ün Sovyetlerle*, p. 407.
[94] Extract from the transcript of the meeting between Mustafa Kemal and Comrade Esba, the Propaganda and Action Officer for the Eastern Peoples (January 29, 1921):
"If we gain control of the Caliph, we can use him as a weapon to unite all the Muslim People against the West. This issue also requires the reinterpretation of Islamic ideas so that they do not contrast with the principles of revolution. I think that once all the Muslim states gain their independence and taste popular sovereignty, their devotion to the Caliph will disappear ... Us Turks are among the most mistreated peoples of the world. Therefore, the International [sic] can count on our support. With our struggle against Western imperialism, we support the 3rd International's [sic] ideas in action." *Ibid.*

intervention. We are sincere in this promise; this is not a game."[95] The Bolsheviks returned Mustafa Kemal's enthusiasm by giving the Anatolian resistance military and monetary support. Furthermore, they lobbied for Ankara's inclusion in international conferences.[96]

After the Republic was proclaimed, the Ankara government did not adopt socialism, preferring a mixed economy in state planning. In foreign relations, however, the two states remained close at first. Turkey consulted with the Soviet Union over important foreign policy decisions, such as the decision to join the League of Nations in 1932. However, by the 1930s, these relations had started to show signs of strain.

Soviet emissaries reported[97] the repeated pronouncements of Mustafa Kemal that the two regimes should become more similar. However, by the 1930s, the Republic of Turkey had been around for almost a decade and had not yet delivered on any of its substantial promises to Moscow. A telegram by the Soviet Ambassador in November 1933 expresses his suspicion that Turkey was using the Soviet card to strengthen her power in the West and to improve her standing in the Balkans.[98] A meeting between the Soviet Representative Comrade Karahan and Mustafa Kemal on November 29, 1935, was symptomatic of this tension in the relationship. In his top-secret report to Stalin, Comrade Rozengolts relayed the following scene from this meeting:

Kemal ... asked why he was not congratulated on the anniversary of Turkish independence ... Karahan reminded him of the congratulatory telegram sent by Comrade Kalinin. Kemal, with a resentful voice, said "Yes, I am aware of that and have even replied to it, but I am not talking about messages brought by middlemen. I am not only the President of Turkey, but also the leader of the Turkish People." And looking at Karahan, he asked: "Who is your leader?" Karahan replied that Comrade Stalin was our leader. "Then why did he not send me the telegram personally? Everybody else did. He is trying to show that he does not want to recognize me." Karahan told him that it was not acceptable for Comrade Stalin to send congratulatory

---

[95] Aras, *Atatürk'ün*, p. 205.   [96] *Ibid.*

[97] Telegram from Soviet Ambassador Astahov to People's Commissariat of Foreign Relations (April 3, 1933) in Perinçek, *Atatürk'ün Sovyetlerle.*

[98] Telegram from Soviet Ambassador Astahov to People's Commissariat of Foreign Relations (November 10, 1933). *Ibid.*

messages ... Kemal, still resentful, told him that he was a great friend of the Soviet Union, that this friendship would continue as long as he lived, but that he would honor this friendship only if it was a relationship of equals, that the middlemen hurt all this ... [Karahan tried to reassure him] ... Kemal interrupted Karahan ...: "I will accept this friendship only if there are equal relations; I will not accept any other kind. You might have a powerful and well-equipped army, but I am not afraid of it. I am not afraid of anybody in this world, you included ..."

Both sides had stopped trusting each other. In October 1939, Turkey signed a mutual cooperation treaty with Britain and France about which Moscow was very displeased. The treaty marked the de facto end of the friendship between the Soviet Union and Turkey, only a year after Mustafa Kemal's death.

European views regarding modern Turkey

After the Lausanne Conference, relations between Turkey and Western powers, especially Britain, were lukewarm. First, there was the unsettled dispute over the status of the Mosul province.[99] Second, Western observers were skeptical of the domestic reforms the Ankara government was pushing through in Turkey at great speed. Diplomatic relations would not be improved until after the settlement of the Mosul question in 1926. Perceptions about the durability of Turkish reforms also started to change toward the 1930s.

After the proclamation of the Republic in 1923, the Ankara government started pushing drastic reforms in every aspect of life in Turkey. These changes were meant to help Turkey join the community of "civilized nations." Originally, the European press were skeptical of these reforms, especially because they were being imposed from above. In the early years, it is possible to see two kinds of views reflected in the press and books about Turkey. The first view argued

---

[99] Britain claimed that Mosul province belonged to Iraq – a British mandate – for geographical and strategic reasons. Turkey argued that the province had a Turkish majority and, therefore, belonged in Turkey. The League of Nations recommended that the Mosul province stay with Iraq at least for a 25-year mandate period and asked that the Kurds in the region be given some local autonomy. One day after the Mosul decision of the League of Nations Council, Turkey signed a new friendship treaty with Moscow. See e.g. Dilan, *Türkiye'nin*, p. 38.

that modernization efforts would not succeed[100] and that Mustafa Kemal was being oppressive and authoritarian[101] in his efforts; the second, friendlier view thought that Turkey should be congratulated for trying[102] (again with the implication that the reforms would likely fall short).[103] The British press in general viewed Turkey's foreign policy before the settlement of the Mosul dispute as revisionist and no different than the strategy of the Young Turks.[104] That judgment softened somewhat after the Ankara Treaty resolving the Turkey–Iraq border dispute.

For instance, the *Daily Telegraph* (December 31, 1927) noted that the new Turkey had full independence and was pleased about its military prestige. However, according to the *Telegraph*, Turkey wanted more, because Turkey had become the leader of an Asian movement that resisted European influence and it claimed full equality with Europe. Moreover, Turkey wanted her leadership to be recognized by the Muslim world. *The Times*, on the other hand, was of the opinion that Turkey had already attained a special place between Europe and Asia thanks to her own efforts. Turkey was perceived in Asia as an ambassador of Western European civilization. In the meantime, Europe, *The Times* said, admired, with some reservations, what the country had accomplished.[105] The eminent British historian Arnold Toynbee concurred: "The fundamental fact in modern Turkish history is that the Turks, starting from an historical background and a social system far removed from ours, have latterly been coming on to our ground as fast as it has been humanly possible for them to travel over the rough country that intervenes."[106]

By the 1930s, the coverage in Europe regarding Turkey had become even more positive. For instance, in 1930, the *Contemporary Review* argued that Turkey and Japan were the most modern countries of Asia. In an article published on November 2, 1933, *Near East and India* observed that Turkey had made the transition from the Middle

---

[100] *The Spectator* (March 8, 1924); *The Spectator* (August 5, 1925) in Yılmaz, *İngiliz*, pp. 75, 78.
[101] *The Morning Post* (July 23, 1926). *Ibid*, p. 79.
[102] *The Times* (October 17, 1925). *Ibid*, p. 77.
[103] See *ibid*. for other examples and a detailed discussion of trends. Also see Toynbee and Ross, "Modernisation of the Middle East," for a discussion among British scholars about the developments in Turkey.
[104] Yılmaz, *İngiliz*, p. 157.   [105] July 25, 1928, p. 13.
[106] Toynbee, *Turkey*, p. 8.

Ages to modernity in only a decade, and that now Turkey was a strong "border guard" in the Near and Middle East. Indeed, throughout the 1930s, Turkey was seen as a devoted facilitator of international peace.[107] In 1937, *The Morning Post*[108] declared Turkey to be the most peaceful country in Europe. Thus, by the time of Atatürk's death in November 1938, the days when Lord Balfour called Atatürk the "most terrible of all the terrible Turks"[109] and deemed Turkey a country of brigands[110] were in the past.

The League of Nations

Despite the unfavorable rulings of the League of Nations on matters concerning Turkey in the 1920s,[111] Turkey accepted the League's invitation to join in the work of the Preparatory Commission for the Disarmament Conference in 1928. Turkey also ratified the Briand–Kellogg Pact in 1929, participated in the International Opium Convention, and implemented several humanitarian and legal measures recommended by the League.[112] Having established such friendly relations with the League, a question arose in the early 1930s as to why Turkey had not joined the League. In 1931, the view expressed by Foreign Affairs Minister Aras was that Turkey could not join the League yet, because it was not clear if Turkey could be a member of the Council of the League of Nations: this situation violated the equal rights and treatment principle that had been the cornerstone of Turkish policy since independence. A year later, however, Aras observed that Turkey would be happy to join the League if it was

---

[107] *The Times*, October 29, 1932, p. 9; *Daily Telegraph*, December 1, 1933, p. 21; *The Listener*, November 29, 1933, p. 820; *The Economist*, April 8, 1936, p. 122; *Fortnightly Review*, v141, March 1937, pp. 328–9; in Yılmaz, *İngiliz.*

[108] March 24, 1937, p. 12.

[109] *Time Magazine* (November 21, 1938): Obituary of Atatürk.

[110] Güçlü, "Turkey's Entrance."

[111] In this period, Turkey viewed the League with great suspicion. See e.g. extract from Isaac F. Marcosson's Mustafa Kemal interview, *Saturday Evening Post* (July 13, 1923): "Mustafa Kemal: The biggest mistake of the League is its separation of nations into those who have the right to rule and those who deserve to be ruled over." In Uğurlu, *Yabancı Gözüyle.* The main points of contention were: the population exchange issue; the "Etabli" problem; and the Mosul dispute. See Güçlü, "Turkey's Entrance."

[112] Here's an example of how such reforms were received:

thought that Turkish foreign policy was compatible with the League's principles.

Following Aras's suggestion, the Special July Session of the League of Nations Assembly unanimously voted to invite Turkey to join. All the members spoke in favor of admitting Turkey, emphasizing the country's strategic importance between Europe and Asia.[113] Thus, Turkey was elected to the Council in 1934 and became a very active member, committed to keeping the status quo and peace in Europe.

After Turkey joined the League in 1932, she entered a rapprochement period with the Western powers, especially Britain and France. Britain supported Turkey in the Montreux Conference in 1936, and helped settle the question of the status of the Straits in Turkey's favor. The same year, King Edward VIII visited Istanbul and signed a trade agreement. As the situation in Europe grew tense in 1938, Turkey started negotiating alliances with Britain and France. Finally, despite Germany's threats of withholding products and credit from Turkey, a tripartite agreement was signed in 1939, which put Turkey in the Allied camp.

Shaping modern Turkey

Turkey lost 85 percent of its territories and 75 percent of its population between 1870 and 1920.[114] This fact and the experience of the Ottoman Empire with the intervention of Western powers in domestic affairs had two effects on the Turkish mindset after 1923: a discernible paranoia about territorial integrity and a strong desire to be respected in the international system. In the interwar period, these two attitudes were – and had to be – intimately connected. However, in the beginning Turks themselves were divided on how best to achieve the status the country so desired.

"One other example of progress is that Japan has just raised her marriage age to sixteen, and Turkey has raised her marriage age to fifteen for boys and girls. That is not at all a bad example for certain European countries, who retain the marriage age of twelve, comforting themselves with the reflection that marriages at such an age very seldom take place, quite forgetting the effect *their example* may have on smaller or *less civilized* countries." Crowdy, "Humanitarian Activities," 161 (italics added).

[113] Güçlü, "Turkey's Entrance."
[114] *Ottoman Archives.*

In the first session of the Turkish Parliament during the Independence War, there were three main divisions in the Assembly. The largest group, headed by Mustafa Kemal, favored a pragmatic approach, negotiating with both the West and Russia as conditions required. A second group favored Eastward expansion. The smallest group wanted Turkey to become an active influence in the Turkic Republics of Central Asia, with Moscow's assistance.[115] These groups roughly corresponded to the three dominant ideological movements in the late Ottoman Empire: Turkish nationalism with selective Westernization (i.e. the Japanese model), Pan-Islamism, and Pan-Turanism. Mustafa Kemal rejected both Pan-Islamism and Pan-Turanism because he found their aspirations unrealistic.[116]

After the military victory, the main division in the Parliament regarding domestic policy was between, on the one hand, those who favored keeping the old Ottoman system, either entirely or partially intact, and, on the other, those who favored adopting a new, Western system.[117] In the end, the Westernizing forces won out. There are two reasons for this: first, Mustafa Kemal's personal influence; and second, the fact that the Westernizing camp made a more compelling case, given Turkey's previous experience in the international system and the contemporary standards of international society.

In mainstream approaches to history in Turkey, Mustafa Kemal (Atatürk) gets almost exclusive credit as the driving force behind Turkish domestic reforms. While exaggerated, this view has some basis in reality. Atatürk had consolidated his power as the leader of the new Turkish nation during the Independence War. The war-time Parliament made him executive-in-chief and gave him wide latitude in his powers. After the Republic was established, he was elected President. Leaving aside assassination attempts and two brief forays into a multi-party system, Atatürk did not face substantial opposition. Therefore, the fact that he personally was committed to Westernization, and that most of these reforms were planned and implemented by him personally, is important in explaining why Turkey chose the path of Westernization.

---

[115] Report of the General Officer Commanding in Chief, Allied Forces, Constantinople; No. C.R.A.F. 543, October 5, 1921, in Şimşir, *İngiliz Belgelerinde.*
[116] Atatürk, *Söylev.*   [117] Demirel, *Birinci Meclis'te Muhalefet*, p. 34.

However, Atatürk's personal biases are not an adequate causal explanation for this choice. First of all, attributing everything to Atatürk's power – as the official account in Turkey has been wont to do since his death – leaves open the question of why Atatürk himself favored this path. Second, such an account also misses the complexity of Turkish politics in that era. Atatürk was no Stalin and the early sessions of the Parliament are notable for lively discussion and debates despite the absence of formal party structures.[118] While the system was not democratic, Atatürk preferred to rule by persuasion rather than persecution. This is why, for instance, he drafted *The Speech* and read it to the Turkish Parliament over the course of three months. *The Speech* chronicles Atatürk's motivations, plans, and decisions from the end of World War I to 1927.[119] It is a very detailed account that aimed to justify and legitimize his actions to his contemporaries and to future generations. Therefore, we must ask why Atatürk's audience found the program of Westernization compelling. Furthermore, they did not merely come on board; the general population was very much energized by Atatürk's program, and continued on the same path even after Atatürk's death – so much so that even contemporary Turkey is still marked by the worldview of the interwar period. They did so because Westernization/modernization were presented to skeptics and detractors as the only way to exist and thrive in the international system. In the debates over and justifications of each of the proposed reforms, there is a common thread: the Westernization camp always made an intimate connection between (Western) civilization on the one hand, and autonomy, sovereignty, and power on the other hand. It was argued that a country could not have the latter without the former.

"There Is Only One Civilization"

In 1923, the idea that all laws and rules should follow the Western model gained traction not only in the Cabinet (and the Parliament at large) but also among the leaders of influential groups such as the *Türk Ocakları*[120] ("The Turkish Hearth") organization.[121] The principle that

---

[118] *Ibid.*   [119] Atatürk, *Söylev.*
[120] *Türk Ocakları* was a neighborhood organization for youth with a clear purpose of nation-building. Üstel, *Türk Ocakları.*
[121] Atay, *Çankaya*; Demirel, *Birinci Meclis'te Muhalefet*; Özer, *Osmanlıdan Cumhuriyete*; Berkes, *Türkiye'de Çağdaşlaşma*; Özer, *Avrupa Yolunda.*

this was the only way a state could survive in the international system became the centerpiece of Turkish policy.[122]

For instance, the Minister of Justice, Mahmut Esat, said in 1924: "The Turkish Nation, who is committed to following the path to join Modern civilization, cannot modify Modern civilization according to its needs; it has to adapt to the demands of this civilization whatever the cost."[123] Modern civilization, according to Turkish Westernizers, was based on principles of rationality and enlightenment. Any Ottoman institution that did not embody these two principles had to be left behind. The Sultanate had to go, because it was against the popular will. The Caliphate was an office that could only exist in a theocratic system – and religion clearly was not rational,[124] so the Caliphate also had to be abolished. Religion had to be forced into the private realm, as it was in Europe. Religious clothes were banned in public, and religious schools and organizations were closed. Basically, everything from the alphabet to the education system, from the civil code to clothing had to change and become "rational," "practical," and "modern," just as it was in Europe.[125]

The noteworthy aspect of the rationalizations for these reforms is how they were simultaneously grounded in nationalist rhetoric. The nationalist *Türk Ocakları* organization was supposed to operate according to the dual principles of nationalism and Westernization. Their founder, Hamdullah Suphi, explains this duality:

Türk Ocağı ... is progressive and contemporary. [A member] knows that this organization is an ambassador of the West in the East. Türk Ocağı ... is Westernizing. We only became aware of our Turkishness when we approached Europeanness, and we will be Turks as long as we feel European. There is only one civilization though it varies in form. However, Türk Ocağı aspires to the Western form of civilization.[126]

---

[122] Berkes, *Türkiye'de Çağdaşlaşma*, p. 469.

[123] *Ibid.*, p. 470.

[124] Especially Islam, which, in addition to being non-rational, was also "Eastern" and "backward."

[125] Berkes, *Türkiye'de Çağdaşlaşma*, p. 607.

[126] Suphi, "Irk ve Milliyet," 7.

The same sentiment was echoed in the organization's activity program issued in 1926. The program claimed that Eastern civilization was in ruins and that Turkey was now an ambassador of the West in the East.[127]

Atatürk resorted to similar themes to justify the reforms. In *The Speech*, he said that the essential principle was that the Turkish nation should live with dignity and pride, which could only happen with full autonomy: "However rich and strong a nation may be, if she is not fully independent, she will be viewed as a servant by the civilized people."[128] According to Atatürk, the Ottoman Empire had lost all dignity and was viewed as a subjugate for this reason.[129] Furthermore, he argued that foreign policy[130] had to be compatible with domestic form[131] and vice versa.[132] Atatürk's official biographer and friend

---

[127] See *Türk Ocakları Mesai Programı* in Üstel, *Türk Ocakları*.

[128] Atatürk, *Nutuk (Söylev): Belgeler*, p. 43.

[129] "Atatürk's briefing of the *Neue Freie Presse* Reporter about the Republic (22/9/1923): ... Suppose you have two men before you; one of them is rich and has all kinds of vehicles at his disposal; the other is poor and has nothing in his hands. Apart from this material difference, the latter is no different or deficient in moral spirit. This is the situation of Turkey against Europe. Apart from defining us as a tribe that is doomed to backwardness, the West has done everything to hasten our ruin. When West and East appear to clash, it is best to look toward Europe to find the source of conflict." Uğurlu, *Yabancı Gözüyle*.

[130] "Atatürk's interview with French reporter Maurice Pernot on the eve of the creation of the New Republic (29/9/1923): There are many countries, but there is only one civilization; for a nation to progress, it needs to join in this one and only civilization ... We have always walked from the East towards West. If we seem to have changed our course recently, you must admit that it was through no fault of our own. You made us do it. However, even if our bodies are in the East, our opinions look toward the West. We want to modernize our country. Our only goal is to constitute a modern, and therefore Western, state in Turkey." Uğurlu, *Yabancı Gözüyle*.

[131] "Gentlemen! Our nation will demonstrate her intrinsic qualities in this new state and prove that the Republic of Turkey rightfully belongs among the independent, civilized states of the world." Atatürk, *Söylev*, p. 380.

[132] "Atatürk's Speech to Turkish Parliament regarding the Proclamation of the Republican Regime (29/9/1923): Gentlemen! For centuries our nation has been victimized and unjustly treated in the East because it was thought that the Turkish nation was lacking in certain qualities. In the recent years, our nation has demonstrated, with advancements in education, tendencies and faculties, that those who passed judgments of Turkey were people easily deceived by appearances and lacked critical analysis skills. Thanks to the

Atay remarks that Atatürk did not believe in the mermaid myth.[133] Atatürk and the Westernizing camp in the early republican period were convinced that no problem could be solved without making a clear choice about which civilization Turkey belonged to. According to them, Turkey deserved to be independent, autonomous, and well respected, but first she had to prove this to the world by demonstrating she was civilized.[134]

Religion, particularly the fact that Turkey's was Islam, was seen as the biggest obstacle to joining "Civilization." This is the reason why the Caliphate had to be abolished, despite the costs to Turkey's relationships with Muslim communities in India. Those in domestic politics who were in favor of keeping the Caliphate thought that the regime could be changed to a theocracy with minimal effort, with the Parliament acting as an advisory council to the Caliph.[135] They argued that this would put Turkey in a spiritual leadership position in the world, especially if the Caliph was backed by a Parliament representing the popular will.[136]

Atatürk and the Westernizing camp based their argument on two main points: one, a theocracy could not join the community of civilization; two, having the Caliph in Turkey would decrease, not increase, Turkey's stature.[137] Atatürk argued that a Westernized, modern Turkey that had joined the community of civilization would have a higher stature in the Muslim world as the messenger/ambassador of the West and Western values, than would a theocratic state harkening

---

new regime, it will be even easier for Turkey to prove her qualities to the civilized world. Turkey will prove with her masterpieces that she deserves the status she has heretofore occupied in the world." *Atatürk'ün Bütün Eserleri.*

[133] Atay, *Çankaya*, p. 434.

[134] "A Speech delivered by Atatürk on the 2nd Anniversary of the Victory Day (30/8/1924): Gentlemen! Our nation's goal, our nation's purpose, is to be a civilized nation as recognized by the entire world. As you know, the existence, the worth, the right to independence and sovereignty of every tribe in the world is correlated with its possession and its ability to provide products of civilization. If a tribe cannot produce masterpieces of civilization, they are condemned to live without their independence and sovereignty. The history of humankind proves this point. Walking on the path of civilization is a life-or-death matter. Those who falter or turn back on this path will be doomed to drown under the powerful floods of civilization." *Atatürk'ün Bütün Eserleri.*

[135] Berkes, *Türkiye'de Çağdaşlaşma*, p. 449.

[136] *Ibid.*, p. 456.   [137] Atatürk, *Söylev*, pp. 347–84.

back to a bygone era.[138] It was with this same logic that the religious lodges were banned. Explaining that decision, Atatürk said:

the Republic of Turkey cannot be a country of dervishes, cult followers and religious fanatics. The most righteous, the most real cult (path) is the cult of civilization. Doing what civilization requires and demands is enough to be human. Leaders of cults will understand the truth of my words and will immediately shut down their lodges of their own accord, and accept the fact that their followers have now reached this level of maturity.[139]

Once religion was forced into the private realm, everything else reminiscent of the old religious order had to follow suit.

Turkish leaders were also of the opinion that one of the main reasons the West had been so prejudicial against Turkey in the past was because of the difference in costume. Therefore, one of the first reforms to be implemented had to do with adapting the Turkish costume, for both women and men, to the European standard. Hats received particular attention, and the European-style felt hat became the symbol of the new regime.[140] Atatürk himself argued that the fez was a symbol of ignorance, backwardness, fundamentalism, and hatred of civilization. By throwing it away, Turkey would show that there was nothing separating the Turkish nation from civilized nations.[141]

In 1924, the education system was centralized. Subsequently, in 1926, civil law was changed almost entirely, and the new civil code was modeled on the French and Swiss civil codes. The criminal code was based on the Italian model. Islamic courts were abolished and polygamy was banned. The equality of sexes was recognized. In 1928, the new Turkish alphabet was adopted. This was derived from

---

[138] *Ibid.*, p. 392.

[139] Kastamonu speech, August 30, 1925, Erüreten, *Türkiye Cumhuriyeti*, p. 86.

[140] Law on Wearing Top Hats (Şapka) November 25, 1925 – Preamble, The reasoning for the law:

"Even though the hat issue is of no real concern on its own, because Turkey plans to join the family of modern and civilized nations, for us it has special significance. Until now the fez and the turban were marks segregating Turkey from other civilized nations. It has become apparent that all civilized and modern nations have the top hat in common. Our mighty nation will be a model for everyone by wearing this modern and civilized headpiece as well." *Ibid.*, p. 6

[141] Atatürk, *Söylev*, p. 409.

the Latin alphabet, whereas the old one had used Arabic script. The lunar Islamic calendar was exchanged for the Western calendar, and Islamic measurement units were replaced by the metric system. In 1934, legislation introduced Turkish citizens to surnames. Finally, in 1935, women were given the right to vote and compete in elections. Throughout his tenure, Atatürk personally encouraged women to get into professions that traditionally were not open to women, including politics, aviation, and the natural sciences. He also supported Turkish women's entry to international beauty pageants,[142] with the expressed purpose of showing the world how civilized Turkish women were under the new Republic.[143]

Heads and tails: stigmatization, national habitus, and sovereignty

Your opinion that Turkey carries an important role in the fate of Eastern nations is entirely right. I think that Turkey plays an interesting role due to its geographical location on the borders of the Eastern and Western worlds. This situation is beneficial on the one hand, but perilous on the other. Because we are able to stop the spread of Western imperialism to the East, we have gained sympathy of Eastern peoples who view Turkey as a model. On the other hand, this situation is dangerous for us because it places the entirety of the burden of the aggression towards the East on our shoulders. All of Western hatred is focused on us. Turkey is proud of its position and is happy to fulfill this duty for the East. (Mustafa Kemal, speaking with Comrade Esba, January 29, 1921)

---

[142] The first beauty pageant in Turkey was organized by the *Cumhuriyet* newspaper in 1929. The 1930 pageant was held with the purpose of sending the winner to the European Beauty Pageant in Paris. The newspaper claimed that this would show the world how modern Turkey was, how beautiful Turkish women were, and that Turks belonged to the white race. A true Turkish beauty would have the following qualities: character, health, smartly applied make-up, moral aptitude, proper hygiene, a sweet demeanor, a taste in clothing, sincerity, genuineness, and abstinence from any exercise or diet that would unnaturally enhance the body, quoted in *Resimli Ay* (January 26, 1930). Özer, *Avrupa Yolunda*, p. 304.

[143] The first beauty queen of Turkey was sent to Europe with much fanfare. The following year's queen, Keriman Halis, was declared Miss Universe. Turkey had now proved to the world how "modern" Turkish women were. Thankfully, after her victory, Turkey took a break from beauty pageants for several decades.

Turkey now defends the European civilization at the gates of Asia. But at the same time, Turkey is protecting Asia against all of Europe's imperialist desires. (Herbert Melzig, *Atatürk*)

In the previous section, I explained how, in less than a decade, Turkey went from being perceived as a great threat to the West, especially Britain, to a state perceived as committed to peace and order. In the interwar period, Turkey came to be respected by both the West and the East for both its foreign policy and domestic reforms, at least compared to its recent past. It is not possible to explain this outcome without understanding the significant degree to which the concern for status in the international system shaped the domestic and foreign strategies of Turkey after World War I.

In the 1920s, Turkey chose a domestic system because of concerns over its status in the international system. The choice was made in the context of a normative ideal that placed a premium on "modernity" and tied the right to be independent to the level of civilization. Those domestic choices, in turn, brought Turkey closer to the West in the 1930s. This is not to say that material constraints did not play any role, but ultimately what tipped the outcome in favor of the West was Turkey's obsession with attaining membership in the community of civilized nations, thereby guaranteeing its independence. Having won on the battleground against Western powers and their allies, Turkey's independence was not in danger because of any threat of military occupation, but because of its stigmatized status as an outsider in the international system. This is the condition the Turkish leaders wanted to rectify.

Turkey sought equal status with the West because the new Turkish nation's habitus was shaped by an imperial past. In the case of former empires, the domestic expectations about international recognition are especially high, because maintaining ontological security requires preserving continuity in relationships to the world to the degree that is possible. Empires have hierarchical worldviews.[144] After the nineteenth century, Turkey's ontological security was continuously threatened by not having a prestigious (or "normal") position in the international system, and the Ottoman Empire's defeat and collapse only made this

---

[144] For Turkish views of their place in the Ottoman world, see Bozkurt, *Azınlık Imtiyazları*, pp. 60–1; Lewis, *The Emergence of Modern Turkey*, p. 127; Akçam, *Türkiye'yi Yeniden Düşünmek*, p. 191.

problem more acute. As the heir of the Ottoman Empire, the new regime in Turkey had to justify its legitimacy to a domestic audience united by the common belief that Turkey should have a higher stature in the international system, even if they disagreed on the best way to attain such stature.

As the successor state to the Ottoman Empire, the domestic audience (or at least the intelligentsia) in Turkey was acutely aware that Europe and the West did not apply status standards to Eastern states uniformly or objectively. The experience of the Ottoman Empire with capitulations and foreign interventions on behalf of minorities had taught the leaders of Turkey that these standards were used to deny Turkey her sovereign rights and to weaken her material power. In other words, there was a general sense that the treatment of the Ottoman Empire in the nineteenth century was unjust and discriminatory. This belief is evident in all of the arguments of the Turkish delegation at Lausanne and Turkey's insistence that all residual institutions of foreign presence be removed from the country. Furthermore, stigmatization of Turkey was not only something Turkish leaders had dreamed up as a justification for their failure to stop the empire from unraveling, or as an excuse for their future shortcomings. Turks were very much aware that *a priori* nations as discussed by Toynbee (see above, pp. 120–2) were the number one obstacle to their normal functioning and ontological security in the international system.

Turkey accepted that it had to prove to the West that it deserved to belong to the family of civilized nations through actual, visible steps, but simultaneously asserted that this was a choice Turkey was making and, moreover, was capable of making. Turks wanted to believe that they had been wrongly denied respect in the past for superficial, not intrinsic, reasons: the stigma of civilizational backwardness did not reflect an incorrigible defect. The leaders and the population of Turkey embraced the modernity standards of the early twentieth century, because implicit in the idea of modernity was the principle that "the most deserving" would advance.[145] Because of the promise held out by this logic, the content of the normative ideal was not

---

[145] As Bauman also notes, "ethnic-religious-cultural strangers are all too often tempted to embrace the liberal vision of group emancipation (erasing of a collective stigma) as a reward for individual efforts of self-improvement and self-transformation." *Modernity and Ambivalence*, p. 71.

questioned. Turkish leaders insisted on the moral and intrinsic equality of the Turkish nation with the West, and presented Turkey's lower
stature and defeat as resulting from a combination of factors such as
historical happenstance, the fault of the West, and the exaggerated
influence of religion in Ottoman affairs.

The obsession with cosmetic changes, such as the hat law, makes
sense when seen in this light. It was as if Turkey were a man who
intrinsically, *naturally*, belonged in the family of "civilized nations"
and he was marginalized only because he happened to be wearing
the wrong kind of hat. All of the Westernizing reforms were justified
to the domestic public with the logic that all of the powerful, civilized countries were doing things in this particular way, and that since
Turkey naturally belonged in that group, Turks should also adopt the
same ways. This is exactly the kind of strategy Goffman describes
when he talks about stigmatized individuals "correcting" their discrediting attribute.

As the above discussions make clear, there is no explanation besides
Turkey's obsession with joining the community of civilized states that
explains the lengths Turkey went to in transforming its domestic system. The Caliphate was relinquished because a theocracy was not
compatible with (Western) civilization and principles of modernity.
Turkish women went from the private domain to walking around on
stages in their bathing suits within five years, because Turkey had to
prove that it was a modern state and it did not deserve to be stigmatized. Every domestic reform was undertaken with this goal.

Realists argue that material competition produces like units, so
they may attribute Turkey's transformation to military defeat alone.
However, such an explanation overlooks the fact that in the Turkish
case, the Turkish Army, which would be the main factor in a competition of material strength, was already modernized to a great extent,
even if it lacked resources. It was the first Ottoman institution to
import European teachers and adopt European standards; German
officers had trained its officers throughout the nineteenth century.
When Turkey won the Independence War in 1922 and the Republic
was created in 1923, the army was the unit most "like" its Western
counterparts. Furthermore, it had proven itself in battle against
unlikely odds. If military competition or security was the only factor driving Turkish policy, Turkey could have stopped there. There
would have been no need to completely uproot the entire gamut of

the country's traditions and institutions. The domestic reforms, as is made clear in numerous speeches cited above, were very clearly driven by the quest for stature and civilization.

The choice to socialize, and to pursue socialization to this degree, was a strategic choice for the new regime: yet it was sustainable because it promised the domestic society the kind of respect its national habitus had conditioned it to expect, but could not attain through military means. The fact that Turkey had come perilously close to losing its sovereignty meant that the distance to the established "old village" was great, and the degree of emulation it had to go through to prove its right to an equal standing was high. The dominant norm of sovereignty also required comprehensive changes, since the modernity standard was a simple abstraction away from the civilization standard.

Any argument that Turkey's socialization was an accident or imposed from outside is mistaken. There were some groups in society that had internalized the normative ideal of the international system, but many people in key places had not. The leaders of the new regime – notably, Atatürk – were mostly soldiers. They had Westernized military training and were familiar with European literature, but had not spent much time in Europe or had any extended contact with Europeans besides German military officers during World War I. Very few of them had traveled abroad after 1918. Despite Atatürk's quest to gain Turkish entry into "civilization," it is clear from his speeches that he was not a particularly fervent admirer of Europe.[146] If the leaders were somewhat skeptical about the normative demands of Europe, the domestic population was even more so, many groups preferring their traditional ways. Because Turkey had won the Independence War and had her terms accepted at the Lausanne Conference, there were very few foreigners in Turkey after 1923. To sum up, in Turkey's case, it is not possible to speak of the

---

[146] He liked to drink and he was a womanizer, though he pushed reforms that he thought were necessary for the country but that he could not personally adapt to. For instance, it is reported that he would only listen to Turkish classical and folk music in private, but he diverted Turkey's entire budget for the arts into the creation of operas and Western-style music. Similarly, in public he was a strong force for the equality of women, arguing that a nation with half of its population behind curtains cannot be civilized: but in private he was patriarchal. His only marriage was short-lived because Latife Hanım was too opinionated and outspoken. Calışlar, *Latife Hanım*.

socializing influence of "victorious" powers. The decision to completely Westernize might have been top-down, but it was also organic.
A majority of the reforms were undertaken in the 1920s when Turkey
was almost isolated from the West and her only powerful "friend"
was the Soviet Union. The evidence permits no other interpretation
besides strategic socialization to overcome stigmatization within an
international system that was marked very clearly by an established-
outsider dynamic.

Turkey's decision to commit itself to a wholehearted Westernization/
modernization/civilization project in its domestic realm is what ultimately brought it closer to the West in terms of military alliances, and
drove it away from the Soviet Union. Furthermore, Turkey's insistence
on its own sovereign recognition as a civilized nation was the underlying principle driving Turkey's arrangements with Eastern states.

Turkey could have chosen to align herself entirely with the Soviet
Union, and in fact there were strong material incentives to do so.
However, Turkey's priority was always acceptance and equal treat-
ment by the West. On several occasions, Atatürk said to his colleagues
they would join Moscow if necessary, but he always made it sound
as if this was the less preferable option. The Soviet Union before
World War II was not yet a superpower, but it was more powerful
than Turkey and some of the European states. Why was the Soviet
Union's friendship and military support not enough for Turkey? The
Soviet Union had been isolated from international society after the
Bolsheviks took over, and aligning with the Soviet Union completely
would mean finding a place in a "new world order"; it was unpredictable how this world order would rank compared to the existing one.
In addition, the more Turkey wanted to become recognized as a civilized nation and took the steps to bring about this outcome, the closer
it became ideologically to states that the Soviet Union had distanced
itself from. There is also the sense that since the Soviet Union had
taken itself out of this status game, its stature had lessened in the eyes
of Turkey; in the confrontation between Mustafa Kemal and Comrade
Karahan cited above, Mustafa Kemal is not acting as if he is dealing
with a country that is considerably stronger than Turkey. The Soviet
Union at the time was openly claiming the mantle of "Easternness" in
an attempt to challenge the normative power of the established core.
Moscow's strategy no doubt held some initial appeal for Turkey – the
life of the discreditable requires a much higher degree of information

management than the life of the discredited. As Goffman observes, "[A stigmatized individual] can voluntarily disclose himself, thereby radically transforming his situation from that of an individual with information to manage to that of an individual with uneasy social situations to manage."[147] Nevertheless, as Goffman notes, disclosure requires the willingness to take on uncomfortable encounters – and the memory of such were much fresher in Turks' minds in the interwar years than they were for the Russians. At some level, therefore, the Russians' flaunting of the Eastern label bothered the Turkish leaders and decreased their willingness to be associated with the Soviet Union: "a person who wishes to conceal his disability will notice disability-revealing mannerisms in another person. Moreover, he is likely to resent those mannerisms that advertise the fact of disability, for in wishing to conceal his identity he wishes others to conceal theirs."[148] This would actually establish patterns of treatment that Turkey would adapt in the future vis-à-vis all "Eastern" nations.

Ultimately, Turkey joined the League of Nations, even though the League, as an instrument of European power, had not treated Turkey favorably at all. Turkey worked very hard to maintain the status quo in the Balkans and the Near East, instead of actively fighting against Western imperialism, as had been predicted in the early 1920s. While Turkey was against the mandate regime in principle, she was actually a transmitter of Western norms into mandated regions. By her own constant attempts to prove that she deserved to join the community of civilized, modern nations, Turkey legitimized the norm that sovereignty was something that needed to be earned, and that a nation needed to prove itself to the world community before it could become fully independent. When Turkey encouraged Eastern nations to organize around popular sovereignty movements and win their independence, it was because she wanted to lead the way for the nations of the East. In effect, for all of the anti-imperialist rhetoric of the war years, Turkey turned out to be the best emissary for imperialist norms – if it was possible for Turkey to successfully transform itself, the implication was that there was no inherent structural problem with civilization standards. Of course, Turkey took it even further. Under the guise of an "anti-imperialist" rhetoric, Turkey

---

[147] Goffman, *Stigma*, p. 100.   [148] *Ibid.*, p. 86.

actively encouraged other "outsider" countries to commit to the same advancement strategy. This strategy should not be taken lightly, for as Toynbee remarked, Turkey was seen as something of a test case for Westernization: "in studying the Westernization process in Turkey, we are increasing our understanding of the human world in which we ourselves live and move and have our being; for the issues with the West are confronting other non-Western peoples the world over."[149] The fact that Turkey's actions ended up affirming the normative order of the established-outsider dynamic definitely had something to do with Turkey's positive reception by the West in the 1930s.

Conclusion

I believe that the best policy is to be as powerful as possible in every field. Do not think that being powerful refers only to force of arms. On the contrary, I believe that this force comes last among the factors which constitute the whole. I believe that being powerful means being strong in the scientific, technical and moral areas. For if a nation is devoid of these values, even if we imagine all its members are equipped with the most advanced arms, it would be wrong to regard it as powerful. To be armed is not sufficient to take one's place as a human being in today's community of humanity ... I believe that for my country ... to achieve the progress of which I am well aware and of which we have gone without, it is necessary to work hard and continuously – in peace and tranquility, and above all while establishing freedom and independence. (Mustafa Kemal Atatürk, Ataturk'un Butun Eserleri, p. 288. Speech given on August 30, 1924)

The point of this chapter has been to illustrate that every step that Turkey and Turkish leaders took in the fateful years between 1918 and 1938 had an alternative. The choices they ended up making, taken together, can only be explained by the established-outsider dynamic that had been effective in the international system up until and during that time, as well as by the Turkish leaders' awareness of, adherence to, and, at times, resistance against this structure. Turkey is independent, sovereign, and confused about its identity today because of this dynamic and its desire to seek normalcy within it.

In the summer of 2007, hundreds of thousands of people marched on the streets of Turkey's major cities against the purported Islamization

---

[149] Toynbee, *Turkey*, p. 300.

of the Republic. The trigger for these marches was the fact that the wife of the then presidential candidate, Abdullah Gül, wears a headscarf. It has since come to light that these marches may have been organized by an underground organization of ex-military men, journalists, and bureaucrats bent on provoking the military to stage a coup to unseat the Justice and Development Party (AKP) government. Nevertheless, the majority of the hundreds of thousands of people who marched were sincere in their fears that there was something very troubling about the presidential candidate. Many Turks continue to believe that a president whose wife wears a headscarf would be worse for Turkey's image abroad than a military junta regime. Among the many slogans expressed on these marches were: "The spirit of the 1920s lights our way," "Just because you like the Rose,[150] we cannot tolerate his thorn." What is especially interesting about these developments is the fact that at the time of the marches, the AKP had been in power for almost five years. What brought things to a head (literally) was the realization that the headscarf, which is a symbol with incredible power in Turkey, was about to be attached to the head of state, which only has symbolic power. Even today, many Turks believe that respect in the international system can only be attained through Westernization, which they understand as being synonymous with displaying the superficial attitudes and markers of modernity. In the case of Turkey, the decision after defeat to overcome outsider status by following a strategy of stigma correction has taken on a life of its own, and has come to definitively shape the state identity around feelings of inferiority against the West and superiority toward the East. It is this decision around which all domestic cleavages are still organized.

Problems of the present day can all be traced back to the strategy Turkey settled on after the collapse of the Ottoman Empire. The Turkish modern state identity was a deliberate construction in direct response to the lessons drawn from the international interactions of the nineteenth and early twentieth centuries, and not an endogenous manifestation exclusively emanating from dynamics within state borders. When the Ottoman Empire was replaced by Turkey, the new regime took it upon itself to fashion a domestic strategy that would allow the state to feel ontologically more secure in its relations with

---

[150] A play on words: the presidential candidate's last name means rose. I assume his wife is supposed to be the thorn.

the West. The goal was to change the hierarchical, stigmatizing relationship between Turkey and Europe, and join the circle of the "established" states, but the republican regime constructed their strategy around a worldview that was based in the internalized lessons from *the normative structure of the nineteenth- and early-twentieth-century* international system. For instance, the Turkish state borrowed its understanding of secularism from the 1920s French model; in fact even the term is the same: *laicism*. This is the understanding that was incorporated into the modern Turkish state identity. Because this particular understanding of secularism is linked with Turkish understanding of "modernity," questioning it creates great anxiety for most secular Turks. Their understanding of the concepts of "nation" and "state," for instance, also remain firmly rooted in the normative ideals of the 1920s. Therefore, any demands for freedom of religious observation and/or accommodation of ethnic minority identities are interpreted as threats to Turkey's "modern" identity. While there is hardly any consensus in the West as to how best to accommodate group rights, to argue that such things are un-*modern* is to skip over almost a century of developments in Western identity politics.[151] Every hot-button issue in contemporary politics, from the inflexible definition of secularism employed by establishment Turks to the resistance to Kurdish efforts for recognition to the Armenian genocide, is rooted in Turkey's post-defeat quest for "civilization," and is therefore an unfortunate side effect of Turkey's responses to its stigmatized position.

Those were formative years for modern Turkey, and the aspirations as well as the psychoses of that period continue to shape the Turkish mindset. I think it would be fair to argue that, while the fall from grace as a great empire and the humiliating years of foreign intervention that the Ottoman Empire had to endure as a member of so-called "semi-civilized" humanity are a thing of the past, the wounds they have inflicted are still open. The European Union path on which Turkey has willingly set itself recycles many of these same issues, and Turkey's present-day attempts to place itself as a model of a secular or a moderate Muslim country, or as a mediator in Middle Eastern conflicts, echoes Turkey's earlier attempts to regain its lost status by

---

[151] For an excellent discussion of secular Turks' static understanding of "modernity" and the "West," see Özyürek, *Nostalgia for the Modern.*

trying to be a leader in the movement against imperialism at the exact same moment the country was wholeheartedly emulating the civilization of the imperialists.

Even in its most isolationist periods, the citizens and leaders of the Republic of Turkey have never stopped playing to an imagined audience that is constantly assessing how civilized and modern Turkey is.[152] Turks resent this intrusive gaze but crave its approval, and suspect the approval when it is dispensed, yet sense discrimination when it is not. While secular, urbanized Turks feel the effects of this gaze most strongly, even the most reactionary Turks are not immune to its penetration. Unlike in most "developing" countries, Turkey's choices have not been dictated from outside, but have been propelled through Turkey's seemingly inconsistent exercise of auto-Orientalism on the one hand and belief in its own intrinsic greatness on the other hand. This experience is something Turkey shares with Japan and Russia, and there is some solace to be found in that fact, and also in the knowledge that, given the realities of the international system, this path has served Turkey better than the alternatives. However, there is something particularly corrosive to the soul about always seeing oneself from others' eyes – it is not good for the individual psyche, and it is even worse for groups.

There is an apocryphal story about the first Turkish Miss Universe, Keriman Halis, who represented Turkey in the competition which was held in Belgium in 1932. In crowning Keriman, the head of the jury supposedly said:

Dear members of the jury, today we celebrate the victory of the European Christian civilization. Islam, which has been dominating the world for

---

[152] Here is but a recent example:

"Michelle Obama may have been the star of the US President's European show, but Turks were deprived of the chance to see her when she chose to return to her children ... The Turkish media have been following Michelle Obama's European visit with interest, carrying stories of her dress and exploits ... A picture of her at the G20 summit in London, standing next to Emine Erdogan, the wife of the Prime Minister, Tayyip Erdogan, attracted mixed emotions, however, since Mrs Erdogan's Muslim headscarf is viewed with distaste by secular Turkey's establishment ... 'I bet she decided not to come because she didn't want to be involved with our headscarved crowd,' said Cigdem, 39, an accountant. 'Who would? I'm glad we don't have to watch her posing side by side with them here.'" Erdem, "Disappointment".

1600 years, is now finished. Europe has finished it. Miss Turkey, Keriman, the representative of all Muslim women who once upon a time looked out to the world from behind curtains, is now among us in a bathing suit … This year we are not only selecting Miss Universe. We are celebrating the victory of Europe. The granddaughter of Suleiman the Magnificent … wants us to admire her. And we admire this girl because she has adapted to our ways. We select her as Miss Universe with the hope that all Muslims will follow in her footsteps. We will raise our glasses in honor of the victory of Europe.

Unfortunately, despite numerous references to this speech in conservative Turkish sources, I could not verify its authenticity from any Western source, and if it is real, it was also downplayed in mainstream Turkish newspapers of the time. However, even if it is only a figment of the imagination of Turkish conservatives, as it may very well be, I find it a suitable note to end this chapter with. Pursuit of status, regardless of the advantages it brings to the individual lower-ranking agent, makes those who have higher status stronger by legitimizing and normalizing their arbitrary normative order.

4 | *"The children": Japan (1945–1974)*

First there was silence, then sobs of grief.[1] The humiliation was almost too much to bear. Once again Japanese manhood had been put to the test against superior Western force, and once again it had been found wanting. But then an extraordinary thing happened. Moments after his victory, Dutch fans tried to rush to the mat to congratulate their hero. Immediately, however, Geesink raised his hand to stop them and turned to Kaminaga to make his bow. The Japanese audience rose to applaud this traditional gesture of respect. And they never forgot it. Geesink, the big Dutch victor in Tokyo who had shown the Japanese what skill as well as bulk could achieve, would be treated as a hero in Japan forever after.

Ian Buruma, Inventing Japan

Introduction

Japan has been a pacifist country and a reliable ally of the West for more than half a century. Today, most casual observers take this situation for granted, and generally assume that Japan's defeat and subsequent occupation by the United States left the country with virtually no other option.[2] It is true that Japan had limited options – the country was officially occupied for seven years and, later, Cold War dynamics narrowed Japan's room for maneuver. However, a careful look at Japan in the decades after the crushing defeat of 1945 reveals a country that not only made some unexpected choices and stuck to them, but also a state that was as preoccupied with its international stature as it had been before the war. The unexpected choices that Japan has made, from its resistance

---

[1] 1964 Tokyo Olympics, Judo Championship match.
[2] Ikenberry and Kupchan, "Socialization and Hegemonic Power," 305; Owen, "Transnational Liberalism," 131.

160

to remilitarization to its economic model, are intimately connected with Japan's desire to (re)gain the respect and recognition of the international community.

In this chapter, I explore Japan's choices and follow the same organization as Chapter 3. First, I provide a brief historical account of Japan, starting with the Meiji Restoration, and continuing on to the motivations of Imperial Japan. Second, I make the case that Japan made her own choices after 1945 despite the constraints of the post-World War II international system. In the third section of the chapter, I analyze those choices within the context of the stigmatization theory outlined in Chapters 1 and 2.

The European civilization standard and Japan: *Bunmei Kaika*[3]

"Civilization and Enlightenment" always was more a cultural than a political slogan, a matter of style and appearances. But appearances count for a lot in Japan. There was a satirical Meiji saying that went: "Knock a head without a top-knot, and you hear the sound of Bunmei Kaika." As if wearing one's hair in the European style were a sign of superior breeding. Some Meiji leaders seriously believed that a display of European manners would persuade Western powers to give up the unequal treaties. (Ian Buruma, *Inventing Japan*, p. 31)

Japan Westernized much later than Russia, but more comprehensively than Ottoman Turkey.[4] Despite the emergence of a backlash toward the end of the nineteenth century, the Meiji Restoration allowed Japan to retain its independence and made her a rising power in Asia in the early twentieth century.[5]

The Meiji Restoration takes its name from the claim that it restored the ancient form of Japanese rule.[6] The impetus was the encroaching European threat, just as in the *Tanzimat* reforms in the Ottoman Empire. Unlike the Ottomans, however, the Japanese had the "advantage" of dealing with an ethnically homogeneous society, relatively speaking, and also the benefit of geography.

---

[3] Civilization and Enlightenment.
[4] Bull and Watson, *Expansion of International Society*, p. 74.
[5] Watson, "Introduction," pp. 29–30.
[6] Buruma, *Inventing Japan*, p. 22.

As an island state, Japan had entered the nineteenth century in isolation. Over the nineteenth century, several outside events forced Japan to confront the reality of expanding European power. One of these factors was the increasing number of Russian probes south to the Kuril Islands.[7] Another was the realization of the developments occurring in China. The Opium War of 1839 and the subsequent 1842 Treaty of Nanking had forced China into capitulatory arrangements, which in effect signaled the loss of Chinese sovereignty.[8] This served as a wake-up call for the Japanese, who feared they might be next: "Bravery alone is not sufficient, the art of war demands something more. No outlandish power can compete with a European one, as can be seen by the great realm of China which has been conquered by only four thousand men."[9] Then came the Perry expedition in 1853.

The American commander, who arrived with four heavily armed black ships, demanded to deal only with the highest officials[10] of Japan.[11] After formal ceremonies, he departed, only to return six months later. Americans demanded trade privileges, arguing that the Chinese had found extending similar privileges very profitable; finally a compromise was reached whereby the Americans could use two Japanese ports for supplies.[12] Japan was unprepared for a coastal defense, but had nevertheless escaped the fate of China for the moment.

Soon other countries started pressing for what was granted to the United States. By 1855, the British and the Russians had their own privileged treaties. The Americans, for their turn, came back asking for more. American negotiations were helped by the fact that the British, with the aid of France, were inflicting even more humiliations on China at the time.[13] As the Japanese chief negotiator was backed into a corner, he signed the treaty. However, this act signaled the beginning of a period of unrest, as the weak Edo government was

---

[7] Jansen, *Emergence of Meiji Japan*, p. 260.
[8] *Ibid.*, p. 270.
[9] Boxer, *Jan Compagnie in Japan*, p. 186.
[10] Until this point, the Japanese were sending foreign emissaries to a tiny island off the shore of Nagasaki.
[11] Jansen, *Emergence of Meiji Japan*, p. 278; Buruma, *Inventing Japan*, p. 1; also see Totman, *History of Japan*.
[12] Jansen, *Emergence of Meiji Japan*, p. 278; Buruma, *Inventing Japan*, p. 2.
[13] Jansen, *Emergence of Meiji Japan*, p. 283.

blamed for foreign intrusions. The negotiator was assassinated two years later by a group of samurai[14] and a decade after the treaty, the Tokugawa dynasty fell. The Meiji Restoration War, which began as a coup organized by officials, was over in 1869.[15]

What did the Meiji Restoration bring? To begin with: the end of feudalism and a very centralized state.[16] In a document called "The Charter Oath," the emperor promised the establishment of deliberative councils, the freedom for each individual to pursue their own calling, abandonment of evil past traditions, and the search for knowledge throughout the world.[17] The military was completely reformed. Economic readjustment was also a top priority for the Meiji state. For instance, government expenditure was reduced and state industries were privatized.[18] A new constitution, modeled on Prussia's, was introduced in 1889, and the first national elections were held in 1890.[19] It should be noted that many of these reforms were undertaken with the West very much in mind; it was necessary for the West to look upon Japan favorably in order to get the trade and port treaties revised. It was also believed that these reforms were necessary for Japan to compete in the modern world. Despite the existence of a parliament, the political reforms did not go very far.[20] The constitution had placed sovereignty in imperial hands. Yet, it was the cultural reforms, from the fashionable consumption of meat to the wearing of frocks, that attracted the most attention from the West, but perhaps not in the way the Japanese had hoped. Pierre Loti[21] observed of Japan: "They danced quite properly, my Japanese in Parisian gowns.

---

[14] Buruma, *Inventing Japan*, p. 16.
[15] Jansen, *Emergence of Meiji Japan*, p. 336.
[16] *Ibid.*, p. 335. This was something Turkey could not/would not accomplish until the Kemalist "revolution" in 1923.
[17] Tsunoda, *Sources of the Japanese Tradition*, p. 644. Note the similarities to the *Tanzimat* Declaration.
[18] Jansen, *Emergence of Meiji Japan*, p. 376. This was one of the several ways the Meiji reforms were superior to the Ottoman *Tanzimat*. The Ottoman observers seem to have missed the importance of the economy in competing with the West; even in their observations about Japan, their attention is on military and cultural matters. See Worringer, "'Sick Man of Europe'."
[19] Again, note the similarities with the *Tanzimat* reforms.
[20] Buruma, *Inventing Japan*, p. 29.
[21] Pierre Loti, coincidentally, was an Orientalist who spent considerable time in Constantinople, romanticizing the "backward" ways of the East.

But one senses that it is something *drilled into* them that they perform like automatons, without any personal initiative."[22]

Nevertheless, the economic reforms were quite successful. As a consequence, from the 1880s onwards, "foreign trade established itself as a serious objective of the Meiji state."[23] If cultural equality with the West remained elusive, attaining the Western model of economic dominance seemed more within Japan's grasp. The example of the West convinced the Meiji period thinkers that trade and expansion were aspects of a healthy state.[24] Meiji writers such as Fukuzawa Yukichi were convinced that it was important for Japan to signal to the West that it was not a "backward" state like Korea. Moreover, Foreign Minister Inoue recommended that Japan set up a Western-style empire in Asia, before Western encroachment was complete.[25]

It is important to note this feature of Imperial Japan: later it would legitimize its actions as the defender of Asia against Western imperialism, but Japan's own behavior was very much modeled after Western imperialism.[26] During the Meiji period, Japanese attitudes to Asia underwent a significant shift, which in itself was a consequence of Japan's efforts to redefine itself in the new world which seemed to have Europe at both its center and its pinnacle. This shift was reflected in the introduction of new terms and concepts to define Japan's relations with its neighbors. For instance, *shina* replaced *chugoku* (Middle Kingdom) as the most commonly used appellation for China.[27] This term (along with the usage of the term *Nippon*) reflected the new-found need in Japan to define both itself and its neighborhood in terms of territorial, nation-state entities; and quickly *shina* became "a word that signified China as a troubled place mired in its past, in contrast to Japan, a modern Asian nation."[28] Another term which acquired a new meaning and currency in the Meiji era was *toyo*, which came to

[22] From *Madame Chrysanthème*, as quoted by Buruma, *Inventing Japan*, p. 33.
[23] Iriye, *Japan and the New Asia*, p. 758.
[24] Jansen, *Emergence of Meiji Japan*, p. 426.
[25] *Ibid.*, p. 427.
[26] See also Suzuki, "Japan's Socialisation," as well as *Civilization and Empire*, pp. 3–4
[27] Tanaka, *Japan's Orient*, p. 3.
[28] *Ibid.*, p. 4. See also Suganami, "Japan's Entry into International Society," pp. 196–8, for a comparison of Japan's and China's relationship with the European society of states in the nineteenth century.

mean "that which was not the Occident,"[29] and was used to indicate a distinct culture of the East, an Oriental civilization.

The East as *toyo* was idealized: it was characterized by "its gentleness, moral ethics, harmony and communalism."[30] Japan was seen as the one Asian country which not only embodied the best aspects of *toyo* but had adapted to the modern world. It is important to note that the *nihonjinron* discourse about Japan's uniqueness also dates back to this same period. The term was used in Ariga Chonan's 1888 book *Kokka Tetsuron* (Philosophical Discourses of the State),[31] which tried to explain Japanese uniqueness vis-à-vis the West scientifically by attributing it to the 300 years of Tokugawa rule.[32] This is a perfect example of the elite-level internalization of the modernist ontology discussed in Chapter 1. The Japanese elite had not bought into the European theory of racial inferiority, but did accept the fact of comparative backwardness, and went about disputing it through *scientific* means. In other words, they accepted the validity of the scientific method and they internalized a worldview where everything and everyone could be compared "objectively" with everything else.

Stefan Tanaka remarks that in the early twentieth century, Japanese scholars, "having accepted a progressive and scientific conception of knowledge ... increasingly faced the problematic of 'de-objectifying' Japan – and Asia – from a unilinear concept of progress that confirmed Japan's place as ... Europe's past and without history."[33] The "sweeping views of world development introduced from Europe" were accepted; it was Japan's place in that view that produced problems.[34] To put it in another way, the scientific method had produced the desired material results through the Meiji Restoration: Japan had been able to industrialize, to renegotiate unequal treaties, and even defeat a major "European" power in the Russo-Japanese War (1904–5). Yet Japan still did not have actual equality with the European society of states, because of Japan's placement in Asia, which was cast as Europe's past in this new modernist ontology. In order for Japan to gain equal respect, this conclusion would have to be challenged.[35] However, as

---

[29] Tanaka, *Japan's Orient*, p. 4.   [30] *Ibid.*, p. 13.

[31] Leheny, *Rules of Play*, p. 38.

[32] *Ibid.* Leheny's reference here is Hiroshi, *Nihonjinron*, pp. 15–43.

[33] Tanaka, *Japan's Orient*, p. 17.

[34] *Ibid.* See also Aydın, *Anti-Westernism in Asia*, pp. 25–30.

[35] Vincent, "Racial Equality," p. 244.

Tanaka notes, there was an inherent paradox in these efforts: "For in the process of adaptation and regeneration, these historians were seeking to prove that they were not 'Oriental,' as defined by the West, by using the same epistemology of the West."[36]

I had noted in Chapter 2 that the stigmatized actor – assuming that by this point he has already internalized the standards of stigma framework – faces two kinds of problems: he requires acceptance from wider society and also from himself. Japanese historian and elite efforts to cast Japan as something other than "Oriental," as defined by the West, by rethinking Japan's relationship with Asia should be understood in this light. In other words, these efforts were not undertaken only with an eye on getting equal respect from the West, but so that Japanese could come to accept their identity as viewed through the lens of this new worldview. Japan could no longer be left alone in its own "world"; but neither could she accept her new position among the stigmatized East – so she had to rethink her standing in comparison to *toyo*.

Thus, having accepted the modernist epistemology, the Japanese went on to apply it to their relations with Asia.[37] The success of the Meiji Restoration, especially in the economic realm, meant that Japan "objectively" ranked higher on the historical development plane than the rest of Asia, which remained trapped in history. Therefore, it was Japan's destiny and duty to revive Asia and lead it into the new age. *Shina* as part of the civilizational space of *toyo* naturally fell under Japan's manifest destiny.[38]

Imperial Japan

The Imperial Family of Japan is the parent, not only of her sixty millions, but of all mankind on earth. In the eyes of the Imperial Family all races are one and the same. It is above all racial considerations ... The League of Nations, proposed to save mankind from the horrors of war, can attain its real object only by placing the Imperial Family of Japan at its head; for to attain its object the League must have a strong punitive force and a supernational and superracial character; and this force can only be found in the

---

[36] *Ibid.*, p. 244.   [37] See *ibid.*, pp. 45–9.
[38] For an excellent discussion of the link between Japanese modernization and imperialism, see also Suzuki, *Civilisation and Empire*.

Imperial Family of Japan. (Translated *Niroku* editorial, as printed in the *Japan Advertiser* (May 9, 1919)[39])

The first step toward Japanese imperialism was the manifestation of the tension with China over Korea. In 1884, Japan and China had come to an agreement about the mutual backing-off of Korea. In the meantime, Japanese efforts toward Westernization had borne some fruit in relations with the West: in 1894, a new treaty with Great Britain dissolved consular courts, and tariff autonomy soon followed thereafter.[40] Once this was accomplished, Japan returned its gaze to Korea, and decided that China was gaining too much influence there. In a strategic move, Japan asked China to join in demanding that Korea undergo reforms very similar to those enacted by the Meiji state: a specialized bureaucracy, a new judiciary, a reformed tax system, and a modernized military.[41] China declined the offer. Tokyo declared war against China in 1894, and completely destroyed the Chinese navy, delivering a humiliating defeat. China had to sign a treaty that forced her to hand over territory (e.g. the island of Taiwan and the Liaotung Peninsula), economic privileges, and a degree of her sovereignty (the Treaty of Shimonoseki). Europe was impressed – it had been predicted that China would prevail – but despite, or perhaps because of, this favorable impression, Germany, Russia, and France asked Japan to withdraw from some of the newly acquired territory. The withdrawal was quite humiliating for Japan, especially considering the ever-growing presence of Russia and the United States in what Japan saw as her own turf.[42]

The high point of Japanese militarism came a little later, in the war against Russia. Japan struck the Russian fleet in 1904; the Russians were completely unprepared as they thought the Japanese would never dare to attack a major Western power. It was a relatively even match, with casualties on both sides numbering tens of

---

[39] And surprisingly enough, as quoted in Syngman Rhee's 1941 volume: *Japan Inside Out*, p. 14.

[40] Jansen, *Emergence of Meiji Japan*, p. 426.

[41] *Ibid.*, p. 431; Totman, *History of Japan*, p. 442. Even at this early stage, Japan was acting as a vassal carrying international society norms to peripheral areas.

[42] Buruma, *Inventing Japan*, p. 44. Japan had struck an alliance with Great Britain in 1902.

thousands.[43] At the end, however, Japan emerged victorious, regaining the Liaotung Peninsula and the Manchurian railways.[44] Korea came under Protectorate status in 1905, relinquishing control over her foreign relations. Japan was emerging as an Asian great power.

Japan's rise to power was aided by the outbreak of World War I in Europe, which weakened European states. Japan was even able to grab some German territories in Asia. It is therefore not surprising that Japanese leaders did not really grasp the significance of changes in Europe: empires tumbling down, self-determination and international cooperation on the rise.[45] Yet, Japan was a rising power; it was succeeding at a time where everybody else seemed to be flailing (or merely isolated, as in the case of the United States).

In the early decades of the twentieth century, Japan continued to be preoccupied with China. This was not purely materialistic aggression; as discussed above, many sincerely bought into the theory that the Meiji state could provide a template for success in China. Others were more interested in gaining parity with the West through the "European way." In the end, the second group prevailed, and Japan's special status in China was reaffirmed through a series of treaties in 1907 and 1908 with Great Britain, France, Russia, and the United States. Japan was playing great power politics – the timing was off, but for the moment, Japan, among all Westernizing Asian nations, seemed to be the one who broke the barrier most successfully.[46]

As noted above, views of China in Japan had undergone a significant revision during the Meiji period. By the time of the Republican

---

[43] For a point of comparison, please refer to the Turko-Russian War of 1877–8. It is remarkable that the advancement of these outsider powers was always at the expense of one another, and never a European power.

[44] Buruma, *Inventing Japan*, p. 45.

[45] Jansen, *Emergence of Meiji Japan*, p. 512. The obvious point of comparison is the position Russia's Tsar Nicholas found himself in after the Napoleonic Wars.

[46] "Throughout Asia the fact that Japan had defeated a major imperialist power attracted the admiration of nationalists of many stripes. Sun Yat-sen, the first president of the Chinese Republic, later recalled how, in going through the Suez Canal, he had encountered an Arab who asked him if he was Japanese. The Arab had 'observed vast armies of Russian soldiers being shipped back to Russia from the Far East,' which seemed to him a sure sign of Russia's defeat. 'The joy of this Arab,' wrote Sun, 'as a member of the great Asiatic race, seemed to know no bounds.'" See Jansen, *Emergence of Meiji Japan*, p. 441.

Revolution of 1911, which signaled the end of Chinese imperial dynasty, the view that China was not "a state but merely a civilization" was well established. Japan was not pleased with these developments and in 1915 issued a list of demands to China ("The Twenty-One Demands"[47]), to which China reluctantly agreed.[48] The irony here should be underlined: it was China's lack of "development" – in a way, her lack of shame over being Europe's past – which had led the Japanese to conclude that China was still mired in history. Yet, China's efforts to dust off the remnants of said history were condemned by Japan, and only led to the deepening of the conclusion that China was merely a civilization.[49]

Japan's demands were humiliating to the new government of China, which had the backing of the Americans. World War I ended before the issue could be fully resolved, but the Japanese kept pressing. The Japanese leaders were in no mood to be dissuaded by Western powers, having been denied racial equality in the League of Nations Charter. In the meantime, the Koreans, encouraged by Wilson's principles, staged a demonstration, which was swiftly and brutally crushed by Japan.

Japan participated in the League of Nations, but many Japanese had doubts about the new international order. The new order seemed to favor the status quo, at the expense of latecomers such as Japan. Japan soon found an excuse to act: rising Chinese nationalism of the 1920s.

The sparks first flew in Manchuria, where the Japanese army was already stationed. The army generals had the idea that another war was coming,[50] and they wanted to take full control of Manchuria. The

"The Japanese had attained great power status in a very short time. This was because their first move was to get rid of Chinese schools and Westernization." Turkish writer Atay, *Çankaya*, p. 392.

[47] E.g. Group 1, Article 1: "The Chinese Government engage to give full assent to all matters that the Japanese Government may hereafter agree with the German Government respecting the disposition of all the rights, interests and concessions, which, in virtue of treaties or otherwise, Germany possesses vis-à-vis China in relation to the province of Shantung."

[48] China was saved from implementing them for a brief while by the intervention of the Washington Conference of 1921–2.

[49] Miwa, "Japanese Policies."

[50] Jansen, *Emergence of Meiji Japan*.

military was also critical of the government in Tokyo, and the general mood was not helped at all by the worldwide economic slump. The officers planted a bomb on the railways, and used that as an excuse to take over Manchuria. The government's hands were tied, and subsequently the prime minister was assassinated in 1932. Imperial Japan had entered its last stage. Generals, bureaucrats, and the court now drove Japanese decisions and the Parliament turned into a "rubber stamp" endeavor. Full-scale invasion of China followed in 1937, a year made infamous by the Nanking massacre.[51]

These aggressive moves were underpinned by the "New Order in East Asia" policy, openly enunciated in 1938. By that year, Japan had found itself increasingly isolated in the world, especially since its departure from the League of Nations over the League's condemnation of the Manchurian incident. Yet Pan-Asianism (*Dai Ajiashugi*) was not an innovation of late-1930s Japan. It was a policy which had developed in direct response to Japan's stigmatization by Europe. I noted above that by the end of the Meiji period, there was a great frustration among Japanese intellectuals about both Japan's temporal placement vis-à-vis Europe and the fact that Japan's material prosperity had not translated into equal social capital. While some historians, as described above, had tried to overcome this problem by challenging the conclusion of the analysis which defined Japan as an "Oriental" nation *only*, others rejected the premise of relations with Europe altogether. For instance, in 1916, Odera Kenkichi wrote:

Is it not strange that in the [sic] Europe which has come to control or overwhelm Asia the talk of the Yellow Peril is boisterously heard, whereas from among the colored peoples who have been conquered or intimidated by the white nations little has been spoken out loud about the White Peril? This, when the Yellow Peril is no more than an illusion while the White Peril is real ... Some people denounce Greater Asianism as being based on a narrow racist frame of mind. But racial prejudices are what the white nations have taught us. This trait is more especially pronounced among them. The fact that their arguments about the Yellow Peril are provocative and disdainful is proof enough, and the fact that in the New World discriminatory treatment is being dealt out steadfastly [to non-white ethnic groups] is substantial evidence. To speak of the White Peril and to advocate Greater Asianism cannot touch the malicious propagation by Europeans

---

[51] It is unclear whether the massacre was ordered by Tokyo.

and Americans of the Yellow Peril and their calls for a white alliance. While the former is defensive, passive, and pacifist, the latter is offensive, aggressive, and imperialistic.[52]

As Japan's isolation grew, such views became more popular. I had noted in Chapter 2 that there are only a few recourses of strategic action open to the stigmatized actor. What Kenkichi was advocating here is a variation on the "sour-grapes" strategy: embracing Western approaches to international relations – including racial prejudice – but refusing to play ball with the West. As discussed above, there was always this strain in the Japanese reconceptualization of state identity: the stigmatized position Japan found itself in as a result of its encounter with modernity made it impossible to embrace the Western worldview as a whole because that would mean conceding Japan's inferior standing vis-à-vis the West. Nor could it be rejected in its entirety, so each reaction had to fall along a spectrum which has using Western methods to ingratiate oneself to the West at the one end, and denouncing Western methods to fight the West at the other (whereas true rejection would be aloofness). This is the same dilemma that the stigmatized individual faces in domestic society.

The attempts during the Meiji period to recast Japan first as a variant of Europe which happened to be in Asia and second as a country which was both modern and Oriental (in other words, as a country which had successfully overcome its justifiably stigmatized past) resemble strategies of passing and correction (which is the preferred method of the upwardly mobile *arriviste*). The more these strategies failed to achieve the desired result of obliterating Japan's stigma, the more attractive the strategies of rejection became. Both the "sour-grapes" and *ressentiment* approaches fall under that heading. In fact, in the decades following the publication of Kenkichi's book, the trajectory of the Japanese worldview gradually became even more reactionary. For instance, in 1919, Yanagida Kunio criticized the Japanese government for trying to place Japan at the same level as the white race and "charged his countrymen with having little interest in establishing solidarity with other Asians who had experienced racial discrimination

---

[52] From the introduction to his 1916 book *Dai Ajiashugi ron* (*On Greater Asianism*), as quoted by Miwa, "Japanese Policies," pp. 138–9.

similar to that faced by the Japanese."[53] Such a *ressentiment* attitude was also exemplified by the writings of Nakayama Masaru, the man who drafted "The New Order in East Asia Proclamation."[54] Masaru idealized the Japanese peasants and the traditional way of life. He wrote that agrarian villages had to be preserved at all costs because they contained the best of the Japanese race.[55] Miwa notes that, by the end of the 1930s, such calls for the restoration of agrarian life had become the prototype for the new order Japan was supposed to establish in Asia:

> It was a call to return to a classical East Asia, a new-found antithesis to the modern industrial society of the West. And it could be accomplished by first destroying that order of international law of the European system of nation-states which had been forced upon East Asian countries since the mid-nineteenth century, and then by replacing it with an "international new order" in accordance with the "real force of history."[56]

Japan was supposed to be a "third civilization,"[57] standing for new values, capable of rescuing both the East and the West from themselves. It was very much assumed that the peoples of Asia, especially the Chinese, were on board with this plan.[58] This was the context in which the concept of the Greater East Asia Co-Prosperity Sphere was articulated and announced in 1940. Of course, just as in European imperialism, there was a strong economic motive accompanying the civilization rhetoric. Sanctions from the West forced a deeper realization in Japan over its dependence on imported resources.[59] Also in the same year, political parties were dissolved and replaced by the Imperial Rule Association, partly because the Japanese thought an alliance with Germany could help them break out of this isolation.[60]

The factors that pushed Japan into World War II have been explored in detail elsewhere.[61] In retrospect, it seems clear that various Japanese

---

[53] Matsuda, *Soft Power*, p. 55.
[54] Miwa, "Japanese Policies," p. 140.
[55] As quoted by Miwa, "Japanese Policies," pp. 141–2.
[56] *Ibid.*, p. 142.   [57] *Ibid.*   [58] *Ibid.*, p. 139.
[59] Jansen, *Emergence of Meiji Japan*, p. 627.
[60] Furthermore, Japan's actions in China had brought Japan face to face with the United States.
[61] See e.g. Van der Vat, *Pacific Campaign*; Churchill, *Memoirs*; Ludwig, *World at Arms*.

actions during World War II, which seemed so shocking to the Western world at the time, had their basis in the Japanese mindset which had developed gradually during the prewar years. For instance, there was the historical precedent of Japan successfully taking on a bigger Western power in the form of the Russo-Japanese War of 1904–5.[62] Some observers have also noted that the war against the West gave the Japanese people the sense of purpose that the war in China had been lacking: "there was a sense of euphoria that we'd done it at last; we'd landed a punch on those arrogant great powers Britain and America, on those white fellows ... Never in our history had we Japanese felt such pride in ourselves as a race as we did then."[63] The initial victories were greeted with great enthusiasm.

Japan termed the conflict the "Great Asian War" and claimed that she was freeing Asia from Western oppression: "The Japanese way of life was ineffably superior to that of the West, based on individualism, and that of China, based on familialism. Other Asian races looked upon the Europeans and Americans as somehow superior, but it was now up to Nippon to show how wrong they were."[64] This propaganda was carried into the war years, as the Japanese needed something besides brute force to solidify their grasp on Asia.[65]

By 1942, the situation was deteriorating and by 1944, after colossal loss of Japanese territories, the Japanese leaders had realized that the war could not be won.[66] Nevertheless, the official propaganda encouraged fighting until death and emphasized that there would be no surrender. Mass suicide became widespread.[67] The emperor made some overtures to Stalin for peace, but the military preparations to fight to the end continued.

---

[62] Hosoya, "Characteristics of the Foreign Policy," 354. Obviously, an argument could be made that at the time it was defeated by Japan, Russia was neither Western nor a major power, but that is not how the lesson was perceived in Japan.

[63] Okuna Takao, as quoted in Buruma, *Inventing Japan*, p. 90; see also Jansen, *Emergence of Meiji Japan*, p. 642, for various eyewitness accounts of reactions to the war.

[64] Tokotomi Soho in 1934 from Tsunoda, *Sources of the Japanese Tradition*, pp. 798–801.

[65] Buruma, *Inventing Japan*, p. 99. Obviously, even eyewitness recollections of wartime memories can be and are contested, and at least some are, in part, post hoc rationalizations of events. However, even if that is the case, the particular normative framework chosen for such rationalizations is telling.

[66] Buruma, *Inventing Japan*, p. 100.   [67] *Ibid.*, p. 101.

How the war ended is well known. The United States dropped the atomic bomb on Hiroshima on August 6, 1945, and, two days later, on Nagasaki. The emperor read his surrender speech on August 15. Japan would never be the same again.

Comparisons with Turkey

Ironically, it was the Japanese delegate who most vehemently opposed Turkish demands for the lifting of capitulations. The Japanese delegate, Hayachi, told İsmet Pasha that Japan, too, had suffered from capitulations, and so he sympathized with Turkish demands. However, not even in Japan had the capitulations been lifted before the implementation of necessary administrative and legal reforms! (Notes from 1923 Lausanne Proceedings[68])

Before continuing with the postwar chapter of Japanese history, a few comparisons with Turkey should be underlined, considering that the events covered so far were coterminous with the events described in Chapter 3.

First, one cannot but be struck by similarities that stem from the fact that, in the nineteenth century, Ottoman Turkey and Japan occupied the same social space vis-à-vis the European society of states, despite their geographical distance. They were both outsiders in the emerging international society. Therefore, they had very similar reactions to European intrusion;[69] going through the same motions of superficial emulation and constitutional reforms and the same pleas for equal treatment in trade treaties, and roughly around the same time. The *Tanzimat* reforms were issued in 1856 – only a decade before the fall of the Tokugawa dynasty. The Ottoman Empire adopted a constitutional regime in 1876 and Japan's Restoration began in 1870. Furthermore, while the economic treaties with Western powers were a great threat to sovereignty, the main source of territorial aggression against both countries was Russia, which, as we shall see in Chapter 5, was itself a liminal power.

Nonetheless, several differences explain the temporary success of Japan in its quest for status and power during the Meiji Restoration,

---

[68] Karacan, *Lozan*, as translated and discussed in Chapter 3.
[69] Aydın's *Anti-Westernism in Asia* marshals evidence for this argument in great detail.

whereas the comparable reform efforts in the Ottoman Empire foundered. First, as a multiethnic empire, the Ottomans spent a considerable amount of time and resources unsuccessfully fighting the nationalist separatist movements, which were also encouraged by the European powers. Geography was also a factor; there were no natural barriers between the Ottoman Empire and European infiltration. Furthermore, the Ottomans had an early history of dealing with Europe successfully, which blinded them to the urgency of the situation, at least initially. The Japanese would not achieve the Ottoman level of arrogance until the 1930s. For all these reasons, Japan was able to embark on a more successful and comprehensive Westernization program, and sustain the new state with military advances until World War II. The Ottomans never finished the project they began, until they were defeated.

Finally, attention needs to be paid to the fact that the Russian advancement between the seventeenth and nineteenth centuries had come at the expense of the Ottomans, while the Japanese proved their rising power status at the expense of the Russians at the turn of the twentieth century.[70] One cannot but be struck by this fact – it is almost as if there was only one spot open for outsider states at the great powers' table. While there are of course perfectly reasonable geographical explanations for this development, we should also note that this pattern is well observed in the established-outsider stigmatization dynamics in domestic society: for instance, the advances of younger women or people of color in business settings often come at the expense of people from their own sub-group.

Japan makes the best of defeat

Embracing the defeat: 1945–1952

"We all thought the emperor was going to ask us to fight to the death," said Kumasaki. "We dreaded it, but we prepared ourselves for that. Of course, we would have obeyed." (Russell Brines, *MacArthur's Japan*)

MacArthur's remark in 1951, that in terms of modern civilization the Japanese were like a twelve-year-old boy, was typical of his thinking ...

---

[70] China was another semi-power whose geographical proximity and state decline proved advantageous for Japan.

MacArthur, was comparing Japan to Germany. The Germans, he said, were a "mature race." The Japanese were still in "a very tuitionary condition." … The Germans did not have to be tutored in the ways of another civilization. (MacArthur did not mean this as a compliment; in his view the Germans were all the more despicable because they should have known better.) The Japanese, on the other hand, had behaved like the children they were. They had, in MacArthur's version of events, "stumbled" into militarism because they did not know any better. (Ian Buruma, *Inventing Japan*, p. 108)

Japan's choices in the postwar era are associated primarily with two men: General MacArthur and Yoshida Shigeru.[71] General MacArthur was the Supreme Commander of the Allied Powers (SCAP) and headed its office in Japan from 1945 to 1951. Yoshida served five short terms[72] as prime minister, most of them during the occupation years. He is credited with shaping the postwar direction of Japan under what is known as the "Yoshida Doctrine." This doctrine held that Japan should concentrate on and prioritize economic reconstruction and development, and leave security matters to the United States.[73]

Americans had expected resistance to the occupation,[74] but upon taking over the country with relative ease, MacArthur immediately set about the task of reforming the existing system, which in his mind had brought out the worst tendencies of a "childlike" people.[75] The general ordered that certain reforms be undertaken immediately: emancipating women through enfranchisement; encouraging the unionization of labor; liberalizing schools; abolishing "systems which through secret inquisition and abuse have people in constant fear"; and democratizing economic institutions.[76] The original plan of SCAP was to treat Japan as a laboratory for Asian democracy, a plan that was also fed by the New Deal in the United States.[77]

However, after the war was over, it quickly became evident to MacArthur and SCAP that the Soviet Union factor needed to be taken seriously. He and his office believed that if traditional institutions

---

[71] Although, arguably, Kishi played a more significant role than Yoshida in entrenching what came to be known as the Yoshida Doctrine.

[72] May 22, 1946–May 24, 1947; October 15, 1948–February 16, 1949; February 16, 1949–October 30, 1952; October 30, 1952–May 21, 1953; May 21, 1953–December 10, 1954.

[73] Klien, *Rethinking Japan's Identity*, p. 69.

[74] Brines, *MacArthur's Japan*, p. 23.

[75] *Ibid.*, p. 107.   [76] *Ibid.*, p. 48.   [77] Totman, *History of Japan*, p. 443.

were dismantled entirely, the Soviet Union would step in to fill the
vacuum.[78] As a result, the idea that Japan should be a bulwark against
communism started to take precedence over the idea of Japan as an
equitable democracy.[79] Consequently, the goal of economic reconstruction was prioritized and by 1947, American policy had shifted
its focus from punishment to development.[80]

Only two of the planned reforms were enacted in the way originally envisioned: the new Japanese constitution and land reform. The
results of reform in the sectors of labor, education, and local government were mixed and the plan to break up the *zaibatsu* monopolies
was a failure.[81]

The new constitution enumerated the rights and liberties of citizens
and strengthened the Parliament. Article 1 emphasized that sovereignty
resided with the people and that the emperor derived his position from
the will of the people. Article 9 declared that Japan was renouncing
war as a sovereign right and that military forces to that end would not
be maintained. Article 9 would become a source of future controversy
and would go on to frustrate neorealist scholars for many years, but it
was rather well received by the Japanese: "Most Japanese were quite
content never to have to fight another war. Besides, Article 9 allowed
them to bask in the glow of moral satisfaction: the first pacifist nation
in history."[82] The Yoshida government, initially reluctant, accepted the
constitution because it was partly believed that the fate of the emperor
rested on its adoption.[83] The chambers of the Diet passed the constitution on October 6, 1946, and the emperor approved it on November
3 of the same year.

Also in 1946, a study group composed of Japan's economic experts
issued a report that declared Japan should proceed "from a broad
global and developmental standpoint" in formulating its economic
policies; that Japan "must discern the course of progress of human
society, its present state and future trends, and second, understand
the nature of the world environment in which Japan now stands, and

[78] Brines, *MacArthur's Japan*, p. 51.
[79] Allinson, *Japan's Postwar History*, p. 45; Pempel, "Japanese Foreign
    Economic Policy," 731.
[80] Totman, *A History of Japan*, p. 445; Allinson, *Japan's Postwar History*, p. 53.
[81] Allinson, *Japan's Postwar History*, p. 63.
[82] Buruma, *Inventing Japan*, p. 118.
[83] Jansen, *Emergence of Meiji Japan*, p. 685.

in which it will stand in the future."[84] As Jansen notes, there was no defeatism in this new economic outlook.

In the meantime, labor leaders became restless, partly in response to the influence of communists within the unions, and they called for a general strike in the winter of 1946. It was assumed that this would be at least tolerated by SCAP. This turned out to be a mistake, as MacArthur banned the strike, declaring that he would not allow such "a deadly weapon" to be used in the context of impoverished Japan.[85] MacArthur launched a campaign for an early peace treaty in 1947 and followed it with steps to end the economic blockade.[86]

Nevertheless, labor leaders kept the pressure up. They demanded and achieved the removal of the Yoshida Cabinet, calling Yoshida a representative of the industrialists[87] and a "SCAP toady."[88] In the subsequent elections of 1947, leaders of all major labor organizations were elected to the Diet.[89]

As the 1940s drew to a close, SCAP became increasingly worried about communist infiltration of Japan, and the outbreak of the Korean War did not help matters.[90] Initially, many American observers had been skeptical that the reforms would work[91] and there was a general concern that Japanese society had an affinity toward authoritarian regimes.[92] Since the Soviet Union had an outward policy of disinterest or even hostility toward Japan, it had been barred from participating in the occupation by the United States.[93] When the Soviet Union signed a treaty of friendship with China in 1950, Japan was singled out as a potential aggressor.[94] Nevertheless, the United States suspected the Soviets of covert propaganda in Japan: bookstores were filled with Soviet magazines and books.[95] Not every leftist or union organizer was a communist, but there was enough sympathy for the viewpoint to cause SCAP and Washington headaches. The left demanded complete independence from the United States.[96] They also looked up to

---

[84] *Ibid.*, p. 693.   [85] *Ibid.*, p. 698; Brines, *MacArthur's Japan*, p. 165.
[86] Brines, *MacArthur's Japan*, p. 79.   [87] *Ibid.*, p. 165.
[88] Buruma, *Inventing Japan*, p. 129.   [89] Brines, *MacArthur's Japan*, p. 178.
[90] Jansen, *Emergence of Meiji Japan*, p. 699; Brines, *MacArthur's Japan*, pp. 206, 254.
[91] Morley, "Between Two Eras," p. 1.
[92] Brines, *MacArthur's Japan*, p. 258; Buruma, *Inventing Japan*, p. 107.
[93] Hellmann, *Japanese Foreign Policy*, p. 30.
[94] *Ibid.*, p. 31.   [95] Brines, *MacArthur's Japan*, p. 261.
[96] *Ibid.*, p. 263.

the Soviet Union and felt "a kind of guilt-ridden solidarity with the Chinese communists."[97] The leftists argued that any security arrangements with the United States would compound the historic mistake Japan made by trying to be a Western-style imperialist power. They thought that Japan should stand in alliance with Asian neighbors who were fighting imperialism.[98]

At the same time, especially in Asia, there were fears that Japan was going to revert to its old imperialistic ways once it gathered its strength.[99] The fact that many militarists went unpunished did little to quell these fears. In the 1940s, the people resented militarists but many remained unconvinced that Japan was wrong in wanting an empire.[100] Given this attitude and this history, it was not surprising that many Asian nations protested American support for the Japanese economy.[101] This support included bringing in a Detroit banker named Joseph Dodge who drew up a monetary stabilization program ("The Dodge Line").[102] Among his recommendations was one that suggested Japanese workers and consumers should make sacrifices for the national good.[103] Subsequently, many layoffs followed. In addition, in 1950, purge orders were issued by SCAP against alleged communists in media and labor organizations and nearly 20,000 people were forced from their jobs.[104]

It was in this context that the peace treaty was negotiated. After a brief interruption, Yoshida was prime minister again. However, MacArthur was out. The Korean War had erupted, supplying the Japanese economy with much needed demand, and MacArthur invoked Truman's wrath by threatening to take the war into China.[105] However, the Japanese were against becoming entangled in another conflict. MacArthur was replaced by Dulles, who wanted Japan to remilitarize[106] so that it could be counted on for its own defense.[107] He wanted a Japanese army of 350,000 troops[108] and Japan to limit its

[97] Buruma, *Inventing Japan*, p. 130.   [98] *Ibid.*
[99] Brines, *MacArthur's Japan*, p. 140.   [100] *Ibid.*, p. 124.[101] *Ibid.*, p. 150.
[102] Allinson, *Japan's Postwar History*, p. 77.
[103] Buruma, *Inventing Japan*, p. 124.
[104] Allinson, *Japan's Postwar History*, p. 55; Buruma, *Inventing Japan*, p. 24.
[105] Buruma, *Inventing Japan*, p. 125.
[106] A small force called the Japanese Defense Forces was created in 1950.
[107] Jansen, *Emergence of Meiji Japan*, p. 701.
[108] Buruma, *Inventing Japan*, p. 129.

commercial relations to dealing only with those in the "free world."[109]
Yoshida was entirely against the remilitarization of Japan and did not
want to bypass Article 9 or burden the Japanese economy.[110]

Yoshida negotiated skillfully[111] and argued that establishing a formal military would antagonize the socialist opposition. There are
reports that he secretly encouraged the socialists to demonstrate in
front of his office in order to strengthen his hand.[112] In the end, he
prevailed. In the compromise that was reached, access to Okinawa
was given to the United States to create a military base. It was promised that in some distant day in the future Japan would assume
responsibility for its own defense. Until then, the United States would
be responsible for Japan's security and Japan would be free to prioritize economic development.[113] On the negative side, Japan, by recognizing the Republic of China in Taiwan, had to forgo its trade with
the People's Republic of China,[114] which was starting to redevelop.[115]
A peace treaty and a security treaty were signed simultaneously in San
Francisco, in September 1951. Also as part of this arrangement, Japan
recognized the independence of Korea and renounced all claims to

[109] Holsti, "Politics in Command," 649.
[110] Jansen, *Emergence of Meiji Japan*, p. 701.
[111] "Looking back over the origins and development of Japan's postwar defense
policy, it seems clear that this policy was not cooked up in Washington
and swallowed whole in Tokyo. On the contrary, Prime Minister Yoshida's
feelers and Foreign Minister Ashida's memorandum on security policy in
1947 are strong evidence that the Japanese leaders had a well-thought-out
defense policy, based on their strategic views, several years before the United
States Government formulated its Far Eastern security policy." Weinstein,
Japan's Postwar Defense Policy, p. 128.
[112] Jansen, *Emergence of Meiji Japan*, p. 701; Buruma, *Inventing Japan*, p. 129.
[113] Buruma, *Inventing Japan*, p. 130; Jansen, *Emergence of Meiji Japan*, p. 701;
Chai, "Entrenching the Yoshida Defense Doctrine," 397.
[114] 1950 resolution passed by a large majority in the Upper House of the Diet:

Before the war about 65 percent of our trade was with Asia, and most
of that with China. These facts are particularly significant in light of the
steadily diminishing U.S. economic aid. Business and trading circles and
the Japanese people urgently desire the renewal of direct trade relations
with China in order to relieve the stagnation in trade and commerce ...
Japan absolutely cannot exist unless trade is promoted. The government
should leave aside ideological and political differences and look at the purely
economic problems, exchange economic missions with the new China,
restore trade with her immediately, and set forth a bold course of action. (As
quoted in Holsti, "Politics in Command," 651)

[115] *Ibid.*

Taiwan and the other Pacific Islands it had invaded during World War I.[116] The treaty went into effect in 1952. Japan was sovereign again.

Dulles's part in these developments should not be entirely discounted, especially because he seems to have had an intuitive understanding of the effect of stigmatization on Japan's national habitus, and used that understanding to his advantage. As Takeshi Matsuda notes, "Dulles recognized that historically the Japanese wanted to be counted among the members of the Western world, but if only they were received on terms of approximate equality."[117] Furthermore, Dulles was disposed "to capitalize on the Japanese feeling of racial and social superiority to the Chinese, Koreans, and Russians, and to convince them as part of the free world they would be in equal fellowship with a group which was superior to the members of the communist world."[118] Dulles had observed that "the Japanese were particularly sensitive to the assumption that they were 'backward' or 'undeveloped' because Japanese felt that their own advancement was beyond the general levels of civilization in Asia."[119] Dulles realized that a long-term Western alliance with Japan could only be sustained if the West realized Japan's hunger for status and equal respect in the international system and played along.

Yoshida's own memoirs corroborate Dulles's impressions. In the following passage, Yoshida dismisses the argument that Japan's plight bears any resemblance whatsoever to that of other Asian nations and argues instead that Japan's destiny is to be a role model and norm mediator (I quote at length from this passage because of its pertinence to the argument of the book):

According to some people, Japan too gained – or rather, regained – her independence in 1952 after seven years of foreign occupation, and, our plight being therefore much the same as those of other countries of Asia and Africa, we should throw in our lot with them in opposition to such "colonial" powers as the United States, Great Britain, and France. Such a view seems to be completely at variance with actual facts. Apart from the few years of foreign occupation following the termination of the Pacific War, Japan has been an independent state throughout its long history and we cannot conceive of our country occupying any other status than that of a completely independent and sovereign nation. In the fields of government,

---

[116] Jansen, *Emergence of Meiji Japan*, p. 701.
[117] Matsuda, *Soft Power*, p. 55.   [118] *Ibid.*   [119] *Ibid.*

economy, industry, and social development, also, Japan is more Western than Asian – at least insofar as the levels attained by us in those spheres are concerned – whereas many of the other countries of Asia and Africa are still undeveloped, or under-developed, industrially and economically, and their peoples have still to attain the standards of living to which modern civilization entitles them to aspire. In short, they are what we are forced to recognize as *backward nations* ... We can both understand and sympathize with their present policies, but that is not to say that we should rate them as being more important – internationally – than they actually are, and still less that Japan should model its foreign policy on their largely negative philosophy. I have stated that we Japanese are in many respects more European than Asian; nevertheless, Japan is geographically an Asian nation and economically an integral part of the continent and, as such, better equipped than are most Western peoples to understand Asia. Racially speaking, also, other Asian and African nations tend to feel a greater sense of kinship towards Japan than towards the peoples of the West. This fact coupled with our superior economic development, should, it seems to me, leave us in little doubt as to the role which Japan must play in international affairs in the future ... It is our duty to aid the peoples of Asia and Africa in their *economic development and thus foster an awareness in the countries concerned that the political institutions and way of life of the free nations of the earth are best suited to bring prosperity to their nations and happiness to the peoples therein.*[120]

The passage is striking in several ways. First, Yoshida seems intent on situating Japan apart from and above the rest of the "East" while acknowledging that geographically and racially Japan bears an affinity to the newly independent former colonies (which would soon be grouped under the category of the "Third World"). The reader will notice that, in spirit, this line of argument is not that different than the Meiji Era constructions of Japan as the leader of Asia and a country on equal footing with the West. Second, Yoshida explicitly makes the argument that Japan should take an active role in leading Asia and Africa by convincing them that "the political institutions and way of life of the free nations ... are best suited to bring prosperity ... and happiness." If we compare this with the earlier rhetoric of the Greater Asian Prosperity Sphere, we see that the way Yoshida situates Japan and its mission vis-à-vis the

---

[120] Shigeru, *Last Meiji Man*, pp. 10–12 (italics added).

other nations of Asia is not substantially different. What have been substituted, however, are Japan's claims to have invented a better values system compared to the West. In Yoshida's rephrasing, Japan is now a missionary for Western values, and one that is better at selling those values even than the West.

In other words, several responses of the stigmatized individual discussed in Chapter 2 are clearly visible in this passage; especially on display are the strategies of stratifying against one's own stigma group and seeing one's affinity with the stigma group as a mixed blessing. Finally, what is remarkable about the passage is the ease with which Yoshida is using the norm rhetoric of the postwar years discussed in Chapter 2. He has no problem labeling the newly independent nations of Asia and Africa as "backward" and there are several references to economic development. This passage is evidence of the clear intent behind the policy Japan pursued during the Cold War years: fighting stigmatization through an emphasis on economic development and pursuing a strategy of playing up Third World connections in order to get respect from the West.

A new Japan

Because it has been constrained from becoming a political and military superpower ... Japan's business and foreign policy activities in East Asia are intensely market-centered ... Japan's foreign policy is thus built on foreign trade ... This market orientation is natural for Japan as long as its foreign policy uses economic affluence and manufacturing competitiveness as ways to influence other countries. (Takashi Inoguchi, "Japan's Foreign Policy in Asia", p. 409)

Within the incubator of the patron–client relationship, Japan slowly redefined its foreign policy orientation. Having failed internationally with militarism and domestically with totalitarianism, and having no real commitment to the larger strategic goals of the Cold War, Japan looked elsewhere for foreign policy direction. Consistent with its perennial desire to achieve international stature, Japan emphasized economic relations. (Louis D. Hayes, *Japan and the Security of Asia*, p. xv)

Yoshida had been more successful than his American counterparts in dictating the outcome of the San Francisco Treaty. The most important achievement was that Japan could decide for itself when and how (and if) it was going to re-arm.[121] This would allow Japan to focus entirely on economic recovery and growth. Furthermore, its strong ties with the United States gave Japan access to the largest market. Yoshida refused his critics' argument that the security arrangement had made Japan subservient to the United States, and commented that there was no reason to feel "a colonial sense of inferiority."[122] This worldview would later become entrenched in Japanese foreign policy as the "Yoshida Doctrine." However, it would be a mistake to conclude that it had unconditional support from the beginning.

Students and workers, supported by the Communist Party, labor unions, and leftist intelligentsia, staged massive demonstrations against the security treaty in May 1952.[123] They were against "American imperialism" and did not want Japan to be part of it. On September 12, 1954, Soviet Foreign Minister Molotov announced that "the Soviet Union was ready to normalize relations, provided that Japan showed a similar willingness."[124] With the help of the socialists, the Democrats brought down the Yoshida government.[125] Going into the 1954 elections, it seemed that the socialists might have a chance of winning when various factions overcame their differences and merged. However, in response, the conservatives, formerly represented by the Democrat and the Liberal parties, also merged, forming the Liberal Democrat Party (LDP).[126] The LDP came to power, first under the leadership of Hatoyama Ichiro, who immediately announced that normalization of relations with the Soviet Union and the People's Republic of China was a priority.[127] However, the plan to restore diplomatic relations with China was quickly abandoned.[128]

One of the major developments under Hatoyama's leadership was Japan's enthusiastic entry into the United Nations. In the admittance speech, the Japanese foreign minister declared that "possessing a cultural, political and economic system that fused both Western and

---

[121] Jansen, *Emergence of Meiji Japan*, p. 703.
[122] Shigeru, *Yoshida Memoirs*, p. 4.
[123] Buruma, *Inventing Japan*, p. 130.
[124] Hellmann, *Japanese Foreign Policy*, p. 2.
[125] *Ibid.*, p. 32.   [126] Buruma, *Inventing Japan*, p. 133.
[127] *Yomiuri shimbun*, December 10, 1954; *Asahi shimbun*, December 13, 1954, both quoted in Hellmann, *Japanese Foreign Policy*, p. 32.
[128] *Asahi shimbun*, January 22, 1955, as quoted in Hellmann, *Japanese Foreign Policy*, p. 32.

Eastern civilizations, Japan could very well become a bridge between East and West."[129] Japan also achieved GATT membership the same year, but European countries, and even the United States, remained reluctant to lift restrictions on Japanese trade for almost a decade.[130]

In 1957, Kishi Nobusuke became prime minister and served until 1960. Kishi was a conservative, and had even spent three years in prison as a war criminal. On economic matters, he was in favor of state control and a planned economy. He, too, had problems with the security treaty. The right-wingers maintained that Japan's war had been just: they wanted to revise Articles 1 and 9 of the constitution, to restore the emperor's divinity, and for Japan to actively join the war against communism.[131] Kishi wanted to change the security treaty as well: "The security treaty, which gave the United States a free hand on Japanese soil, reminded many Japanese, on the Right and the Left, of the unequal treaties in the 1860s."[132] Therefore, Kishi wanted Japan to be more assertive.

To achieve that result, he went on a tour of Southeast Asia and apologized for past atrocities. He also went to Washington, but secured only a minor promise that Japan would be consulted in future deployments. On this visit, Kishi also recommended the establishment of a Southeast Asian development fund: "The biggest problem the Asian countries are being faced with for the time being is how to add economic independence to their political independence ... Our country is willing to cooperate with these countries in various fields for their economic development."[133] Japan's potential as a role model for developing countries in Asia and Africa had already been observed at the 1955 Bandung Conference.[134]

However, on the home front, Kishi could not secure the support of the socialists for revisions in the security treaty. They were suspicious of him because of his nationalist past, and they thought the changes were merely cosmetic:

By the end of 1959, radical students were rushing toward the Diet and pissing on its doors. First tens of thousands, then hundreds of thousands

[129] Klien, *Rethinking Japan's Identity*, p. 73.
[130] Austin and Harris, *Japan and Greater China*, p. 33.
[131] Buruma, *Inventing Japan*, p. 130.   [132] *Ibid.*, p. 135.
[133] As quoted in Klien, *Rethinking Japan's Identity*, p. 73.
[134] *Ibid.*

joined the demonstrations. Police barricades were crushed … Soon almost a million people were in the streets, screaming – in English – "Yankee go home!" … For a moment it looked as if revolution might be at hand. All the hatred and distrust of the old order, and the United States, which was blamed, not without reason, for supporting it, gathered like a storm in the streets of Tokyo.[135]

The Diet was divided over the controversial ratification of the treaty. For instance, the socialists locked up the Diet Speaker in his office, who called the riot police, and, while the LDP held the ratification vote without the socialists, Kishi had to resign.[136] He was replaced by Ikeda Hayato, who oversaw Japan's re-entry onto the world stage.

The period between the end of World War II and Kishi's resignation in 1960 can be viewed as the period when Japan made its decisions about the kind of country it wanted to be.[137] Within this period, despite the occupation, there was considerable debate within Japan about the US partnership.[138] There were three sides to the debate: first, pragmatic conservatives, such as Yoshida, wanted to make the best of a constraining situation; second, nationalists like Kishi desired Japan to be more autonomous in its relations with the United States and remilitarize;[139] third, the left and the socialists wanted the United States to leave and Japan to forge better relations with China and other oppressed peoples of Asia. Japan in this period could not be described as a monolithic society that had been cowed into submission. To the contrary, it was a very divided society until the radicalized left and the nationalist right took each other's eyes out in 1960,[140] leaving the ground open to the more moderate pragmatists represented by Ikeda. Ikeda cemented support for the Yoshida Doctrine by announcing and delivering on the income-doubling plan of 1960–70.[141] Of course, the doctrine was successful with the people because it also delivered ontological security by raising Japan's profile in the world.

---

[135] Buruma, *Inventing Japan*, p. 136.
[136] *Ibid.*, p. 137; Jansen, *Emergence of Meiji Japan*, p. 708.
[137] This also squares with Kissinger's observation that Japan changed its foreign policy every 15 years. Inoguchi, *Japanese Politics*, p. 178.
[138] *Ibid.*, p. 179.   [139] *Ibid.*
[140] Totman, *History of Japan*, p. 450.
[141] Inoguchi, *Japanese Politics*, p. 179.

It is possible to interpret the mass riots of 1960 as a symptom of the growing confidence of the Japanese people.[142] That confidence reached a new high in 1964, the year Japan hosted the Olympics: "No longer a defeated nation in disgrace, Japan was respectable now ... To the Japanese, always acutely conscious of their ranking among nations, sporting victories were one way to soothe memories of wartime defeat."[143] This was also the year Japan joined the International Monetary Fund and the Organization for Economic Cooperation and Development, clubs that marked "Japan's rise from a developing country to a member of the industrialized world."[144] Thus, the 1960s were a good decade for Japan. Trade with South Korea and Taiwan increased substantially[145] and the GNP kept rising, as did Japan's influence, at least in the way Japanese now perceived the world.[146] One of the catch-phrases of the decade was "US–Japan equal partnership": Japan had reached a point where it envisioned itself as on a par with most industrialized countries in the West.

Nonetheless, Japan encountered some problems in the 1960s. For instance, there was still resistance from Europe to Japanese trade. On a trip to France, Ikeda was called "a transistor radio salesman" and was made fun of for his short stature by Charles de Gaulle.[147] It took many years for Japan to receive respectable treatment in the international organizations of which it was a member.

Every policy in this decade was subordinated to macro-level economic growth, a big part of which was achieved through foreign economic policies: "As such, Japanese foreign economic policy has been neither isolated from, nor contradictory to, domestic economic policies. Nor has it been directed more fundamentally to achieving security, military, or other external political and noneconomic aims ... International glory was domesticated and treated as measurable through increases in GNP."[148] Perhaps for this reason, despite a high degree of commitment to pacifism and peace, Japan pursued trade

---

[142] Packard, "Living with the Real Japan," p. 38.
[143] Buruma, *Inventing Japan*, pp. vii–viii; see also Inoguchi, "Japan: Reassessing the Relationship," p. 246.
[144] Klien, *Rethinking Japan's Identity*, p. 77.
[145] Inoguchi, "Asia and the Pacific Since 1945," p. 916.
[146] See Inoguchi, *Japanese Politics*, p. 39.
[147] Klien, *Rethinking Japan's Identity*, p. 78.
[148] Pempel, "Japanese Foreign Economic Policy," 741.

rather aggressively. China, for instance, viewed Japanese trade as a political weapon and attached difficult conditions to all trade agreements with Japan, in effect curtailing most exchange.[149] Others also criticized Japan for practicing a new kind of imperialism through trade in Asia.[150]

As the 1960s drew to a close, Japan re-emerged as a major presence in Asia, but observers were baffled by the question of what her future direction in foreign policy would be. Some thought that Japan would become more active in the economic and political affairs of Southeast Asia, or perhaps lead the nonaligned states.[151] The role of mediator was also frequently offered.[152] The Americans desired that Japan re-arm and more actively support American policies in Vietnam in particular and Asia in general.[153] Writing in 1968, Badgley keenly observed that the Japanese government seemed "to be developing a new principle in foreign policy, one that might accommodate the free-world orientation, dominant for the past two decades, and the Asian orientation, held both by those with progressive ideological beliefs and by those with conservative cultural attachments."[154] This would be the principle of "regional development," with Japan getting more involved in the political and economic affairs of Asian states. Japan could be a model of success by adopting Western technology while keeping her Asian identity.[155] Badgley also suggested that this policy was a result of Japan's historical tendency to seek influence and status in Asia.[156] He added that "although Japan's ability to play a leading role in Southeast Asian affairs rests on its demonstration of successful modernization as an Asian state, the country's influence over its neighbors will flow from the most dramatic outward manifestation of that success: its economic power and interests and the reciprocity these activities have created and will foster among its trading partners."[157] Japan had already taken concrete steps in this direction by joining the Asian Development Bank in 1966.

---

[149] Holsti, "Politics in Command," 653.
[150] Steven, *Japan's New Imperialism*, p. 244.
[151] Osgood, "Japan and the United States in Asia," p. 9.
[152] Badgley, "Necessity and Choice," p. 150.
[153] Packard, "Living with the Real Japan," p. 36.
[154] Badgley, "Japan's Nonmilitary Road," p. 51.
[155] *Ibid.*, p. 56.   [156] *Ibid.*, p. 55.   [157] *Ibid.*, p. 57.

Following the United States' lead, Japan normalized its relations with China in 1972. By this time, Japanese GNP had risen to be second only to the United States. Japan had maintained a peaceful profile for more than two decades. Nevertheless, Japan had not yet earned the full trust of the American public. Annual opinion polls conducted by the Japanese Foreign Ministry consistently showed trust for Japan in the United States hovering around 40 percent. Asian countries, especially those that had been colonized by Japan in the past, remained even more skeptical.[158] In 1973, Japan unsuccessfully sought a permanent seat on the UN Security Council.[159]

Whatever outside observers might think, since the 1970s, Japan has not wavered substantively from the path Yoshida chose. The Japanese learned to take pleasure in their GNP. As Matsuyama comments: "Why is the Japanese GNP so highly publicized? I presume that one reason is that the Japanese, who had lost confidence and had been suffering from an inferiority complex since the end of the war, have finally found delight in the GNP as a means of competing with and surpassing other powers, this satisfying the national pride."[160] Or, as Maull has put it, Japan was on its way to becoming a civilian power.[161]

For the sake of comprehensiveness, however, let me note that the more things have changed, the more things have remained the same in Japanese foreign policy.

On the one hand, there is no doubt that the end of the Cold War has rejuvenated identity debates in Japan, and many have raised questions about what Japan's responsibilities are to the East and the West.[162] But the very fact that there are still identity debates to be had points to the continued impact of Japan's prewar stigmatization in shaping Japanese responses. Despite all of Japan's economic successes, the country still remains an outsider at some level. As noted in Chapter 2, pursuing a strategy intended to correct stigmatizing attributes can never succeed entirely in solving ontological security problems: the taint of once having had the discreditable attribute remains (hinting at the possibility that one can easily fall back) and a sense of inauthenticity

[158] Matsuyama, "Outlook for U.S. Japan Relations," pp. 48, 57.
[159] Soroos, "Global Interdependence," 220.
[160] Matsuyama, "Outlook for U.S. Japan Relations," p. 51.
[161] See Maull, "Germany and Japan."
[162] See Klien, *Rethinking Japan's Identity.*

(externally imposed and internally felt) threatens ontological security. Japan has tried to complement its "corrective" strategy by positioning itself as a bridge between West and East. However, because Japan's ultimate goal is to garner equal respect from the West, it has not been able to commit entirely to the Asian prong of this strategy, not only picking Western interests over the Eastern ones when the two seemed to conflict but also often undermining its own efforts in the region by questionable actions such as ex-Prime Minister Koizumi's 2001 visit to the Yasukini War Shrine. By trying to play up both aspects of its identity, but not being able to guarantee one and commit to the other, at some level, Japan remains mired in its own history of outsiderness. I will have more to say about this in the concluding chapter.

On the other hand, Japan continues to devote a very small percentage of its GDP to defense expenditure, despite the *absence* of evidence suggesting that "the Japanese public perceives that their country has unusual immunity from military threat"[163] and opinion polls showing that only "49 percent believe that the United States would provide assistance if Japan were attacked."[164] Despite these beliefs, less than 10 percent of those polled support an increase in military spending. This reluctance has puzzled many IR experts, especially realists, who inevitably end up arguing that this unnatural state of affairs will end sooner or later.[165] As Katzenstein and Sil note,[166] most of the 1990s was characterized by this type of scholarship on East Asia, advancing the argument that the continent, including Japan, was "ripe for rivalry" and violent conflict.[167] Yet neither Asia in general nor Japan has reassumed an aggressive foreign policy posture. Liberal approaches[168] may attribute Japanese unwillingness to re-arm to the

---

[163] Chai, "Entrenching the Yoshida Defense Doctrine," 392.

[164] *Nihon Keizai Shimbun* poll as reported in Chai, "Entrenching the Yoshida Defense Doctrine," 392.

[165] For a review of this literature, see e.g. Katzenstein and Okawara, "Japan, Asian-Pacific Security," 154–6, 167, 169, 178–80; Kang, "Getting Asia Wrong," 61–2.

[166] "Rethinking Asian Security," p. 1. This article also provides compelling critiques of both realist and liberal readings of Asian international relations.

[167] E.g. Bracken, *Fire in the East*; Betts, "Wealth, Power and Instability"; Friedberg, "Ripe for Rivalry."

[168] Owen, "Transnational Liberalism," 130. To be fair, Owen argues the same logic applies to Western Europe as well, but he never demonstrates why liberalism makes Japan particularly pacifist.

nature of the Japanese post-World War II system, but it is not clear why a liberal domestic system should have such a singular effect only on Japan, or why Japan should be so conflicted about foreign policy in the post-Cold War world.

Many observers are rightly skeptical that traditional theories can predict outcomes in Asia. For instance, Kang argues that traditional theories derived from the experience of European states fail to account for the Asian system and that Japan does not re-arm to the level it could because it has no intention of challenging the United States.[169] Let us now see if introducing concern for status as a variable helps us make better sense of Japan's behavior, especially in the decades immediately following the humiliating defeat of 1945.

From Kamikaze pilots to radio salesmen: changing status standards

Japan has been considered by outsiders and especially by Westerners to be an enigmatic country. (Takashi Inoguchi and Kinhide Mushakoji, "The Japanese Image of the Future," p. 217)

Despite numerous differences in the details, the overarching narrative in Japan's transformation post-World War II is strikingly similar to the case of Turkey as discussed in Chapter 3. Here, too, we are faced with a country that went from being perceived as a threat to the West to being a peaceful participant in the international system and its institutions. It is often assumed, mistakenly, that seven years of US occupation and the subsequent security alliance with Japan explains all that there is to know about Japan's postwar policy choices. It is beyond a doubt that these were formative experiences for Japan; nevertheless, the Japan that has emerged from the postwar period is not necessarily one that the Americans imagined or desired. Japan has kept making her own choices, with Japanese leaders skillfully navigating the constraints imposed by both the occupation and the San Francisco system. It is not possible to explain this outcome without understanding how the concern for status in the international system significantly shaped the domestic and foreign policy strategies of Japan after World War II.

---

[169] Kang, "Getting Asia Wrong," 77.

We saw in the first section of this chapter how prewar Japan was motivated by the same desire to overcome the civilization standards that plagued Turkey's behavior. By the time World War II broke out, these standards – at least in their explicit, quasi-legalized form (through the League of Nations) – were becoming obsolete, making way for a more teleological view of human development and progress centered on the concept of modernity. Old-fashioned justifications for imperialism focused on a civilizing mission had first been discarded for the tutelage justifications of the League of Nations, but even before the war, anti-colonialism movements had been causing the Western imperial powers headaches in Palestine, Algeria, India, and elsewhere.

Japan, however, seemed to have missed the memo about overseas imperial enterprises being on their last legs. Japan's quest for inclusion in the civilization of Western powers, which had started as an attempt to save itself from the fate of colonization, reached a feverish nationalist-imperialist pitch in the interwar period. This was a Japan that was manifesting the worst aspects of Western civilization – i.e. imperialism and condescension – through a military regime duly propped up and legitimized at home by reference to how the West had been acting until then, on the one hand, and also by the emperor divinity cult, on the other. It should also be acknowledged, however, that part of the reason that Japan's actions seemed so beyond the pale, with all due respect to the Asian countries' suffering under Japan's advances, had something to do with the fact that the civilization standards and the norms of the international system had shifted. Interwar Japan was an anachronism. There is something understandable about the joy the average Japanese felt about a declaration of war with the United States. Moreover, the juxtaposition of that irrational exuberance with the feelings of regret and skepticism about Japan's advance in China, which were much more rational from a materialistic point of view, is telling. The particular evolution of the international system has often allowed the West to create monsters in its own image,[170] and saddle them with all of the guilt. This is rather an ironic by-product of the

---

[170] I am not claiming that Western civilization is the inventor of aggressive expansion. However, the particular kind of imperialism that Japan was manifesting was a European-style imperialism, with aggressiveness of colonization justified with a rhetoric of civilizing mission.

established-outsider dynamic in the international system. This is not to say that Japan does not deserve blame, but rather points to a larger causal complexity that constantly favors early rule-makers of the system over latecomers in assigning blame.

The way Japan was defeated separates this case from the cases of Turkey and Russia. The utter and complete destruction wrought by the two atomic bombs humiliated and traumatized Japan in a way that we do not see in the other two cases. Some observers, including several in Japan, have concluded from this defeat and Japan's early experience with Perry's black ships that it requires foreign intervention to shake itself out of institutionalized impasses. There is some truth in this observation if it is interpreted not to mean that Japan is beholden to foreign powers, but rather to point to a pattern we see in other cases. The pattern is that because of the particular way Japan entered this international system, the judgment of the West has always been a motivating factor in domestic debates and foreign policy decisions. Interestingly enough, in a 1973 article Johan Galtung also observed that Japan's willingness to cooperate with the American occupation itself had something to do with status concerns (using a very questionable analogy to make an otherwise valid point): "she was occupied by somebody very high up. Occupation is not unlike rape: it becomes almost an honor if only the status gap is sufficient and positive ... Had the situation been somewhat different, had Chiang-Kai-Shek been the occupier of Japan in 1945, we would have hypothesized a stream of incidents and rebellion."[171] I believe he is correct about speculation of a hypothetical Chinese invasion. What helped along Japanese cooperation with the West, as represented by the United States, was the worldview that Japanese had internalized long before US troops arrived in Japan. As Japanese scholar Harumi Befu has observed, Japan suffers from "auto-Orientalism" or "do-it-yourself Orientalism," just like Turkey and Russia: "Said, of course, focused on the Middle East for the Orientalized people, but a similar Orientalizing process took place in other parts of the world, including Japan ... where the Japanese accepted the Western-centric scheme of the universe and believed in Westerners' value judgments about Japan's backwardness."[172]

[171] Galtung, "Japan and Future World Politics," 366.
[172] Befu, "Geopolitics, Geoeconomics, and the Japanese Identity," as quoted in Klien, *Rethinking Japan's Identity*, p. 7.

In any case, while the defeat itself was traumatic, it did not end Japan's quest for status; it merely transformed its dominant manifestation. Almost every scholar who writes about anything related to Japan mentions that the Japanese care deeply (and always have) about their ranking among nations.[173] Other themes that constantly emerge from the postwar literature are, how disillusioned the Japanese were until their GNP carried them to a top rank; how the 1964 Tokyo Olympics marked a definite shift in the mood of the country; and how important international organization memberships were for Japan.[174]

The economy-first doctrine of Yoshida was chosen deliberately. Besides the obvious benefits of economic development, emphasizing economic growth and trade was the only way a country could advance, status-wise, within an international system dominated by two powers. Furthermore, this choice was very much in line with the dominating normative discourse in the international system, which had shifted from civilization to development. It also allowed Japan to increase its stature by presenting itself as a model of successful Asian development. This course was sustainable and had legitimacy because it delivered the kind of power-prestige that the domestic audience demanded. The new state identity delivered ontological security by allowing the Japanese people to hold onto their hierarchical worldview[175] and their view of Japan's right to a high stature without utilizing military strategies.

Despite the constraints, it should not be assumed that Japan had no other choice. As noted above, what came to be called the Yoshida Doctrine was very controversial from 1945 until 1960. Those on the left favored a greater distance from the United States, and desired to stand in solidarity with China and possibly even the Soviet Union. In terms of curbing the influence of the left, the socialists and the communists, the American occupation played a definite role, first through MacArthur's ban on labor strikes, and second through the "Red Purge" of the early 1950s. Nevertheless, the popularity of these views, prior to 1960, which were demonstrated rather frequently through work stoppages and riots, should not be summarily dismissed. On

---

[173] Buruma, *Inventing Japan*; Islam, *Yen for Development*.

[174] Jansen, *Emergence of Meiji Japan*; Buruma, *Inventing Japan*; Klien, *Rethinking Japan's Identity*.

[175] Galtung also observes this about the Japanese on p. 362.

the flip side, the conservative nationalists, who were pro-capitalism, but also supported more autonomy for Japan on security matters and re-armament, had considerably more breathing room. This kind of thinking was clearly more in line with US policies during the Cold War years, and it is hard to imagine that as long as it kept cooperating with the United States, a capitalist government made up of nationalists who were unapologetic to a communist China for past deeds would have much to fear from the United States. The United States would have been happy to see a re-armed Japan that was unapologetically participating in American endeavors in Asia. But that is not what emerged.

The point is not that such a government might have ended up being a threat to US interests, but rather that the United States did not have the willpower to stop it from emerging. In fact, the observations of scholars are that the 1945–60 period is filled with fears and concerns that Japan would either turn too much to the right or to the left. Just as American soldiers expected a fight when they landed in Japan in 1945, for many years afterwards many outsiders did not stop fearing that Japan would revert to its authoritarian ways. That Japan did not take either of these paths is even more remarkable.

In the end, there are compelling reasons to think that what made the middle-ground Yoshida Doctrine – as well as pacifism – popular and worth sacrifice is what made Kemal's Europeanization and secularization project compelling in Turkey three decades before. Both strategies tapped into the thirst for and obsession with international power-prestige, which is a constant for the populations of these semi-peripheral, insider-but-outsider countries with imperial pasts. Obviously, the economy-first doctrine delivered material benefits as well, but it is not for naught that the Japanese were more interested in the relative ranking of their GNP than in their absolute purchasing powers or objective living conditions.[176] It was this rank that allowed Japan to re-enter the world stage with her head held high. And to extend the analysis into the present day, as long as the power-prestige needs are met at that level, support for re-armament in Japan will continue to fail to garner popular support.

---

[176] Badgley, "Japan's Nonmilitary Road"; Bailey, *Postwar Japan*; Clesse, *Vitality of Japan*.

Furthermore, in the Japanese case, a side strategy for status enhancement has revolved around attempts to position the country in a mediator or bridging role between the East and the West. Here we see an even clearer example of the strategy whereby one inserts oneself between the haves and have-nots, as holding the definitive interpretation of the norms of inclusion. From the 1950s onward, Japan did start to formulate a clear strategy of influence in Asia through trade, but also presented itself to both the United States and Asian countries as *the* Asian model for economic success. All of Japan's involvement in Asia bear this point out, from the Bandung Conference of 1955 to the Asian Development Bank. Such a strategy is often framed as progressive and beneficent, but it in fact reinforces the status hierarchies in the international system, and assured for Japan a more privileged position vis-à-vis their Asian neighbors, at least during the Cold War. That Asian countries received this offer of assistance with some skepticism is further evidence of that fact.

Of the three cases under investigation, Japan is the most successful example of charting an alternative route to high stature by exemplifying dominant norms of the international system, though how well Russia will do in the future remains to be seen. If Turkey's commitment to its post-defeat identity has proven the most durable, Japan's commitment has proven to be the most fruitful. Part of this has to do with the international context that Japan was operating in. Japan was certainly helped by the Cold War dynamics in this endeavor.

During the process of writing this book, I had the occasion to tell many Turkish acquaintances about my subject-matter and case selection. Almost without fail, I would get one of two responses (I am paraphrasing): "Why Japan? Surely they do not have the same insecurities we do!"[177] and "The Japanese did it the right way: they developed economically without compromising their identity. We should have followed their model!" I find these responses rather interesting, and I suspect that Japan specialists would find them amusing. Given the foreign origins of Japan's constitution, let alone things such as the beef-eating fashions of the Meiji period, it is difficult to claim that Japan's identity has never been "compromised." Yet I believe that these casual comments are picking up a major difference between the Turkish and Japanese cases, and that difference is mostly traceable to

---

[177] Nobody objected to the inclusion of Russia for some reason.

the fact that Japan was defeated at a later period than the Ottoman Empire.

Japan's relative distance to the "established" core before defeat was not unlike the Ottoman Empire's: grudgingly recognized by the international society as a great power, but not treated equally because of differences in inherent characteristics such as race (and religion). The material conditions Japan faced after defeat were even worse than Turkey: a devastated economy, a country in ruins, and occupation by US forces. Despite the heavy level of American interference, Japan was able to fashion a successful strategy out of these conditions. As discussed in Chapter 2, the normative criteria for respect in the international system had changed by the time World War II was over. The emphasis had shifted from displaying signs and markers of modern civilization to displaying markers of economic success and "development." This allowed Japan to pursue a strategy of emulation that left more room for preserving surviving Japanese social traits. In other words, while the Turkish strategy of emulation ("correction") hinged on wholesale reformulation of all sorts of cultural practices that fell under the rubric of state authority (in an attempt to convince the Western powers of Turkey's "inherent" greatness and fitness for "civilization"), after World War II, Japan was able to focus status-enhancement efforts on economic practices.

Japan's ascent on the status ladder was helped by the emergence of two distinct camps in the international system in the Cold War period. As far as general state behavior was concerned, the assimilatory pull of the ideal-typical Westphalian state norm had remained intact from the previous period, but especially as far as the economic practices of this ideal state were concerned, there were two competing ideologies. This allowed, on the one hand, Japan to improve its status quickly, for it is easier to rise in a smaller group, and on the other hand, gave maneuvering room to Japan to parlay its new alliance into social capital by taking the role of a norm transmitter. Of the three cases, Japan used tactics for status advancement most successfully, quite deliberately attempting to position itself as a role model for Asian countries and/or newly independent colonies. Turkey's similar efforts in the interwar period to position itself as an Asian/Muslim power that had succeeded in joining "civilization" could only be directed to the very limited number of sovereign states which could learn such lessons.

The end of the Cold War has hurt this balance, but has not destroyed it. The two problems that Japan has faced in the post-Cold War period are the emerging normative criteria which are moving away from pure traditional understanding of economic development to more postmodern values, and the convergence of the two Cold War camps, which has increased the number of countries with access to core privileges. However, I would argue that having succeeded in largely erasing its postwar stigmas, Japan is unlikely to experience any radical ruptures in foreign policy in the future. Despite the growing domestic demand for Japan to take a more prominent role in international affairs, the analysis here supports the predictions of constructivist scholarship on Japan that any such expansion in the future will not take a military turn.[178]

Nevertheless, the fact that Japan still does not have the stature commensurate with its material power is a demonstration of the reality that Japan still feels the effects of the historical established-outsider dynamic of the international system. Ironically, Japan's insecurities are partly to blame for this prestige gap. One of the main current threats to Japan's status in the international system stems from an issue not unlike those faced by contemporary Turkey: namely Japan's trouble with facing its past crimes, especially the atrocities of World War II. Japan's reluctance to take full responsibility for its wartime actions remains a source of tension in its relationships with both Asia and the West. In 2007, much to Japan's consternation, the US House of Representatives passed a resolution condemning Japan for crimes of sexual exploitation committed by the Japanese military during World War II.

That crimes of World War II remain an issue for Japan should be surprising given the much greater lengths Japan has gone to, to face its past compared to Turkey. Japanese military leaders were brought to trial and punished after World War II, and Japan had formally apologized for many of its actions, including the now controversial sex slaves issue. When controversies flare over "comfort women" or visits to the Yasukuni war shrine, Japanese leaders are actually *retracting* apologies for actions Japan has accepted guilt over previously. Given

---

[178] See also Katzenstein and Okawara, "Japan, Asian-Pacific Security"; Katzenstein and Sil, "Rethinking Asian Security"; as well as Katzenstein, *Cultural Norms*.

Japanese postwar commitment to pacifism, these retractions are especially puzzling.

Japanese nationalists who cling onto a whitewashed version of Japanese history might represent only a minority, but controversies over Japan's wartime behavior would not be flaring up with such frequency if the construction demonstrated in the above resolution did not resonate with Japanese national identity. An interesting point of contrast is with Germany; oppositional groups in Japan who push for a more critical examination of the state's past often draw upon the German example: "Japan, it was held, had not sufficiently 'mastered the past' and should look to [Germany] as a model ... Even the term for 'mastering the past' (*kako no kokufuku*) was invented in 1992 to translate the German *Vergangenheishewaltigung*."[179] Despite arguably being the less malevolent of the pair during the war, a present-day comparison ends with the conclusion that Japan has not been able to deal with the stigmatization accompanying its wartime actions as well as Germany. Germany's reconciliation efforts, however, have to be contextualized against Germany's reintegration into Europe.[180] Whereas Japan's exact placement between East and West still remains open to question, the postwar trajectory of Germany has been securely anchored in Europe. Whatever difficulties Germany has had reconstructing its national identity have been tempered by the affirmation provided by the European identity of Germany. There is an obvious irony here in the fact that even in such a context-specific historical matter, the established-outsider dynamic and the pattern of evaluating oneself (and coming up short) according to Western standards is perpetuated.

Unlike Germany, Japan, despite its economic stature, is securely anchored neither in Asia nor among the great powers of the international system.[181] Japan stands apart from colonized Asia as a former colonizer. At the same time, Japan is not completely comfortable among Western powers either. As Shogo Suzuki notes, Japan is a "frustrated great power." Frustrated great powers believe that they are not given the social equality and the privileges they deserve.[182] Japan remains a frustrated great power mainly because of its World

---

[179] Konrad, "Entangled Memories," 96.   [180] *Ibid.*, 98.
[181] Klien, *Rethinking Japan's Identity*, p. 6.
[182] Suzuki, "Seeking 'Legitimate'," 49.

War II legacy and subsequent commitment to pacifism. Pacifism, which has gone a long way in obscuring the past stigma of Japanese military aggressiveness, has come at a price: it has kept Japan out of decision-making processes in matters of international security.[183]

The Japanese right consider the anti-militarism of Japanese society a consequence of the "brainwashing" of the occupation years.[184] They believe that Japan was robbed of its sense of national pride and emasculated by a hypocritical West which would not apologize for its own actions. This is why they want to revise Japan's apologies and reconstruct a nation proud of its own history. In their view, only such a nation can once again create a strong military and reassert Japan's significance on the world stage. However, just as in the Turkish case, it is precisely these efforts to recapture Japan's pride which drive Japan away from a position of influence in Asia and, by extension, the international system. Such is the irony of ontological insecurity created by stigmatization: it is a snake which feeds on its own tail. Just like Turkey, Japan has to learn to leave the patterns of the past behind, but if *even Japan* cannot overcome the effects of its stigmatized past, what does that imply for the prospects of others in the international system? I will revisit this question in the concluding chapter.

[183] *Ibid.*, 52.
[184] Suzuki, "Strange Masochism."

5 | The "enigmatic" enemy: Russia (1990–2007)

Russia's identity crisis has made it difficult to formulate and pursue a clear and consistent policy toward the outside world.

Andrei Tsygankov, "From International Institutionalism to Revolutionary Expansionism"

So much of Russian thinking about foreign affairs seems to converge around the idea that there is a conspiracy to prevent Russia resuming its great power status and to halt the "natural" restoration of the Russian imperial complex in some form.

Guardian, March 22, 1997

Boris N. Yeltsin, speaking on Independence Day, told Russians their country remains a great international power, one that is respected instead of feared.

News Service reports, June 13, 1997

Who lost Russia ... our new rival? Neither ally nor partner ...

Washington Times, February 18, 1998

There is enough uncertainty ... about the wisdom of President Vladimir Putin's new pro-western foreign policy. Is he trying to join the west, or is he trying to use it?

Financial Times, April 15, 2002

For the first time, the Russian president directly questioned the legitimacy of the approaches, principles, evaluation criteria and even the very ideology of the West in relations with the rest of the world.

BBC Monitoring Former Soviet Union, December 12, 2004

It's time we start thinking of Vladimir Putin's Russia as an enemy of the United States.

The Wall Street Journal, November 28, 2006

Introduction

Is Russia, the former Soviet Union, an ally of the United States and Europe, an enemy of the West, or neither? The jury is still out, and Russian leaders have been giving out confusing signals since the official end of the Cold War.[1] From Yeltsin's drunken ramblings to the supposed exposure of Putin's soul,[2] Western observers have not been able to figure out a way to read Russia's intentions. Every couple of years, some policy expert definitively proclaims that Russia is a friend. The next year some incident suggests the exact opposite. If Russia was a riddle wrapped in an enigma during Soviet years, it has since then become a *matryoshka* doll of foreign policy gestures.

The goal of this chapter is to analyze the foreign policy choices Russia has made since the downfall of the Soviet Union, and suggest that Russia's actions make sense only in a framework of status-seeking in a socially stratified international society of established and outsiders. The status standards that Russia faces now are quite different than those Russia, Japan, or Turkey faced in the last centuries. Therefore, Russia's behavior in the last decades gives us important clues about the future of international society and the future impact of status-seeking behavior within this society.

As with the previous two chapters, Chapter 5 is divided into three sections. The first section gives an overview of Russia's relationship with international society and its status standards prior to the collapse of the Soviet Union. Both imperial Russia's and the Soviet Union's relationship with international society will be briefly considered as a precursor to the post-Cold War period. The second section offers a narrative of the choices Russia made within the foreign policy sphere after the demise of its empire, as well as the domestic debates about which direction Russia should take to regain its status and overcome its stigmatized position. Of the three cases under investigation, Russia has come closest to dominating international society as a great power, so it is not surprising that Russian domestic debates are the most explicit about status-seeking motivations.

---

[1] Owen, "Transnational Liberalism," 119, 132–5.
[2] President George W. Bush's remark that he looked into Putin's soul. See e.g. Slevin and Baker, "Bush Changing Views," 26.

The third section will analyze this narrative within the framework discussed in Chapter 2 in regard to responses to stigmatization.

Russia and the West: Émile or Caliban?

Thus, Utkin argues, the standard interpretations of Peter's role in Russian history – that he either made Russia part of Europe, or that he destroyed traditional Russia but did not succeed in Europeanizing it – are both misplaced ... Rather, the reforms served as a shield which allowed Russia to maintain its independence and originality while it was at the same time included in the sphere of European culture. (Iver Neumann, *Russia and the Idea of Europe*, p.191)

Russia's "Westernization" project was the first of its kind[3] in the history of the modern states system, and, as we saw in previous chapters, was replicated to some degree by all other premodern empires struggling to withstand European expansion. In fact, Neumann notes that "Trotsky reminds that Russia was one of the first countries to experience the pangs of globalization emanating from the European core ... [The] discovery of Russia by the evolving European state system was part of that era we think of as the 'age of European discovery.'"[4] The initiator of the modernization project conceived in response was Peter the Great,[5] who introduced Western technologies, practices, beliefs, and personnel,[6] changed the language of the state,[7] changed the title of the ruler from tsar to imperator, and moved the capital from Moscow to St. Petersburg.[8] Peter's reforms had the consequence of successfully making Russia a

---

[3] See Watson, "Russia and the European States System," pp. 61–6, for an overview of Russia's political development trajectory until this juncture.

[4] Neumann, "Review," 350.

[5] Reign: 1682–1725. Although, just as in the Ottoman case with Mahmud II, the inception of borrowing from the West pre-dates Peter's efforts, at least as far back as his grandfather Alexis.

[6] And just as in the Ottoman and Japanese cases, Russian attitudes toward the culture which accompanies these innovations were dismissive at first: "They saw that to do this they must learn the military and also the administrative and manufacturing skills of the West, which the Russians disparagingly described as 'khitry,' meaning clever and tricky." Watson, "Russia and the European States System," p. 63.

[7] French became the medium of communication for the upper classes.

[8] Neumann, *Russia and the Idea of Europe*, p. 11.

player of some importance in the European states system. The main rival of Russia at this time was the Ottoman Empire, and it was Peter's desire to forge an anti-Ottoman alliance that led him on his European travels during the first decade of his reign.[9] However, the reforms inspired by these travels first bore fruit in the Russian victory over the Swedes in 1709, leading to Russia's emergence as the predominant Baltic power.[10] His campaigns against the Ottomans were mostly failures.[11]

It would be a mistake to assume that Russia gained entry[12] into the great power club of the eighteenth and nineteenth centuries simply by adopting a few reforms or through military victory alone. What made Russia successful where the Ottoman Empire and Japan failed subsequently was the Russian state's success in challenging the meaning of "Europe." As Neumann demonstrates convincingly, throughout the eighteenth century, "[t]he Russian state formulated, disseminated and insisted upon a geographical definition of Europe as stretching to all the most populous parts of Russia. The idea that Europe ends and Asia begins at the Urals was first presented by a Russian geographer."[13] The Ottoman Empire also attempted something similar in the nineteenth century, with some success – i.e. the Ottoman Empire was also named a *European* power in 1856; however, the Russian project was more successful because the Russians already had the other characteristic necessary for inclusion: Christianity. Especially in the eighteenth century, membership of the Westphalian states system hinged on religion and geography.

However, around the time Russia made its case for inclusion as a European power, Western Europe went through some fundamental changes, starting with the French Revolution. In a way, Russia became an "outsider" inside the new European society of states almost as

---

[9] Watson, "Russia and the European States System," p. 63.

[10] Neumann, *Russia and the Idea of Europe*, p. 11.

[11] Interestingly, Peter the Great is known in Turkish history as Peter the Madman.

[12] In fact, prior to the Westernization efforts of Golitsyin, the chief minister of Regent Sofia (Peter's predecessor), the Russian state was not recognized as part of the system at all – as far as the Europeans were concerned, it was ranked lower than even the Ottoman Empire. Watson, "Russia and the European States System," p. 66.

[13] *Ibid.*, p. 12.

soon as it managed to gain entry to the club.[14] Russia achieved what no other Eastern agrarian empire had managed to achieve by becoming a major participant in the Concert of Europe, but the concert itself was very much a product of eighteenth-century politics – revolving around the idea of dynastic legitimacy and reciprocity. As soon as Russia gained entry to the great-powers club, the ground underneath began to shift as the effects of the French Revolution became more and more discernible in Western Europe.

In hindsight, there was plenty of irony in the developments of the early nineteenth century. Having played a leading role in the defeat of Napoleon, Russians felt somewhat secure[15] about their standing and stature for the first time since their engagement with Europe: "The journalist Nikolai Polevoi wrote, 'How can a European boast of his puny little fist? Only the Russian has a real fist, a fist *comme il faut*, the ideal of a fist. Indeed, there is nothing reprehensible in that fist, nothing base, nothing barbaric. On the contrary, it possesses a great deal of significance, power, and poetry.'"[16] Yet, the same developments which had produced Napoleon were continuing to work in this period of perceived Russian success and undermining Russia's position in Europe as a result. In fact, we may hypothesize that Russia's unexpected success against Napoleon had the effect of shielding the Russian monarchy from criticism from below and delayed the consideration of reforms taking place in Western Europe. Therefore Russia was in some ways a victim of its own brief success. There is

---

[14] Even before the developments of the nineteenth century, many in Europe were skeptical about the success of Russian transformation. The following passage from Rousseau's *Social Contract* (1762) is illustrative of the European mindset vis-à-vis the Russians in the eighteenth century:

"The Russians will never be truly civilized, since they have been civilized too early. Peter had a genius for imitation. He did not have true genius, the kind that creates and makes everything out of nothing. Some of the things he did were good; most of them were out of place. He saw that his people was barbarous; he did not see that it was not ready for civilization. He wanted to civilize it when all it needed was toughening. First he wanted to make Germans and Englishmen, when he should have made Russians. He prevented his subjects from ever becoming what they could have been by persuading them that they were something they are not." See Book 2, Chapter 8

[15] Almost too secure – the boasts of Russians in this period smack of the kind of bravado discussed in the Introduction and Chapter 2.

[16] Polunov, *Russia in the Nineteenth Century*, p. 69.

a similarity between these developments and those that befell Japan leading up to and after World War I. Just as post-World War I Japan, which had briefly caught up with the West in material terms, was an anachronism, displaying the values of an already disappearing imperialist age, post-Napoleonic Wars Russia, unbeknownst to itself, was also quickly becoming a relic from an age of dynastic privileges.

Some in Russia saw the developments in Western Europe as a betrayal of true European ideals as embodied in the *ancien régime*. Nicholas especially was trapped by his failure to understand the significance of these changes. While Nicholas envisioned Russia as the "gendarme of Europe" and himself a noble defender of the status quo, public and elite opinion in Western Europe perceived the actions of Russia, even those against the Ottoman Empire, as barbaric.[17] The Russian state, on the other hand, represented itself as the "true Europe."[18] In the meantime, Europeans continued to look upon Russia as a learner.[19] In that sense, even though imperial Russia, compared to the Ottoman Empire or Japan, was more successful in gaining formal entry to the European society of states, Russia's identity as a European power was never entirely complete: "Doubts about the ability of Russians to internalize [European] values were ... frequently voiced ... Parallels, political or otherwise, were frequently drawn between Russia and the Ottoman Empire."[20] However, Russia stands out among the other cases as the only one whose perceived power was exaggerated rather than downplayed.[21] This was as true of imperial Russia as it was of the Soviet Union.

Nicholas's failure to read the new international system ultimately led to the Russian failure in the Crimean War, because he "did not understand that his personal friendship with conservative English aristocrats such as the Duke of Wellington and Lord Aberdeen, the British prime minister, would not guarantee England's friendly behavior as a state."[22] Historians have observed that "Nicholas lived

---

[17] *Ibid.*, p. 71. For instance, "Lord Clarendon, the British foreign secretary, called the [Crimean] war a struggle for 'the independence of Europe,' for 'civilization' against 'barbarism.'" Britain and France ended up declaring war on Russia on the side of the Ottoman Empire.

[18] Neumann, *Russia and the Idea of Europe*, p. 194.

[19] Neumann, *Russia as Europe's Other*, p. 27.

[20] *Ibid.*, p. 60.   [21] Bunce, "Domestic Reform," 138.

[22] Polunov, *Russia in the Nineteenth Century*, p. 71.

in a world of 'dynastic mythology'[23] and placed excessive reliance on personal contacts and ties of blood and friendship within the European elite."[24] The debacle of the Crimean War, however, gave Westernizers the edge they were hoping for. The Westernizers were also a by-product of the Napoleonic Wars: the officers who took part in the occupation of Paris "were impressed by the contrast between its freedoms and prosperity and the 'bestiality and arbitrariness' that greeted them at home."[25] Despite the external recognition of Russia as a European power, it was becoming apparent domestically that its developmental problems had not been overcome. Many believed Russia to be backward and called for more freedom. The early half of the nineteenth century had been a time of great turmoil domestically for other European powers, as evidenced in the revolutions of 1848. Russia had been spared these revolutions, but temporary escape from this fate only fueled the discontent of disenfranchised parties.[26] Coming off the high of the Napoleonic Wars, Nicholas had been able to suppress the Westernizers, but after the Crimean War, reforms could no longer be put off – and they were implemented by Nicholas's successor Alexander.

This was partly because the Slavophiles, who had high hopes about the outcome of the war, also turned to criticize the Russian state after defeat: "'Sevastopol did not fall by accident,' [Slavophile] Ivan Aksakov wrote to his relatives. 'Its fall was an act of God to expose the true rottenness of the governmental system and all the consequences of repression.'"[27] Of course, as Robert English notes, the Slavophiles were no less Europeanized than their Westernizer counterparts: "Fundamental elements of Slavophilism were indeed borrowed from European, primarily German, thinkers, from the idea of 'organic' nation to reverence for the traditional peasant commune."[28] Moreover, both groups looked to the past selectively to construct their vision of the future.[29] In other words, just as in the Turkish and Japanese cases, the Russian elite had very much internalized

---

[23] See the discussion in Chapter 1.
[24] Polunov, *Russia in the Nineteenth Century*, p. 71.
[25] English, *Russia and the Idea of the West*, p. 20.
[26] See e.g. Kropotkin, *Memoirs of a Revolutionist*.
[27] Polunov, *Russia in the Nineteenth Century*, p. 86.
[28] English, *Russia and the Idea of the West*, p. 20.
[29] Billington, *Russia in Search of Itself*, p. 14.

the worldview emanating from Western Europe: and just as in those cases, Russian disagreements in the nineteenth century were not about the validity of that worldview but about what the right response to Russia's inferior position would be. While the Westernizers held that everything had to be borrowed from the West, the Slavophiles argued Russia had to preserve its unique civilization which was the source of its strength.[30] We have seen the articulation of identical positions in both the Turkish and Japanese cases.

The Westernizing reforms of the previous centuries had not gone far enough to please various sections of the intelligentsia who demanded more. Alexander II tried to address the calls for reform by issuing "The Great Emancipation Statute" in 1861, around the same time the Ottoman Sultan was issuing his *Tanzimat* decrees, and Japan was coming under the Meiji rule. The Statute freed the serfs but compensated the landowners for their loss. Just as in the Ottoman Empire and Japan, the reforms created their own backlash. Neither the peasants nor the landowners were satisfied with the decree.[31] Alexander II, like Mahmud II in Istanbul, also attempted to reform the army, and pushed through several civil and educational reforms. All in all, Alexander's reforms were the most comprehensive since Peter the Great. Nevertheless, they can, at best, be described as stopgap measures intended to ensure the continuity of the system.

In fact, the debates in the nineteenth century for Russia revolved very much around the same identity issues faced by Turkey and Japan (whose debates had commenced at slightly later dates). James Billington makes the same error as the experts in Turkish and Japanese history when he argues that "no nation ever poured more intellectual energy into answering the question of national identity than Russia,"[32] although he is right to draw our attention to the fact that in Russia the two sides, for a while at least, seemed more equally matched.

What originally ignited the debate were two monographs by Peter Chaadaev: *Philosophical Letter* (1836) and *Apology of a Madman* (1837). Describing Moscow as a "Necropolis," Chaadaev (1837)

---

[30] English, *Russia and the Idea of the West*, p. 21; see also Billington, *Russia in Search of Itself*, for specific examples of thought from both sides.

[31] Mikhailov and Shelgunov, *Proclamation to the Younger Generation*; Broido, *Apostles into Terrorists*; Zaionchkovsky and Wobst, *Abolition of Serfdom in Russia*.

[32] Billington, *Russia in Search of Itself*, p. 12.

nevertheless went on to argue that "Russia's very lateness in development would enable her to do better than Western nations."[33] Just
as their Japanese and Ottoman counterparts would argue only a few
decades later, the Slavophiles of Russia tried to find virtue in Russia's
"unique" civilization, "combining the virtues of the Orthodox faith,
Slavic ethnicity, and the communal institutions and decision-making
procedures of an overwhelmingly peasant population."[34] And Russia,
just like Turkey and Japan would be later, was conceived of as a civilization which would not only help itself but one that was uniquely
qualified to resolve the tensions created by modernity.

What distinguishes the Russian debate from the Ottoman and
Japanese ones is the fact that the Slavophiles were advancing these
claims right around the time the Westernizers seemed to be vindicated by the reforms of Alexander II. In the Ottoman and Japanese
cases, we saw such views articulated strongly only after the attempts
to modernize following Western prescriptions – i.e. the *Tanzimat* and
Meiji periods – failed to erase stigmatization. In the Russian case, the
Slavophile position pre-dates the reforms – and was merely subdued
during their enactment. This difference most likely stems from the
longer engagement Russia had with modernization and Westernization
pressures. In any case, the Russian trajectory did converge with the
other cases after Alexander's reforms – not only did they fail to defeat
the previous Slavophile objections, but created their own backlash.[35]

In Russia, too, then, liberalizing reforms and increased political
openness created expectations that could not be met. Just as new
recognitions given to religious minorities in the Ottoman Empire
actually increased the activities of secessionist national liberation
movements, the civil reforms in Russia served as a catalyst for opposition groups who now demanded a written constitution and a parliament. In response, in both countries, the reform period was followed

---

[33] *Ibid.*   [34] *Ibid.*, pp. 12–13.
[35] And the purely materialist reading of these nineteenth-century reforms
is as misplaced in the Russian example as it is in the previous cases. The
Bolsheviks were as guilty of this as anyone else. For instance, Trotsky's
explanation of the 1861 Emancipation Act as a moment of primitive
accumulation misses the identity dynamics involved in the situation (see
History of the Russian Revolution). By that time, these types of reforms had
come to be assessed by the Russian intelligentsia according to a rubric of
comparison with what was known/imagined about the "West."

by a period of backlash and repression. In the Ottoman Empire, the reign of Abdülhamid, which followed immediately after the *Tanzimat* opening and recognition of the equal rights of all subjects, was a period of extreme repression of Christians (e.g. the Armenian massacres of 1887–8). Similarly, in Russia, Alexander's reforms were severely curtailed by his son, Alexander III, and Alexander III's son, Nicholas II, at least until 1905, when Nicholas II reluctantly conceded a parliamentary assembly.[36] However, he was forced to relent because of the growing unification and the increased violence of the opposition following the events of Bloody Sunday, January 9, 1905.[37] None of this did much to help Russia's image abroad: Robert Service points out that no imperial power before World War I was reviled by democrats in Europe as much as the Russian Empire.[38]

In the events leading up to World War I, there were certain similarities between the Russian and the Ottoman cases. As a result of Bloody Sunday, Russia was ruled as a parliamentary monarchy between 1905 and 1917; the Ottomans switched to a similar system in 1908. Both countries entered World War I (on different sides) with the hope of rejuvenating their global positions and stopping the dissolution of their empires. Russia emerged from World War I under Bolshevik control, whereas Kemalist Turkey replaced the Ottoman Empire. However, as discussed in Chapter 3, in terms of foreign policy, the Kemalist government of Ankara followed a very different path than the Bolsheviks in Moscow. This is where the main difference lies, but it should not obscure the fact that both regimes were dealing with the problem of (the stigmatization of) backwardness.

Unlike the Kemalists, the Bolsheviks came to power as a result of a popular, social revolution.[39] Lenin and his comrades were ideologically driven intellectuals, whereas Kemal and his followers were, above all, pragmatist soldiers. In academic parlance, Russia's was

---

[36] Service, *History of Modern Russia*, p. 1.

[37] On that day, marchers, including women and children, were gunned down as they walked to the palace to hand a petition to the tsar [January 22, 1905, in the new style].

[38] Service, *History of Modern Russia*, p. 1. For period examples of Russia being characterized as an Asiatic or Oriental country prior to the revolution, see e.g. Farbman, "Present Situation in Russia"; Grovin, "Soviet Russia."

[39] For a discussion of revolutionary conditions, especially as they pertain to Russia, see Motyl, "Why Empires Reemerge."

a bottom-up revolution, and Turkey's top-down.[40] What I want to emphasize, however, is Georgi Derluguian's point that the revolutionary movements in these countries were not radically different in terms of developmental aspirations. Derluguian observes that "the modern revolutions have a lot to do with the mobility of states in the geographical hierarchy and axial division of labor in the world-system."[41] He also links revolutions to status aspirations: "revolutions have been at the radical extreme of the more usual reform efforts intended to resist the downward decline of one's group position (as a country or putative nation) in the world's ranking order."[42] In other words, revolutions are wholesale attempts at countering "decline and backwardness, or their perceived effects on social, economic, and cultural fields" by "restructuring the state and social composition of national society."[43] Derluguian's point is that, in essence, there is much alike in what happened in Turkey and Russia – both had concerns about "backwardness" which stemmed from the similarity in the social space occupied by these two countries vis-à-vis the West. Whereas "liberal national reformers (who sometimes were revolutionary, as Atatürk) normally adhered to the Hegelian or Durkheimian ideas of historical progress and order," "Marxist-inspired revolutionaries rather saw the answer in the state-creation of industrial proletariat because either ideology associated industrial proletariat with modernity and universal salvation."[44] What both of these ideological programs had in common was the view of the state as the seat of salvation.

The different responses we find to the "developmental" problem in Bolshevik Russia versus Kemalist Turkey are first and foremost attributable to domestic factors such as "the class composition, outlook and administrative capacities of the revolutionary elite."[45] The difference in the ideologies, however, should not lead one to overlook the many similarities between the regimes: "Both pursued shock modernization programs that involved mass mobilization, nation and state building, political centralization, as well as attempts at radical interventions in the realms of society and culture."[46] And whatever differences may have existed in ideologies substance-wise, the

---

[40] Trimberger, *Revolution from Above.*
[41] Derluguian, *Bourdieu's Secret Admirer,* p. 9.
[42] *Ibid.*   [43] *Ibid.*   [44] *Ibid.*   [45] *Ibid.,* p. 315.
[46] Khalid, "Backwardness and the Quest for Civilization," 234.

ideological end-products in the two regimes resemble each other quite a bit: "both regimes produced an official historiography that shared many elements: a glorious foundational moment and a larger-than-life founding figure; leadership by a group with clearly defined goals, to which the founders remained unwaveringly loyal; and a clear break from the past, so that all connections to the old regime were downplayed."[47] Furthermore, what is remarkable is the fact that both regimes went on to forcefully "civilize" peoples in the territories under their control: "Both the Soviet and the Kemalist states had at their disposal the baggage, common to modern European thought, of evolution, backwardness and progress, of ethnic classification of peoples, and, indeed, of orientalism."[48] Where they differed is in the outward projection of the respective ideologies. Whereas the Bolsheviks aimed to position themselves (along the earlier Slavophile lines) as an international regime which was an alternative to the West, the Kemalist regime aimed to claim its "rightful" place among the "civilized" nations of the West.

The divergence of international strategies has to do with differences in levels of ontological security of the new regimes. The Ottoman Empire was defeated, dismantled, and occupied as a result of World War I. The Kemalist regime did not emerge until 1920, and did not gain control of the country until it managed to fight off the occupation. Russia also suffered setbacks during World War I, but that was before the Bolsheviks took control of the state and withdrew[49] the country from the war before it was over. They also managed to keep the territory of the empire intact, and by 1921 had reconquered some of the previously lost territory in the Caucasus.[50] This was a very significant difference – the Russian imperial habitus survived into the Bolshevik era whereas the Turks had to face the loss of their empire. In other words, the new Russian developmentalist regime did not experience the ontological trauma of the humiliation and confusion accompanying military defeat resulting in imperial collapse.

---

[47] *Ibid.*   [48] *Ibid.*, 251.
[49] Some argue that the Russian Army was in a better condition in 1916 than it was in 1914. See Service, *History of Modern Russia*; Service, *Russian Revolution*.
[50] Service, *History of Modern Russia*, p. 128.

Soviet Russia

During the nineteenth century, the Russian state represented itself as a "true Europe" in a situation where the rest of Europe had failed in its own tradition by turning away from the past values of the ancien regimes. During the twentieth century, the Russian state represented itself as "true Europe" in a situation where the rest of Europe had failed the best in its own tradition by not turning to the future values of socialism. (Iver Neumann, *Russia and the Idea of Europe*, p. 194)

The main difference between Soviet Russia and Kemalist Turkey is that Soviet Russia intended to secure its status in the world by pursuing its own unique developmentalist strategy, grounded in socialist state planning. Recognizing the hostility of this strategy, the Western powers initially treated the Soviet Union as an international pariah[51] because "diplomatic recognition could not be granted a regime that was founded on principles antithetical to Western values."[52] European powers supported the Whites during the Russian Civil War.[53] For their part, Bolshevik leaders spoke aggressively about their expectation for workers' revolts in Europe.[54]

However, it would be a mistake to read Bolshevik policies as a complete departure from the constraints of the normative context of the international status hierarchy. The decade after the revolution is remarkable for the pro-market orientation of the New Economic Policy adopted by the Soviet Union.[55] Matching the economic policy on the international front was the Bolsheviks' new-found interest in playing by the normative rules of European diplomacy:[56] "When they arrived in Italy, the Bolshevik delegates were not wearing their old revolutionary uniforms, but instead the frock coats and striped trousers of the traditional international diplomat."[57] Ringmar points out that in this

---

[51] See Ringmar, "On the Ontological Status"; Ringmar, "Recognition Game"; Francis, *Russia from the American Embassy*; Uldricks, *Diplomacy and Ideology*; Debo, *Survival and Consolidation*.

[52] Ringmar, "Recognition Game," 123.

[53] *Ibid.*, 123.   [54] Service, *History of Modern Russia*, p. 120.

[55] *Ibid.*, pp. 123–49, 294.

[56] Even Waltz acknowledges this development (*Theory of International Politics*, pp. 127–8), but never asks the most interesting question about what he observes: what do frock coats have to do with military power?

[57] Laue, "Soviet Diplomacy," p. 24; Trotsky, *Revolution Betrayed*, p. 140; White, *Origins of Détente*; as cited in Ringmar, "Recognition Game," 123.

decade the Bolsheviks were eminently concerned with being perceived as a legitimate state, and followed the rules in order to get this recognition from Europe.[58] To this end, they continued to pursue two sets of policies: presenting a diplomatic face to the West, and a revolutionary face to the East that was supposed to stand as the vanguard of all the oppressed peoples.[59] The main difference here with the strategies implemented by former powers after defeat is that the diplomatic veneer was intended as a cover for revolutionary activities.[60]

Faced with the growing threat of Nazi activities in the early 1930s, the Soviet Union joined the League of Nations in 1934, emphasizing the importance of collective security.[61] Domestically, the developmental project was bearing fruit under Stalin's rule. The repressed economic situation in the world market had rendered the New Economic Policy moot, and the Soviet leaders therefore "embarked on a quest to build a modern industrial base without the capitalists."[62] Derluguian argues that three institutions underwrote the Stalinist military-industrial enterprise: "the centralized and all-encompassing *nomenklatura* system of political-bureaucratic appointment; the forced mobilization of economic resources and manpower for the war effort; and the establishment of national republics."[63] As the military-industrial complex grew, Stalin came increasingly to define the Soviet Union as a great power equal to European powers.[64] According to Ringmar, it was the reluctance of Western powers to recognize the Soviet Union as such[65] that turned Stalin to Nazi Germany.[66] If the Soviet Union had been able to secure great power recognition within the existing system, alignment with Nazi Germany would have been unnecessary, since Stalin viewed the latter as the less preferable option.[67]

---

[58] Ringmar, "Recognition Game," 124.
[59] Kennedy-Pipe, *Russia and the World*, pp. 24–6.
[60] Ringmar, "Recognition Game," 125.   [61] *Ibid.*, 125–6.
[62] Derluguian, *Bourdieu's Secret Admirer*, p. 295.
[63] *Ibid.*
[64] Erickson, *Soviet High Command*, pp. 475–7; Ringmar, "Recognition Game," 125.
[65] See Kennedy-Pipe, *Russia and the World*, pp. 41–3, for a discussion of reasons behind Western reluctance, including the distaste over Stalin's purges.
[66] Ringmar, "Recognition Game," 126.
[67] See Ringmar, "Recognition Game," for a more detailed discussion of the evidence for this reading of events.

After the war, the Soviet Union was a de facto great power. However, as Ringmar demonstrates, the Soviets continued to feel a degree of ontological insecurity vis-à-vis the United States and the Western world.[68] As Larson and Shevchenko point out, "early U.S. acknowledgement of Soviet parity did not extend to the political and diplomatic spheres."[69] As a result, the Soviet Union increasingly withdrew from international activities that were led by the United States, and sought to create its own sphere of alternative recognition. During the Cold War years, the two competing constructions of Russia had resurfaced, but with different emphases. The new manifestation of the perception of Russia as a pupil or learner emphasized the Soviet Union as the barbarian at Europe's gate. This discourse simultaneously exaggerated the military threat posed by the Soviet Union[70] and attributed moral weakness, laziness, and drunkenness to Russians themselves.[71] On the other hand, the view of Russia as "true Europe" also persisted among a minority in the West, and was perpetuated by the Soviet Union. This construction saw Russia as the land of the future, the true resolution of the contradictions of European history.[72] On the whole, however, "the Soviets' impressive coercive capabilities did not persuade Western states to a•cept the Soviet Union as a political and moral equal."[73]

Even the academic discourse on Russia during this period in the West is telling. For instance, Karl A. Wittfogel made a career out of arguing that Russia always had been (and always would be) an objectively "Oriental" society. In a 1950 article, Wittfogel outlines his argument:

On the managerial plane a much greater similarity exists between Oriental despotism and the USSR ... Oriental trends [such as the coercive devices of a strong autocratic state] were by no means absent in pre-Mongol Russia. But these trends were too weak to make early Russia marginally Oriental. Russia crossed the institutional watershed when, under the Mongol rule, from the middle of the thirteenth century to the end of the fifteenth century,

---

[68] *Ibid.*, 128.
[69] Larson and Shevchenko, "Shortcut to Greatness," 94.
[70] Neumann, *Russia as Europe's Other*; Bunce, "Domestic Reform."
[71] Neumann, *Russia as Europe's Other.*
[72] *Ibid.*, p. 13; Neumann, *Russia and the Idea of Europe.*
[73] Larson and Shevchenko, "Shortcut to Greatness," 95.

it was part of a marginal Oriental empire. It was during this lengthy period of the Mongol Yoke – a period which, for a number of reasons, has been slighted by most investigators – that the coercive and acquisitive techniques of Eastern statecraft were vigorously imposed, making possible the consolidation of an Oriental autocratic and bureaucratic system of government and society.[74]

Despite the social scientific language, it is difficult not to come away from this passage with a feeling that it was the (Asian, Eastern, Oriental) Mongols who "ruined" it for the Russians who may otherwise have turned out as all white races are supposed to. The Soviet apparatus is not a product of the various constellations of geographic, ideological, economic, etc. factors but is somehow directly traceable to the Mongolians of the thirteenth century who must have been carrying its prototype in their genes. In a 1963 article,[75] Wittfogel goes further to make a contorted argument that Russia was an Oriental society of the "nonhydraulic" sub-type. Wittfogel was not the only one making such arguments either; George Guins noted in a 1963 article in the *Russian Review* that "[b]asing judgment on the present regime and the international policy of the U.S.S.R, many … scholars believe that Russia belongs more to the East than the West."[76] Given what was pointed out in the previous chapters, this is not particularly surprising: owning or utilizing a stigmatized position, refusing to play the game of the established, and trying to demand equal treatment from a supposed position of strength ultimately end up reproducing and in fact deepening the stigma.

To sum up, the Soviet developmentalist strategy from World War I until the end of the Cold War, while very much being in response to the problem of stigmatization, differed from the *post-defeat* strategies of outsider states in several ways. First, having opted out of World War I, the Bolsheviks were spared the ontological trauma of defeat. Their initial recognition deficit was more akin to the experience of the

---

[74] Wittfogel, "Russia and Asia," 447, 450.
[75] Wittfogel, "Russia and the East."
[76] Guins, "Russia's Place in World History," 361. Guins himself actually makes an interesting and rather prophetic argument, given what happened after Gorbachev came to power: "No nation can unite the whole world – Russia no more than any other. If Russia may be said to have any historical mission, it is to become a bridge between newly awakened Asia and the newly reorganizing West." See 367–8.

Ottoman Empire or Japan in the nineteenth century – the Bolshevik regime was originally denied recognition because the principles it embodied did not match European norms. In other words, because the Russian Empire had not officially suffered defeat, its ontological relationship with the international system moved into the twentieth century with some continuity. This is also true of Japan until 1945. What was different, however, compared to the nineteenth-century situation of semi-sovereign states – including Russia – was the fact that the Bolshevik regime itself had its own ideological program for catching up with the West. Unlike the semi-peripheral powers of the nineteenth century that had sought equal recognition by adopting European manners, the Soviet Union demanded equal recognition during the Cold War years for the success of *its own* domestic system in producing great power capabilities. This equal recognition was sought both by reinterpreting the teleological rhetoric of Western civilization to conclude that the Soviet state represented the final stage[77] and by matching American endeavors in every symbolic gesture associated with superpower status, from nuclear weapons to international chess tournaments.[78] Of course, it bears repeating that in terms of its ontology, the Soviet model was no great break from either modernity or Westernization. Wallerstein puts it best: "Leninism, which posed itself as the radical opponent of Wilsonianism, was in fact its avatar. Anti-imperialism was self-determination clothed in more radical verbiage ... One of the reasons 'Yalta' was possible was that there was less difference in the programs of Wilson and Lenin than official rhetoric maintained."[79] Derluguian also argues that liberalism and Marxism had consensus on a key element: "the identification of a unilinear historical progression moving through objectively existing stages of development."[80] Both ideologies argued (and believed that) "all countries were moving, albeit at different speeds, along the same evolutionary ladder leading towards the final stage of perfection, which would be the end of history, whether in liberal society or in communism."[81] As discussed in Chapter 2, the Soviet model was just as teleological as the modernization paradigm, and therefore very

---

[77] Neumann, *Russia and the Idea of Europe*, p. 14.
[78] Ringmar, "Recognition Game,"129.
[79] Wallerstein, "World-System after the Cold War," 2.
[80] Derluguian, *Bourdieu's Secret Admirer*, p. 69.
[81] *Ibid.*

much a child of the Enlightenment mindset summarized by Gellner and discussed in Chapter 1. Derluguian's conclusion sums it up rather well: "As Bourdieu observed, the strongest orthodoxy does not come in one but usually two varieties, in the presumed antinomy of mutually exclusive positions."[82]

Gorbachev and "new thinking"

In these circumstances, Gorbachev's "new thinking" in foreign affairs and domestic reforms can be understood as an attempt to refurbish the Soviet state's ideological appeal in the world. (Daniel Deudney and John G. Ikenberry, "International Sources," p. 106)

There is an extensive literature within IR that discusses the causes of the dissolution of the Soviet Union and the end of the Cold War.[83] The main point of contention seems to be how much causality should be attributed to the person of Gorbachev, and also how much of the impetus for change came from domestic vs. international factors. A detailed discussion of the reasons why Gorbachev acted the way he did is beyond the scope of this project.[84] However, there are certain aspects to this last period of Soviet thinking that highlight the fact that, despite the Soviet state's unprecedented success in military industrialization in the semi-periphery, the stigmatization problems of this social space were still plaguing the Soviet state.

For some time, it seemed that the Soviet state had found the semi-periphery's answer to the developmental gap and had managed to catch up with the core capitalist countries. In the 1970s, the Soviet economy had the world's second-greatest industrial capacity.[85] However,

---

[82] *Ibid.*, pp. 69–70.

[83] See e.g. Deudney and Ikenberry, "International Sources"; Mendelson, "Internal Battles"; Mendelson, *Changing Course*; Checkel, "Ideas, Institutions"; Checkel, *Ideas and International Political Change*; Arbatov, "Russia's Foreign Policy"; Bunce, "Domestic Reform"; Risse-Kappen, "Ideas Do Not Float Freely"; Koslowski and Kratochwil, "Understanding Change"; Evangelista, "Paradox of State Strength"; Evangelista, "Norms, Heresthetics"; Brown, *Gorbachev Factor*; Herman, "Identity, Norms"; Forsberg, "Power, Interests"; Snyder, "Russia"; Stein, "Political Learning."

[84] See Mendelson, *Changing Course*; Risse-Kappen, "Ideas Do Not Float Freely"; Stein, "Political Learning," for possible explanations of the mechanisms behind the policy shift.

[85] Service, *History of Modern Russia*, p. 397.

the Soviet economy had started running out of steam, and its failures were delayed only because of the unexpected Soviet windfall from the oil crises of that decade. Agricultural policies were highly ineffective, and the living standard of the average citizen was very poor. It need not be pointed out that the Soviet obsession with gaining status parity with the United States had something to do with the mismanagement of resources and the biased attention paid to sectors with symbolic value as great power markers.[86]

Gorbachev's reforms were a response to the disastrous state of the Soviet economy,[87] but the way they were formulated and justified spoke directly to Soviet concerns about international status: "This strategy promised a magic solution, a shortcut to achieving truly prominent status in the international system and political equality vis-à-vis the West."[88] Deudney and Ikenberry point out that "new thinking" is best seen as an attempt "to refurbish the Soviet state's ideological appeal in the world."[89] Unlike the Marxist rhetoric, however, the globalist outlook of the "new thinking" offered a "basis for a cooperative relationship with the Western powers."[90] According to "new thinking," "the Soviet Union would chart a path to better understanding of global problems, interdependence and the need to cooperate, and the priority of 'universal values.'"[91] The similarity between Gorbachev's rhetoric here and the post-defeat discourse of both Atatürk and Yoshida should be apparent to the reader.

Basically, already at this point the Soviet state had started to display a tendency toward the default strategy choice of defeated powers. This does not mean that Gorbachev and his advisers necessarily envisioned the demise of the Soviet Union; in fact, evidence points to the contrary. Gorbachev, at least in the early years of his government, continued to be a firm believer in Marxist-Leninism and had no intention of taking either *glasnost* or *perestroika* to the point they ultimately ended up going.[92] What he did acknowledge, however, is

---

[86] Hazan, *Olympic Sports*.
[87] Deudney and Ikenberry, "International Sources," 76.
[88] Larson and Shevchenko, "Shortcut to Greatness," 97.
[89] Deudney and Ikenberry, "International Sources," 106.
[90] *Ibid.*
[91] Larson and Shevchenko, "Shortcut to Greatness," 97. They are paraphrasing Gorbachev's speech in *FBIS Daily Report-Soviet Union*, February 17, 1987, FBIS-DRSU, 20.
[92] Service, *History of Modern Russia*, pp. 443–8.

what Alexander II or Mahmud II had also admitted almost exactly a century before: the Soviet system was falling short compared to the Western alternative. He knew that the Soviet Union had either lost or was about to lose the military competition. In other words, while imperial collapse had yet to happen, military defeat was already on the table, so it is not surprising that Gorbachev came to see the world in similar terms as Atatürk and Yoshida. Having lost out on the strategies of trying to rearrange the normative order, a corrective strategy of emulation, especially one that built on Soviet strength in the community of the stigmatized, was becoming the more attractive alternative. By introducing reforms, what Gorbachev did was to demand the rearticulation of the Soviet role in the world: instead of being the exclusive leader of the downtrodden, i.e. the stigmatized East and the South, who would lead them to the top by displacing the established, the Soviet Union would now be the bridge, the mediator between the established and the outsiders. The distance between Gorbachev's New Thinking and Yoshida's understanding of Japan's relationship with Asia and Africa is a short one indeed. Furthermore, just as in the Turkish and Japanese cases, despite outside appearances, Gorbachev did not have unwavering support for his vision[93] – he had to earn that support by making a compelling argument that would appeal to the sensitivities of the Russian people.

According to Gorbachev, the problems of the Soviet state would be solved only if it could be reintegrated into the capitalist world economy on honorable terms. This desire further explains why secessionist movements were not repressed by force.[94] In that respect, the impact of Gorbachev and his reforms repeat the story of the previous century: the reforms were implemented in order to save the regime, but brought about its demise instead. Once the Soviet Union collapsed, the second condition for the preference of cooperative stigma strategies was met: loss of imperial status. This brought to the fore an unresolved question: "Long submerged under the czarist and then Soviet empires, the Russians have never before been forced to define precisely who is a Russian and what the proper limits of Russian territory should be; now they must find answers."[95]

[93] Evangelista, "Norms, Heresthetics," 30.
[94] Derluguian, *Bourdieu's Secret Admirer*, p. 128.
[95] Goble, "Russia and Its Neighbors," 79.

After the Soviet Union: foreign policy choices from Gorbachev to Putin

Is there a "right to be great"? Russia is not alone, but it is extreme in claiming this right. What Russia wants is an agreement that it can control the destinies of other nations; an agreement which reflects not its present weakness but its past, its hopes, its future. (*Guardian*, March 22, 1997)

"We don't want superpower status," Mr. Putin told reporters during an interview at his country house. "We believe this status is deliberately fostered within the EU in order to remind [people] that Russia [used to be] the evil Soviet Union." (*Washington Times*, September 12, 2006)

After the ascent of Gorbachev to the General Secretariat in 1985, there emerged three camps within Soviet politics that also shaped Russian politics after the demise of the Soviet Union. First, there was a pro-Western group which had considerable influence over the Foreign Ministry in the last years of the Soviet Union and early years of the Russian Federation under Yeltsin's rule.[96] The pro-Western group of "International Institutionalists"[97] argued that the best option for Russia was political and economic integration.[98] This group believed that Russia is a natural member of Western civilization and that the international environment is, in general, friendly to Russian security:[99] "Its discourse positions the 'normal,' 'civilised' world congruous with the West as the referent for the Russian evolving identity."[100] According to this group, Russia's main priority should be liberalizing its domestic politics and economy.

Those holding "middle-ground" positions were the moderate liberals and moderate conservatives, who may be called "'statists' or 'liberal nationalists'."[101] Moderate liberals also favored a relatively pro-Western policy but emphasized the uniqueness of Russia's geopolitical position.[102] Moderate liberals are sometimes called the "defensive

[96] Arbatov, "Russia's Foreign Policy," 9.
[97] Alternatively described as "liberals, democrats, Westernizers, Atlanticists." Kassianova, "Russia: Still Open to the West?" 533.
[98] Arbatov, "Russia's Foreign Policy," 10; Tsygankov, "From International Institutionalism," 249.
[99] Tsygankov, "From International Institutionalism," 253–8.
[100] Kassianova, "Russia: Still Open to the West?" 824.
[101] *Ibid.*, 825.
[102] Arbatov, "Russia's Foreign Policy," 11. See also Kassianova, "Russia: Still Open to the West?" 825.

realists" of Russia because while they do not believe Western intentions are "inherently hostile," they argue that as a competitor, the West had no interest in preserving Russian strength.[103] They suggested that "Russia's role is as a great Eurasianist power that stabilizes and organizes the 'heartland' of the continent, serving as a buffer between European and non-European civilization."[104]

Moderate conservatives, on the other hand, while not entirely ruling out cooperation with the West, believed that Russia should hold onto its "sphere of influence" as a great power.[105] This group is sometimes called the "aggressive realists" of Russia because they have imperial tendencies, believing the external environment to be generally hostile to Russia's interests.[106] Like the moderate liberals, they emphasized the cultural uniqueness of Russia, and its independent, autarchic, Eurasian civilization that is especially suited for imperial organization.[107]

Finally, there was (and is) an ultra-nationalist group devoted to the revival of the Russian Empire.[108] These "revolutionary expansionists" see Russia as an anti-Western state,[109] and favor Russia's expansion into China, the Muslim world, and Europe:[110] "Their foreign policy discourse exploits highly mythologized narratives of Russian civilisational uniqueness and 'mission.'" In the immediate aftermath of the Cold War, this group was associated with extremists such as Zhirinovsky and some extreme-left communist factions. This group commanded 43 percent of the votes in the 1993 elections but has not been able to match that showing since then. However, in the last two decades, Russia has at times given signals which worry observers that the weight of the opinions of this group in foreign policy circles might be increasing.

Before getting into an account of Russian political developments post-Cold War, it should be noted that these three camps are best

---

[103] Tsygankov, "From International Institutionalism," 258.
[104] *Ibid.*, 254.
[105] Arbatov, "Russia's Foreign Policy," 13. See also Kassianova, "Russia: Still Open to the West?" 825.
[106] Tsygankov, "From International Institutionalism," 259.
[107] *Ibid.*, 225–6.
[108] Arbatov, "Russia's Foreign Policy," 13.
[109] Tsygankov, "From International Institutionalism," 256.
[110] *Ibid.*, 263. See also Kassianova, "Russia: Still Open to the West?" 825.

seen as the current manifestation of a trend that is as old as Russia's involvement in systemic politics. As Neumann has convincingly argued,[111] debates in Russia about which direction the country should take have always been between three positions: those who argue that Russia naturally belongs with Europe and the West (Westernizers of the old days[112]); those who argue that Russia is a Eurasian country with a unique history, and should therefore pursue its policies accordingly (Eurasianists); and finally, those who argue that Russia deserves to be a non-Western superpower/empire/hegemon (Slavophiles). We have also seen that these camps have their counterparts in Turkey and Japan. This repeated pattern of division within domestic debates is a direct consequence of the special social space these countries share within the international system and the relational ontological insecurity they suffer as a result.

In fact, these camps correspond rather well to the stigma-response strategies articulated in Chapter 2. There are those who favor "correction" in hopes of joining the "normal" civilization, and there are those who favor rejecting standards of "normal" society altogether. In the middle are those who want to exploit the stigma, either as a way of gaining influence among the community of the even more stigmatized, or as a characteristic which demands special accommodation. It is not a surprise that we find the same debate repeated over and over again not only in all three countries under investigation, but also across time, and it is especially vibrant in periods which call state identity into question.

In Russia, this time, the debates about identity have lasted longer than they did in Turkey and Japan after their respective defeats. Part of the difference may be that we do not have the benefit of hindsight in this case. In fact, if we bring the analysis up to the present day, it may be plausibly (but not definitively) argued that Russia has finally settled on a steady course (though how that course will be affected by the current global economic crisis remains to be seen). Nevertheless, if there is anything resembling a consensus about the direction of Russia, it is the fact that "the link between the clichéd 'identity crisis' that Russia has been struggling through ever since post-Soviet

---

[111] Neumann, *Russia as Europe's Other*; "Self and Other "; *Russia and the Idea of Europe*.

[112] See the discussion on pp. 208–210 about the nineteenth century.

emancipation and its foreign policy – commonly represented as contradictory, incoherent and lacking strategic vision throughout most of the period – was established early."[113] Russians, just like the Turks and the Japanese, historically have used foreign policy as the principal mechanism of self-identification[114] – as long as debate rages about foreign policy direction, it rages about identity, and vice versa. And while many outside observers are quick to declare Russian intentions to be one thing or the other, the diversity of opinions regarding what Russia is up to these days is itself evidence of the fact that the question is far from settled.

There are several reasons for the differences in the way the Russian debate is playing out compared to the other cases. First, the way Russia fought its war for recognition was different, and therefore its resolution was different. In other words, the Cold War was not like World War I or World War II – it was a *cold* war after all, fought to a greater extent in the realm of symbolic gestures and arms races than on the battlefield. Therefore, defeat did not occur on the battlefield. As argued above, the fact of defeat or the unavoidability of it probably became apparent to the Soviet leadership some time in the 1980s. This had two related consequences: the unraveling of the empire was decoupled from the military defeat and no rival occupied either Russia or its previous spheres of influence. The former factor inevitably lengthened the period of uncertainty about Russia's new identity (as cataclysmic events shaking state identity came in not one but two waves), while the latter gave a degree of breathing room to the rejectionist camp in Russia, the like of which the Japanese or the Turkish reactionary groups never had.

The argument here is that it was much more difficult to *plausibly* make the "let's turn to Asia" argument in after-defeat Turkey or Japan (although there were groups in both countries which did make the argument right after defeat) – both had not only lost most of their imperial possessions but also lost most of them to the influence of their former rivals due to the intervention of the League of Nations and the United Nations, respectively. Russia did lose considerable territory, but not to the same extent. And many states which did gain their

[113] Kassianova, "Russia: Still Open to the West?" 821. Also see Kerr, "New Eurasianism."
[114] Kassianova, "Russia: Still Open to the West?" 821.

independence from Russia were easily brought back under Russian influence,[115] either because they were led by people whose background made them amenable to taking orders from Russia or because they had no other realistic alternatives (or both). This brings me to the second main difference: the international backdrop for the Russian debates is rather different than it was for Turkey and Japan – I will deal with that in more detail in the next chapter, but for now, suffice it to say that it is not a context which makes committing to one side or the other particularly rewarding from a status perspective. When we look at how the identity debate actually progressed in Russia, we can observe that its earlier contours very much resembled those in Turkey and Japan, but the response from the outside was different. Let me explain.

The pro-Western camp dominated Gorbachev's last years and the first years of Yeltsin's government (up until the mid-1990s). These groups pursued policies with the explicit intent of integrating with the West.[116] Indeed, the "new thinking" of the Gorbachev years was formulated with the intent of accomplishing Russia's entry to the West, but as Larson and Shevchenko argue, the rhetoric of "new thinking" was such that Russia was being presented to the world as a leader in collective security matters.[117] This thinking was based in a philosophy of humanistic universalism, and by following it Russia was supposed to assume a new role in tampering with the excesses of the capitalist order while simultaneously joining it.[118] Under the influence of "new thinking" politicians and advisers, Russia made many "unilateral concessions on matters such as UN sanctions on Yugoslavia, Iraq and Libya; the levels and limitations of weapons permitted under START II; controls on missile technology exports to India and arms sales to Iran; the Western position on the rights of Russian minorities in the Baltic; and the dispute with Japan over the South Kurile islands."[119]

The Foreign Policy Concept of 1993 was very much a product of this particular vision, even though it only made one reference to "the innovative contribution of Gorbachev's 'New Political Thinking'."[120] The Concept emphasized the "democratic nature of the new Russian

[115] Lynch, "Realism of Russia's Foreign Policy," 8.
[116] See Larson and Shevchenko, "Shortcut to Greatness."
[117] *Ibid.*, 87.   [118] *Ibid.*, 86.
[119] Arbatov, "Russia's Foreign Policy," 23; see also Forsberg, "Power, Interests."
[120] Kassianova, "Russia: Still Open to the West?" 829.

statehood." The document described the West as "one of the most important centres of the world economy and international relations [and] the global civilisational process." "World's leading democracies," "leading industrially developed states," and "leading economically and democratically developed states" were referenced. The Concept stated that "achieving the main civil and economic characteristics associated with the constitutive qualities and values of 'the West'" was among the top priorities of Russia.[121] While the Concept also discussed possible points of disagreement between Russia and the West, "the overriding importance of shared democratic values and fundamental interests"[122] was repeatedly emphasized. The Concept also declared "the end of the East–West confrontation" and hopefully described a future of collaboration with NATO and support by Western powers. We can note here that the Russian view of the world at this early point after the collapse of the Soviet Union was very much in line with the views expressed by Turkish and Japanese leaders at the corresponding point in the time-lines after their respective defeats.

Such Russian overtures were greeted with skeptical relief by the West:[123] "The Western powers were ready to stop considering Russia as a foe, but politely declined the enthusiastic appeals from Yeltsin and Kozyrev to instantly become allies."[124] This created a backlash within Russian politics, and strengthened the hand of moderate conservatives as well as the nationalists who accused the pro-Western camp of humiliating the country by a conciliatory stance that achieved nothing.

Yeltsin himself wavered between the two camps. He argued that it was time for Russia to join "the civilized world" by adopting principles of the "market economy," but also made remarks that he wished to expand Russia at the expense of the former Soviet Republics.[125] Faced with foreign criticism, he had to back-track. Nevertheless, electoral and political pressures after 1993 forced Yeltsin[126] to adopt an awkward middle

---

[121] The Foreign Policy Concept of 1993 as quoted in Kassianova, "Russia: Still Open to the West?" 829.
[122] *Ibid.*, 830.
[123] Owen, "Transnational Liberalism," 135.
[124] Arbatov, "Russia's Foreign Policy," 23; see also Kissinger, "New Russian Question," 12.
[125] Service, *History of Modern Russia*, p. 520.
[126] Motyl, "Why Empires Reemerge."

ground of pro-Western foreign policy abroad, on the one hand, and increasingly authoritarian "Russia first" rhetoric at home, on the other. Malcolm and Pravda term this policy "Pragmatic Nationalism."[127]

This shift was very much manifested in the 1997 National Security Concept, which had a remarkably different tone and outlook than the 1993 Foreign Policy Concept. References to democracy and the West were dropped with the exception of a single instance of a "warning against the danger of Russia's 'technological dependence on the leading states of the West' and a mention of discriminatory measures against the Russian goods in the 'developed countries of the West.'"[128] Whereas the 1993 Foreign Policy Concept stated that "achieving the main civil and economic characteristics associated with the constitutive qualities and values of 'the West'" was among the top priorities of Russia,[129] the 1997 National Security Concept took "care to maintain equal distancing in relation to the 'global, European and Asian economic and political actors."[130] Kassianova notes that the document was marked by "a strained kind of optimism, at least partly relying on the sense of nuclear potential rather than confidence in the benign character of the external environment."[131]

Even though Yeltsin, as a masterful politician,[132] maintained his tenuous position at the helm well until the end of the decade, by increasingly adding a nationalist veneer to his government – as in the replacement of Kozyrev with Primakov in 1996[133] – he could not do much to ensure the success of his economic liberalization policies.[134] His popularity waned as the Russian economy deteriorated. The economic crisis of 1998 effectively ended the Yeltsin era[135] and in 1999,

---

[127] Malcolm and Pravda, "Democratization and Russian Foreign Policy," 541.
[128] The National Security Concept of 1997 as quoted in Kassianova, "Russia: Still Open to the West?" 831.
[129] The Foreign Policy Concept of 1993 as quoted in Kassianova, "Russia: Still Open to the West?" 829.
[130] The National Security Concept of 1997 as quoted in Kassianova, "Russia: Still Open to the West?" 832.
[131] *Ibid.*
[132] See Service, *History of Modern Russia*, pp. 509–41.
[133] Freedman, "Russia and Israel," 140.
[134] For a discussion of possible reasons why Yeltsin's economic reforms fell short, see e.g. Handelman, *Comrade Criminal*; Roberts and Sherlock, "Bringing the Russian State Back in"; Blasi *et al.*, *Kremlin Capitalism*; Sergeev, *Wild East*; McFaul, *Russia's 1996 Presidential Election.*
[135] Roberts and Sherlock, "Bringing the Russian State Back in," 477.

Yeltsin appointed Putin, a politically unknown figure with a KGB background, as his prime minister and, ultimately, successor. Putin quickly gained popularity during his time as prime minister, helped especially by Russian actions in Chechnya. Within a year, Putin's popularity rating had soared from 2 percent to 50 percent.[136]

During the time he was in power, Yeltsin referred back to themes from the "new thinking" years, arguing that Russia was still a great power, but with the added character of benevolence: "Russia's authority is acknowledged by the world ... [b]ut, for the first time in 80 years, this acknowledgement is based not on fear, as it was under Stalin, Brezhnev, and others. Not on the dread of being buried under the splinters of empire."[137] His policies were closely associated with US recommendations. Nevertheless, some observers in the United States remained unconvinced of Russia's commitment to a Western alliance. For instance, a 1998 editorial from the *Washington Times* remarks that the "direction of Russian foreign policy ... is reminiscent of past Soviet foreign policy ... its function is ... to support anti-American regimes everywhere."[138] The main disagreement between the United States and Russia during the Clinton–Yeltsin years was the Balkan disputes over Bosnia and Kosovo. Toward the end of the Yeltsin era, however, there was growing frustration and disappointment over Russia's failed economy, its constant need for assistance, and desperate clinging to the title of "great power."

Editorials in the Western press made light of Russia's pretensions of mediation in the Balkan disputes and its need to be treated as an equal at the same time as it had its hand out for Western aid: "There is one sense – and only one – in which Russia is a Great Power. It still has a large (though aging) nuclear arsenal. But that's it ... Moscow gets away with stuff ... precisely because the West lets it";[139] "'They so desperately want to be treated as equals. But it's hard to take them seriously when they stamp their feet petulantly and then give in,' says one military source."[140] Perhaps unsurprisingly, Yeltsin's

---

[136] White and McAllister, "Putin and His Supporters," 383.
[137] From Yeltsin's 1997 Independence Day Speech, *News Service Reports* (June 23, 1997).
[138] Perlmutter, "Who Lost Russia ... Our New Rival?" A17.
[139] *Newsweek* (June 21, 1999).
[140] *Christian Science Monitor* (June 21, 1999).

last year in office was marked by an increasingly belligerent rhetoric.[141] He made menacing remarks about Russia's ability to use its nuclear weapons, and denounced American culture and values on a trip to China.[142]

Nevertheless, the Yeltsin years are marked by an important symbolic – and mostly inadvertent – accomplishment. In 1994, during the early years of Yeltsin's rule, Russia was invited to attend G-7 meetings and in 1997, Russia was invited to formally join the organization. It is noteworthy that these goodwill gestures from the West followed two moments of crisis in Yeltsin's rule, during the 1993 and 1996 elections. Yeltsin responded to both by taking another step toward the nationalist direction, which the West rewarded, interestingly enough, by bringing Russia closer to the inner capitalist club: "The idea was to prop up the flailing Boris N. Yeltsin by making Russia look like a member of the club, even though it didn't qualify based on income or economic growth," remarks an editorial in the *Baltimore Sun*.[143] Russia, however, did not really take advantage of this membership until Putin's presidency.

The first decade of the Russian Federation ended as clouded in uncertainty as it was when it began. Allen Lynch notes in 2001 that:

since 1993, in response to the frustration of early Russian aspirations to join the Western (i.e. G-7) economic, political and security communities, Russian diplomacy has moved in a decidedly unilateralist and frequently anti-Western (often anti-US) direction, reflecting the priority of establishing Russia as the integrating power in central Eurasia as opposed to integrating Russia within the broader G-7 world.[144]

He also notes, however, that Russia managed to avoid causing a rupture with the G-7.[145] Lynch reads the new direction of Russian foreign

---

[141] Despite these developments, Michael McFaul remained optimistic about Russia's chances for democratization: "Most Russians now believe that their country must develop a market economy and adhere to the principles of market economy ... most Russians, although disappointed with Western policies toward Russia, still believe that integration with the West is in Russia's national interest ... If a rollback were going to happen, it would have followed Russia's financial meltdown in August 1998." McFaul, "Getting Russia Right," 59–60.

[142] *New York Times* (December 11, 1999). [143] July 14, 2006.

[144] Lynch, "Realism of Russia's Foreign Policy," 7–8.

[145] *Ibid.*, 8.

policy as a realist turn:[146] "It fell first to Kozyrev and then to Primakov to make the adaptations required to reconcile post-Soviet Russia to a subordinate position in the international system in a domestic setting wherein most Russian elites persisted in assuming Russia's great power status."[147] If we take realist to be synonymous with "realistic" that explanation could indeed be classified as realist. However, it is much more plausible to read it as the result of a frustrated corrective strategy – Russia wanted to be included among the "established" and was willing to engage in the necessary stigma corrections by adapting a market economy and democratic institutions, but found the Western community aloof to its overtures.

Even after he became the Russian president, Putin's intentions remained rather opaque to Western observers. Some observers in the West and the former Soviet Republics were skeptical from the start: on June 15, 2000, the Lithuanian deputy speaker described Putin's foreign policy as Stalinist;[148] a Canadian commentator observed that the West should brace itself for the worst as Putin was sure to default on Russia's $160 billion foreign debt.[149] Others did not know what to make of Putin.[150] Yet others were positively "giddy" about what Putin's presidency meant for Russian capitalism.[151] If observers had reached a consensus on any one thing, it was that Putin believed in a strong, paternalist Russian state, and did not reject the legacy of the Soviet period.[152] What they could not agree on was whether this was a good or a bad thing.

Since taking over from Yeltsin, Putin has argued that Russia can take "its rightful place in the world" by restoring its economic strength.[153] In one of his first public speeches, Putin called for a return of Russia's strong state tradition and argued that Russia has to look out for its own national interests: "Several years ago, we fell prey to an illusion that we have no enemies. We have paid dearly for this."[154] After he was sworn in, he emphasized his desire for Russia to become "a rich, strong and civilized country of which its citizens are proud and which is respected in the world."[155]

[146] *Ibid.*, 23.   [147] *Ibid.*, 23–4.
[148] *BBC Monitoring Former Soviet Union* (June 15, 2000).
[149] *National Post* (June 17, 2000).
[150] *Washington Times* (May 7, 2000); *The Wall Street Journal* (July 11, 2000).
[151] Friedman, "Keep Rootin' for Putin," *The New York Times* (December 27, 2001).
[152] Nicholson, "Putin's Russia," 870.   [153] *Ibid.*, 871.
[154] Putin, as reported in *Washington Times* (January 31, 2003).
[155] Putin, as reported in the *Washington Post* (May 8, 2000).

Putin soon unveiled a new foreign policy blueprint that attached great importance to the Group of Eight (G-8) and called for closer cooperation with the European Union.[156] In the Foreign Policy Concept of 2000, the category of the referents for defining Russia's interests and objectives were broadened to "include the 'world community' and 'world economy,' 'market economy methods' and 'values of democratic society,' 'international economic organisations,' and the familiar but very rarely mentioned 'leading states of the world' along with a single reference to 'influential developing states,' all complete with thoroughly depersonalized 'foreign states and interstate associations.'"[157] While calling for cooperation and partnership, the document also expressed growing concern about Russia's inability to influence the structural-economic and legal conditions of the international system.[158]

Putin made good on his word by insisting on equal-partner treatment in the Japan 2000 summit of the G-8.[159] He made a strong and determined showing at the summit, surprising the other leaders in the group who were accustomed to dealing with Yeltsin, whose "clownish antics ... [had] only cemented their perception that Russia – notwithstanding its nuclear arsenal – lacked a government that could be taken seriously."[160] Putin came to the summit bearing news from his visit to North Korea and impressed the leaders by not asking for debt relief. He continued his impressive showing in foreign policy by engaging in a whirlwind tour of world capitals in the first year of his tenure, as well as issuing declarations about every possible strategic relationship of Russia.[161] Of course, Putin was very much helped by Russia's

---

[156] *Washington Post* (July 11, 2000); *South China Morning Post* (July 12, 2000).

[157] The Foreign Policy Concept of 2000 as quoted in Kassianova, "Russia: Still Open to the West?" 832.

[158] *Ibid.*, 833.   [159] *Reuters News Service* (July 13, 2000).

[160] *Washington Post* (July 24, 2000).

[161] See e.g. the following headlines: "Putin's Indian Visit," *ITAR-TASS News Wire* (October 1, 2000); "Putin's Role in Foreign Policy Expands with Serb Crisis," *Washington Times* (October 4, 2000); "Putin Says Long-Term Relations with Iran Important," *BBC Monitoring Middle East* (October 17, 2000); "Asian Countries Still Top Putin's Agenda," *China Daily* (November 10, 2000); "Putin Stresses Cooperation with Asia Pacific," *Xinhua News Agency* (November 9, 2000); "Russia Angles for Bigger Role in Mideast, Israel's Foreign Minister Will Visit Moscow," *Christian Science Monitor* (November 29, 2000); "Putin Says He Will Visit Egypt in 2001," *ITAR-TASS News Wire* (December 25, 2000).

economic recovery, which freed his hands to pursue international contacts.[162]

Putin also capitalized quickly on the events of September 11 by supporting American action in Central Asia in return for Western indulgence for Russia's military campaign in Chechnya.[163] This was interpreted as a dramatic pro-Western shift in Putin's foreign policy, both at home and abroad. Nationalists, especially those within the ranks of the military, initially criticized Putin for these concessions and others, such as the closure of Russia's spy station in Cuba.[164] It was not immediately evident what Russia received in exchange for its unconditional support for US anti-terrorism efforts.[165] At this time, Putin also faced some criticism from Parliament for pursuing a too friendly foreign policy toward the West.[166] Nevertheless, Putin's domestic approval ratings stayed strong, and the strategy played out well by getting some semblance of international legitimacy for Russia's actions in Chechnya. A 2004 article by John O'Loughlin *et al.* gives us an interesting take on this episode: "President Putin sought to represent the event as a 'global Chechnya' … 9–11 provided the occasion for the development of an innovative geopolitical script that asserted the identity opposition 'civilised/barbarian' as a fundamental axis in world politics, (re-) located Russia within the West as a 'civilised power' and gave Russian geoeconomic interests priority over traditional geopolitics."[167] The authors also found that while the Russian public continued to harbor suspicions about US intentions in Central Asia, the above-mentioned shift engineered by Putin had significant support across all groups in Russia.[168] They further note that:

On one hand, most Russian citizens admire the economic, technological and social achievements of Western countries and are persuaded that Russia must and can reduce her laggard status and reach the same level of economic development as the West. On the other hand, they realize how

---

[162] White and McAllister, "Putin and His Supporters," 384.
[163] Service, *History of Modern Russia*, p. 544.
[164] *The Hindu* (November 18, 2001); *BBC Monitoring Former Soviet Union* (November 17, 2001).
[165] *Nezavisimaya Gazete* editorial, as reported in *BBC Monitoring Former Soviet Union* (March 11, 2002); *Financial Times* (April 15, 2002).
[166] *Financial Times* (April 15, 2002).
[167] O'Loughlin *et al.*, "'Risky Westward Turn'?" 4.
[168] *Ibid.*

deep the gap remains and how difficult it is to catch up with "the West." ... Indeed, 71% of respondents to the VTsIOM (All-Russian Centre for Research on Public Opinion) survey held in November 2001 agreed with the statement that Russia belonged to a "Eurasian" civilization and, therefore, the Western model did not suit her, and only 13% accepted that their country was part of European and Western civilization. These ratios are a kind of compensatory reaction based on understanding that the gap separating Russian and Western standards of living remains important.[169]

If we did not factor in Russia's preoccupation with avoiding outsider status, these findings would present a paradox: while the majority of the Russian public in 2001 did not see themselves as part of Western civilization and no longer thought that emulating Western models was a desirable strategy, on average they supported Putin's efforts to utilize 9/11 to recast Russia as one of the "good guys" within the fold of Western civilization. While some of this probably had something to do with Putin's ability to secure support for (or at least indifference to) the Russian campaign in Chechnya as a result, such an outcome is also very much in line with the argument in this book. Regardless of what else Russia has done since the collapse of the Soviet Union, the West remains the main referent it defines its identity against – and any conceptual construction which defines Russia as a member of the "established" club is bound to be satisfying to a Russian public still shaped by an imperial-past national habitus. That Putin was able to achieve this redefinition (however briefly) without actually having to commit to any "corrective" domestic strategies made this strategy even more appealing – the choice presented no dilemmas of inauthenticity in the short run.

In 2002, Putin emphasized his desire for Russia to join the World Trade Organization, and become a rule-making member of the international economic community.[170] He also made frequent references to Russia's "stronger democracy" and "freer economy."[171] However, if Putin seemed to be inching closer to the West abroad, at home he was doing the opposite: rolling back the political, military, and

---

[169] *Ibid.*, 5–6.
[170] Putin's State-of-the-Nation Address, as reported in *BBC Monitoring Former Soviet Union* (April 18, 2002).
[171] *RIA News Agency, Moscow* (June 12, 2002).

legal reforms of Yeltsin and ruling in an increasingly authoritarian manner.[172]

Putin resisted joining the US campaign in Iraq and in 2003, he put more distance between Russia and the United States: "the other reality underlying Mr. Putin's doctrine is that for all its military, economic and political might, the U.S. cannot, and should not, be allowed to run the world as a 'my-way-or-the-highway' cowboy."[173] He started promoting the notion of an "arc of stability" stretching from Europe through the Caucasus and Central Asia to China and Southeast Asia, and concluded military alliances with the former Soviet Republics of Central Asia and the Caucasus.[174]

Following these developments, the United States rediscovered its skepticism about Russia's reliability as a partner toward the end of 2003. President Bush openly criticized Putin for curtailing basic democratic freedoms, in stark contrast to his earlier statements to the contrary.[175] Tensions escalated in 2004, and came to a head over developments in Ukraine.[176] However, economically, Russia benefited from the instability of the world energy markets: "Surging demand from China and India, the costliest natural disaster in U.S. history, a global war on terrorism centered on the Middle East and Central Asia and other events ... rocked energy markets" and spurred Russia into the position of a global energy superpower. As a result, in the 2006 summit of the G-8 nations, Putin put great emphasis on the country's oil and gas exports as a rationale for its inclusion in the club.[177] Western observers grew increasingly concerned: "As Russia's renaissance has progressed, so it has moved away from the European democratic model that its former eastern European satellites have largely embraced."[178] Worries about Russia's authoritarian turn deepened when in 2008 Putin handpicked his successor for the presidency and took for himself the

---

[172] *Los Angeles Times* (September 21, 2003).
[173] *The Hindu* (July 26, 2003).
[174] *Ibid.*
[175] *Washington Post* (December 14, 2003).
[176] *BBC Monitoring Former Soviet Union* (December 12, 2004).
[177] *International Herald Tribune* (February 11, 2006).
[178] *Financial Times* (April 21, 2006).

position of prime minister.[179] Observers have noted, especially during the development of the Russian–Georgian War of 2008, that Putin very much remains the de facto leader of Russia. Whether he will continue to fare as well during the present economic crisis as he has in the last decade remains to be seen.

To sum up, Russia's post-Cold War policy has been shaped by two men – Yeltsin and Putin – neither of whose motivations have been particularly transparent to outside observers. If Yeltsin was difficult to read and predict because he was hotheaded and impulsive, Putin is more so because he is calm, collected, and discreet. However, leaving personalities aside, it is possible to interpret Russia's post-defeat strategies as amorphous and enigmatic precisely because the international adjustment required of it as a former non-Western "great power" is extremely difficult to chart, even compared to the previous cases of Turkey and Japan.

Whither Russia?

And yet, Russia stands out for its 500 year history of always just having being tamed, civilized, just having begun to participate in European politics, just having become part of Europe … Danger resides on the borders, Mary Douglas argues, and so, as long as Russia is constructed as a border case, it will also be inscribed with danger. (Iver Neumann, *Russia as Europe's Other*, p. 46)

In analyzing Russia's post-defeat choices within the status-seeking framework offered in Chapters 1 and 2, we can start by noting that Russia's response to systemic challenges during the Gorbachev years approximated the corrective strategy of the *arriviste*. Russia started with the assumption that after implementing certain reforms it could be smoothly integrated into Europe/the West. This supposition came to influence the New Thinkers of the Gorbachev years (who had been favoring a more mixed strategy earlier on, trying to capitalize on the Soviet Union's access to the developing world) and very much characterized the worldview of the International Institutionalists who

---

[179] Technically, he was nominated by the newly elected President Medvedev, but the outcome was entirely predictable and entirely engineered by Putin.

dominated the first Yeltsin administration. This was also the belief that was very hopefully articulated in the Foreign Policy Concept of 1993. We see here a slightly stronger belief in an affinity with the Western club than we have observed in other cases – the difference is that while Atatürk and Yoshida went to great lengths to make the case for the presence of such an affinity, Gorbachev and his cadre assumed it.

Four factors account for the optimism of the Russian elite at this juncture: first, there was a historically recurring theme in Russian identity narratives that defined Russia as truly belonging in Europe, geographically and culturally; second, Russia was part of the Concert of Europe, which made it possible for historical revisionists to view the "Easternness" of the Soviet Union as an aberration; third, of the three cases, the Soviet Union had come closest to achieving great power parity with the West, and therefore was ontologically more secure; and fourth, the aforementioned chronological gap between military defeat and imperial collapse initially allowed Russian national habitus to shield itself to some degree from the kind of trauma both Turkey and Japan had experienced.

However, despite the presence of these factors, (some) Russian leaders were also aware that the West might not recognize Russia's natural place in Europe and therefore attempted to present the country's new openness as an added value to Western civilization; with its experience in standing up for the "oppressed" peoples of the East, it was supposed to temper the excesses of the capitalist core through its own inclusion. This strategy was popular during the early years of New Thinking, and it gained popularity again as the initial optimism of quickly joining the West faded and the moderate liberals started gaining influence. As noted above, this group still favored close relations with the West but emphasized Russia's unique geopolitical position. Therefore, we can conclude that before 1996, or even 1993, Russia displayed a strategy very much similar to that observed in the previous cases.

The variation after 1996 – in other words, the ascendancy of the views of the Eurasianists, if not the nationalists – can be explained by the changes that had occurred in the international system compared to the 1950s or the 1920s. Straightforward, conciliatory emulation of dominant Western and European norms of democracy and economic liberalization of the early 1990s was not working as a foreign policy strategy because in the international system of the 1990s, following this path would not have accrued Russia any real status gains. We see the disappointment Russian leaders had with the "exclusionary" policies of the West clearly expressed in the Foreign Policy Concept of 1997. In the 1920s, Turkey could adopt norms of modernization, secularization, and Westernization, and hope to be admitted to the privileged club of "civilized countries" who were the only fully sovereign states of the system. In the 1950s, Japan could follow a developmentalist trajectory by adopting a capitalist template and hope to raise its rank in the GNP-conscious sphere of the First World. Russia, however, could achieve very little status gain by blindly following the democratization requirements of Europe and the West. The presence of the European Union and its size concerns essentially meant that Russia could never again be an integral part of Europe. If Russia were going to restore its status, it would have to do it without membership recognition from Europe.

Ironically, the one move the West made in order to assuage Russia's concerns about its status in the new international system also undermined Russian "Westernization" efforts at home. Also considering the fact that Russia cannot join the European Union, both the social disincentives and incentives for Russia have been minimized to a small enough degree to enable Putin and his cadre to conclude that Russia can afford to pick and choose from the socialization menu, and still maintain domestic support. As discussed in Chapter 2, these are the very conditions that fuel rejection strategies – the lower/nominal members of established groups are exactly in the kind of position to attempt status enhancement by leading a charge of outsiders. Resources that would have been used to break the barrier into the inner circle are now freed up to use to influence others.

To put it another way, the very factors which would lead one to intuitively conclude that Russia, among the three cases under discussion, would be the most amenable to a smooth integration with the West are actually the reasons why Russia's path has veered more Eastward than the previous cases. Russia can therefore be thought of as being either the most blessed or the most cursed of the three cases discussed, depending on one's perspective. Its relative cultural proximity to the West and its natural material strength have decreased social constraints on Russia and given breathing room to the more hawkish/hostile elements in Russian society, as compared to both Turkey and Japan after defeat.

For these reasons, the adoption of liberalizing political reforms was doomed. This trajectory was further helped by the United States' increasing emphasis on "security" after 9/11. The shifting normative criteria gave Putin an opening. The "arc of stability" project, if it worked, could allow Russia to secure recognition from both the Third World and possibly even Europe, but most especially from the Muslim world, as a stable and rational alternative to the "bullying" tendencies of the United States. It should be noted, however, doomsday scenarios of a second Cold War notwithstanding, that the post-defeat strategy Russia seems to have settled on is dissimilar to the anti-systemic, hostile development path followed by the Bolsheviks. While the Russia of today is leaning toward what seems once again like the rejection of the ideal norms of the international society, it is not in the position it was in the early twentieth century. For instance, while Russia is not a democracy, it has not altogether rejected the democratic governance[180] discourse emanating from the West: Putin's (and by extension, Medvedev's) Russia is a "semi-authoritarian regime in democratic clothing. That is to say Russia pretends to be democratic"[181] and it is "at once, a regime that offers its citizens consumer rights but not political freedoms, state sovereignty but not individual autonomy, a market economy but not genuine democracy."[182] In other words, for all its protestations of hostility and even at the peak of its post-defeat economic prowess, Russia has not been able to reject the norms of the international order this time around.

There are several reasons why Russia has ended up in this juncture. Russia's ability to pursue its superficially hostile middle-ground strategy has been entirely contingent on its fortunes in the rather fickle energy market, and economically Russia has no choice but to play by the rules of the world market. Finally, the Russian regime cannot muster a normative alternative to the dominant systemic one of Western capitalist triumph. Hence, there is no *ressentiment* strategy on display

---

[180] See Chapter 2.
[181] Shevtsova, "Vladimir Putin," 34.
[182] Krastev, "What Russia Wants," 48.

here. The only real niche Russia can carve is as an alternative enforcer of system norms in a context where many countries cannot or do not want to match the expectations of the United States. All that Russia is doing is to take normative criteria of the West and reinterpret them for Eastern consumption. It is not preposterous, therefore, to conclude that Russia has also become an enforcer of systemic values, however enigmatic, dangerous, or unfriendly it might appear.

6 | *Conclusion: Zealots or Herodians?*

During the last few centuries, our Western society has been intruding upon the other civilizations of the world with greater insistence. First it has drawn them all into the meshes of its economic system; next it has enlarged the borders of its political ascendency almost as far as the borders of its trade; and latterly it has been invading the life of its neighbours on the most intimate plane – the plane of social institutions and of spiritual emotions and ideas. This revolutionary process of Westernization, which at this moment is overtaking the Turks and many of their co-religionists in other Islamic countries, has already proceeded further among the Oriental Christian ex-subjects of the Turks in South-Eastern Europe and among their Oriental Christian ex-enemies in Russia, and it is actively at work among the Hindus and the Far Easterners. Thus, in studying the Westernization process in Turkey, we are increasing our understanding of the human world in which we ourselves live and move and have our being; for the issues with which the Turks have been confronted by their contact with the West are confronting other non-Western peoples the world over. Everywhere these peoples stand at the parting of the ways, with the choice of entering the camp of the Zealots or the camp of the Herodians. They can no longer remain neutral; for the West, in its restless activity, will not let them alone. Shall they accept the civilization of the West and attempt to adjust their own lives to it, or shall they reject it and attempt to cast it out as a devil which is seeking to possess their souls?

Arnold Toynbee, *Turkey*

The title of this chapter comes from the above passage which concludes Toynbee's excellent analysis of Turkey's Westernization efforts in the interwar period. Great observer that he was, Toynbee realized that the changes Turkey was undergoing in the 1920s amounted to neither an aberration nor a historical curiosity, but rather were part of a great structural trend which sooner or later would engulf the majority of peoples around the globe. Unfortunately, the import of

240

this observation was never really acknowledged by the one discipline that should have been most concerned with such a structural
trend: International Relations. For the most part, IR has relegated to
the dustbin of history the choices the majority of the peoples in the
world faced in the presence of the inevitable Westernization of global
relations, and deems their dilemma as irrelevant to modern-day politics. Not only is this problematic from a social scientific perspective,
but it is also dangerous from a policy-making angle.

IR theorists have had the unfortunate habit of treating social dimen-
sions of international interactions as negligible. This is especially
problematic for analyzing the behavior of states outside the West,
whose identities have been shaped by the additional social burdens
they face in the modern international system. Most structural theories in IR ignore the effects of social stratification on state behavior
and are therefore ill-equipped to explain the behavior of the majority
of states in the international system.

Indeed, a cursory survey of IR theories might lead one to the
conclusion that non-Western states are the decorative plants of
modern international society. The treatment non-Western countries
have received at the hands of IR scholars brings to mind Aristotle,
who thought that men were like animals – they acted, they were
doers – whereas women were like plants – they were acted upon,
they stood still. This general theoretical indifference to the non-
West is backed up by the belief that if any of these states attain
any agency, they will act just like their Western counterparts. The
overall thrust of the discipline has been to ignore the non-West in
theory formulation because non-Western states are either assumed
to be static and therefore indistinguishable from the environment,
or assumed to be easily covered by theories extrapolated from the
Western experience.

This state of affairs in the academic study of international relations mirrors the social stratification in actual dynamics, and is
predicted by the stigma theory offered in this book. The greatest privilege that accrues to "normals" in any stratified society is the ability,
the "smugness" to view their own condition as "natural," "objective," and as "matter-of-fact": "His is the state of 'being situated' or
'tuned' (Heidegger), which can feed nothing but the *relativ-naturliche
Weltanschauung* (Max Scheler): that is a natural propensity to view
the conditions otherwise circumscribed, confined to this place here

and this time now, as 'natural' and thus beyond discussion."[1] This is a position of great power because it makes the situations of the outsider, the stranger, the stigmatized their own problem, even though "all the essential determinants of the stranger's plight lie beyond the reach of everything the stranger himself may do."[2] Almost every strategy to remedy this situation leads to reinforcing it: if the stigmatized/the stranger/the outsider attempts to become "normal" through assimilation, he confirms the definition of himself as not "normal"; if he argues with the "normal" view by pointing out that there are other experiences which that normal view does not account for, he draws attention to his "abnormality."

In Toynbee's words, the outsider's choice is between becoming a Zealot or a Herodian, but it is actually the fact that one is faced with this choice, more than the actual choice itself, that reinforces the condition of stature inferiority. To be "normal" is to not have to worry constantly about which is the right choice to make, to not have to think about the world in terms of this choice. To be "normal," to be "established," is to have the luxury of seeing the world as natural, to take it for granted, and to not have to worry about the "construction" of one's own identity, of society, or of international relations. Once those ontological matters are relegated to the realm of "given" facts, the *illusion* of fully realized agency, of sovereignty, of positive freedom in what is inevitably always an ambivalent world becomes much easier to sustain. And for many, that illusion is enough.

The "normals" hold all the power – they do not, and in fact, they would much rather not, have to listen to the outsider whose efforts to belong and speak their language can be as equally strong a reminder of the arbitrariness of their "objective" worldview as her protestations about injustice.[3] To the degree that mainstream, "normal," "objective" social science theories take into account the plight of the outsiders in the international system, this very pattern is almost invariably reproduced. Recall the normative dichotomies invoked in the first chapters of this book: civilized/barbaric, modern/traditional, developed/underdeveloped (or the politer version,

---

[1] Bauman, *Modernity and Ambivalence*, p. 75.
[2] *Ibid.*, p. 77.
[3] "The very awareness of such an outside view makes the natives feel insecure in their home ways and truths." *Ibid.*, p. 78.

"developing"), liberal/illiberal, democratic/authoritarian, etc. It is always the label on the right side that is presented as a problem that needs to be overcome. This casts the issue as a mechanistic dilemma about attaining desirable attributes, as opposed to what it really is: an existential one of delegitimation and stigmatization. What gets obscured in the process is the fact that the left side of the dichotomy cannot exist without the right side: "Despite the appearance to the contrary, it is not the failure to acquire native knowledge which constitutes the outsider as a stranger, but the *incongruent existential constitution* if the stranger, as being neither 'inside' nor 'outside', neither 'friend' nor 'enemy', neither *included* nor *excluded*, which makes the native knowledge unassimilable."[4] In other words, without an understanding of the deep structural properties of established-outsider relationships in the international system, any attempt to address the supposed endogenous "causes" of outsiderness will actually have the opposite effect of entrenching power disparities and affirming the "objectivity" of the hegemonic worldview.

This is precisely why this book attempts to offer a structural view of international stratification and demonstrate how international stigmatization circumscribes the behavior of non-Western actors. I underline the social, the structural, the exogenous nature of stigmatization, inferiority, laggardness, backwardness, barbarity not as an excuse on behalf of the non-West or an accusation against the West, but as a corrective against a literature that allows for the agency of non-Western actors only when they fail to live up to Western standards. In that perspective, what is wrong about the non-West actor is its own fault, and what is right about it is the West's doing or an automatic response to Western stimuli. In this book, through a juxtaposition of the choices Turkey, Japan, and Russia have made in their interactions with the West, I have tried to show that the reality is more the other way around: outcomes taken to be functionally determined by Western observers are often the result of long considered and contested deliberations by local actors, and what are considered to be domestic failures (by both local and international observers) were often much more contingent on international social dynamics than is usually assumed.

---

[4] *Ibid.*, p. 76.

Let me now recap that discussion and say a few words about the choices facing Turkey, Japan, and Russia today – because what is happening with all three of these cases nowadays is pertinent to the concluding point I want to make about how we can improve the international system.

Just as observers of the last two decades are baffled by the actions of Russia, the behaviors of Turkey and Japan after defeat also gave rise to many a misplaced prediction. However, while in the initial decades after defeat the observers of Russia tended to err on the side of optimism about Russia's receptiveness to international norms and alliance potential, assessments in the cases of Turkey and Japan often displayed serious fears about future reversals. This in itself is very telling.

The Ottoman Empire was defeated in World War I, dismantled, partially occupied. It took three years of military struggle, domestic chaos, and some stubborn diplomatic maneuvering at the Lausanne Conference for the new Kemalist regime to establish itself. The reincarnated Turkish state was much smaller than the Ottoman Empire and had depleted most of its military and economic resources. Japan lost its empire in World War II, and was in perhaps an even worse material condition than Turkey at the end of the war due to the devastation wrought by the atomic bombs. The country was occupied by US forces and it was not until 1951 that Japan regained its full autonomy. Russia, on the other hand, was not defeated in open military war, nor occupied, nor subject to any postwar treaty impositions. In other words, the material conditions of Russia's defeat were quite unlike those in the other two cases.

The juxtaposition between how realism would read each of these situations and the actual comparative treatment Turkey, Japan, and Russia got after their respective defeats is jarring. Of these three countries it was *Russia's* ultimate integration to the "civilized" world that was hailed as a sure thing, bringing about declarations of the "End of History." By contrast, both Japan and Turkey, even though each had very limited material room for maneuver, were eyed with considerable suspicion and skepticism, and continued to be so regarded long after they had established a record of cooperation. The stigmatization framework offered in this book predicts this disparity. Bauman's discussion of what happens to the stranger who attempts to assimilate is directly applicable to our understanding of these three cases: "The loyalty which is simply taken for granted in the case of the natives ... calls for suspicious and vigilant scrutiny in the case of yesterday's stranger; and forever so, as his commitment has been compromised from the start and beyond the hope of redemption by the original sin of being freely chosen."[5] Of the three cases, Russia bears the most "familial" resemblance to the original rule-makers of the international society, and is the one that is most like the "natives" of the European/ Western order. This is partly because of the dominant religion of its population and the ethno-racial make-up of the titular nation, and partly because Russia had in fact managed to gain a formal seat in the European society of states in the nineteenth century. Hence, many observers in the 1990s jumped to the conclusion that the Soviet Union was merely a deviation from Russia's natural destiny as a country that *inherently* approximates the original normative ideal of the states system. While realists may claim that Russia's ultimate aggressive turn vindicates the materialist reading of the situation, the fact of the matter is, as explained in Chapter 5, Russia's hostile turn cannot be thought of as independent from the (comparatively) forgiving social treatment it got from the West for a brief while in the 1990s.

Russia's historical and cultural proximity to the core as well as its previous stature as a great power brought it identity assurances at a time it was probably least qualified to receive them. Russia's (inconsistent) turn to a more aggressive rhetoric in foreign policy does not precede but actually follows Russia's admission to the elite power club of international relations. Russia's admission to the G-8 at a time it arguably had not met most of the criteria for membership, coupled with the fact that the country had inherited the Soviet Union's seat on the UN Security Council, momentarily created an illusion of stature satisfying enough to the Russian domestic audience without solving Russia's otherness problem, and counterintuitively weakened the hand of the liberalizers. This development was not unlike the obstacle Russian Westernizers faced in the first half of the nineteenth century when Russia's participation in the Concert of Europe had allowed Nicholas to keep reformers at bay.

I do not intend to downplay the challenges Russia has faced since the collapse of the Soviet Union, but it is important to draw attention to the fact that Russia was given the benefit of the doubt much longer

[5] Bauman, *Modernity and Ambivalence*, p. 78.

post-defeat and rewarded much more easily than both Turkey and
Japan for doing far less than either to be conciliatory. What is more,
this dynamic is prominently at play again. These days, both Turkey
and Japan are struggling to chart a more autonomous foreign policy
course away from the influence of their traditional Western partners,
and despite decades of loyalty to the West, hardly a week goes by
without a proclamation from a Western observer that either country
has been or is about to be "lost."

It is true that the last decade has been an uncharacteristically high-
profile one for Turkey's foreign policy. Under the leadership of the
Justice and Development Party (AKP), Turkey has taken firmer positions in its dealings with its Western allies, on the one hand, and has
displayed an increasing interest in cultivating ties with its Eastern and
Southern neighbors, on the other hand. For instance, after an initial
strong push for Turkey's accession to the European Union, the AKP
government seems to have lost interest in pursuing this trajectory and,
despite the "Obama effect," Turkey's relations with the United States
remain cooler at present than historically has been the case.[6] On the
flip side, Turkey is actively pursuing stronger economic ties with the
Muslim world and Africa, regions mostly ignored throughout the
last century.[7] In other words, after almost a century of commitment
to a staunch Western alliance, Turkey may be modifying its course.[8]
Interestingly, Japan has also recently come under the control of a non-
establishment party, the Democratic Party of Japan (DPJ). Like the
AKP, the DPJ seems uncomfortable with the foreign policy status quo
and has expressed a willingness to take Japan out of the American
orbit in favor of strengthened ties with neighbors in the Eastern hemi-
sphere. Yet neither what Turkey has done thus far nor what the DPJ
government has declared it plans to do comes even remotely close to
cutting ties with the West – so what exactly is the source of all the
hand-wringing by Western commentators?

Moreover, after decades of pursuing Western-friendly policies in
order to gain recognition, neither Turkey nor Japan has been able to
find itself a secure place in the international order. The course charted

---

[6] Grigoriadis, "Friends No More?"; Rachman, "America is Losing the Free
World."

[7] "Turkey: Trade Shifts away from Europe," Oxford Analytica Brief Service,
February 2009, 1.

[8] Bengio, "Altercating Interests"; Abramowitz and Barkey, "Turkey's
Transformers."

by both Turkey and Japan since their respective defeats has until recently been to seek equal acceptance as "normal" states by their Western counterparts. In order to achieve this outcome, they committed themselves to grand strategies that entailed aggressively adopting Western models at home on the one hand, and cooperating with Western powers in foreign policy matters on the other. Both in their own way can be thought of as having successfully pursued this strategy to its logical end (Japan perhaps more so than Turkey) – the problem is, the *arriviste* strategy itself is fundamentally limited: "The best he can be is a former stranger, 'a friend on approval' and permanently on trial, a person vigilantly watched and constantly under pressure to be someone else than he is, told to be ashamed of his guilt of not being what he ought to be."[9] And this is precisely the position both Turkey and Japan have found themselves in. Despite the great lengths they have gone to in order to transform themselves, both countries remain torn between the East and the West.

Given an understanding of international stigmatization, none of this should come as a surprise. Bauman notes that the promise of assimilation is a hollow one. Stigmatized strangers may

go out of their way to get rid of and to suppress everything which makes them distinct from the rightful members of the native community – and hope that a devoted emulation of native ways will render them indistinguishable from the hosts, and by the same token guarantee their reclassification as insiders, entitled to the treatment the friends routinely receive. The harder they try, however, the faster the finishing-line seems to be receding.[10]

In fact, the effort put into socialization is the very thing that makes it impossible for outsider states to achieve the kind of insider recognition they seek: "the very good will of the stranger turns against him; his effort to assimilate sets him further apart, bringing his strangeness into fuller than ever relief and supplying the proof of the threat it contains."[11] This is why despite decades of loyalty and commitment to Western norms, both Turkey and Japan have immediately become suspect, notwithstanding the fact that in both cases the shifts in foreign policy thus far seem to be more rhetorical than actual.

---

[9] Bauman, *Modernity and Ambivalence*, p. 72.
[10] *Ibid.*, p. 71.   [11] *Ibid.*, p. 78.

The ugly truth is that what is the best outcome for the West is not necessarily the best for Turkey or Japan (or Russia). The best outcome for the West is for Turkey and Japan to continue playing along, to keep pursuing belonging, but never really getting the recognition they crave. Sticking with that strategy would continue to affirm the objectivity, the superiority, the desirability of Western-ness. Essentially this is why the goal-post, the bar one has to clear in order to belong, keeps moving, keeps being rearticulated in established-outsider relationships.[12] This pattern is most obvious in the relations between Turkey and the European Union, but Japan's and Russia's relations with the core of the international system are also subtly undermined by the same dynamic: "The rules of the game are changed with little warning. Or, rather, only now the earnestly 'self-refining' strangers discover that what they mistook for a game of emancipation was in fact the game of domination."[13] Given the fact that gaining belonging through assimilation is a fool's errand, it is actually rather rational for Turkey and Japan (and Russia) to experiment with other coping strategies.

The reader may wonder what has taken Turkey (or Japan) so long to discover (assuming they have) that the recognition strategy they were pursuing would never deliver the optimal outcome they were seeking. Why does Charlie Brown keep trying to kick Lucy's ball, even though she yanks it away every time he tries? Lucy's joke draws on the two features of his identity Charlie Brown is most insecure about: friendship and sportsmanship. The fact of the matter is, the offer of recognition through assimilation is extremely seductive to outsiders because it offers an end to what bothers them most: ambivalence, ontological doubt, uncertainty.

The second (ugly) reason why countries like Turkey and Japan have kept at this strategy for so long is because it offered them a degree more recognition than those who were even worse off. As discussed in Chapters 3 and 4, in addition to directly seeking recognition from the West, both Turkey and Japan have pursued side strategies for status enhancement revolving around attempts to position the countries in a

---

[12] "The stranger had been promised that full 'domestication' would follow cultural reform ... The bluff of this promise is called the moment it has been taken seriously and matched with a behaviour it ostensibly required. The real obstacles guarding the entry are now revealed. They prove to be economic, political and above all social ..." *Ibid.*, p. 80. See also Bourdieu, *Distinction*.

[13] Bauman, p. 71.

mediator or bridging role between the East and the West. It is claimed that Turkey and Japan are in unique positions to help their neighbors because they are the first among their "kind" to reconcile the various tensions between local culture and modern norms. Such a strategy is often framed as progressive and beneficent, but it in fact reinforces the status hierarchies in the international system, and ensures for Turkey and Japan a more privileged position vis-à-vis their Asian neighbors. In fact, despite the "bridging" rhetoric often employed by both countries, any regional role has been for the most part a by-product or an afterthought to these countries' quests to gain equal recognition from the West.

Instead of making an effort to regain a more powerful status by committing fully to regional causes (and becoming advocates for regional complaints), both Turkey and Japan have attempted to frame their Western orientation as the reason why they should matter in their regions. Implicit in this attitude was an endorsement and legitimation of the modern/Western ontology of ranking states. Modernization[14] was the right thing to do – Turkey and Japan had something to teach states in their respective regions because they had traveled down that path first, just as they had themselves learned from the West. Or as Goffman put it: "The stigmatized individual exhibits a tendency to stratify his 'own' to the degree to which their stigma is apparent and obtrusive. He can then take up in regard to those who are more evidently stigmatized than himself the attitudes the normals take to him."[15] This kind of attitude was especially evident in Turkish actions in the 1920s. We see a similar dynamic at work with the Japanese actively pushing the Japanese model of development in Asia,[16] and remaining rather aloof to regional and Third World efforts to question the international economic order. In both cases, problems in the "Third World" are severed from their international context and reduced to being responsibilities of various local governments – if Turkey and Japan could solve[17] their modernity problem, so could

[14] Of course, this term meant something other in the 1920s than it did in the 1950s.
[15] Goffman, *Stigma*, p. 107.
[16] Modernization and development with an Asian twist; just as the Turkish model is modernization and secularism within an Islamic context.
[17] I am not claiming that Turkey solved this problem, but rather depicting how the Turks framed the issue.

other disadvantaged states, and if they couldn't, the implication is that it was because they were not as deserving.[18]

It is possible to read the so-called sea-changes in recent Turkish and Japanese foreign policy simply as an extension and an amplification of this previous side strategy. In the post-Cold War international system, the limits of pursuing a strategy of assimilation are becoming harder to ignore. Ironically, this has much to do with the fact that the norms of the international system have become more homogenized due to the past successes of socialization pressures. This is also the second[19] reason why post-Soviet Russia has been much less committed to socialization as a strategy for coping with its stigmatization than either Turkey or Japan were after their defeats.

When the Ottoman Empire was defeated, the international system was not yet truly global. There were still territories without full sovereign recognition; most European powers still had colonies and mandates; and the Bolsheviks were an unknown and unpredictable factor. Western powers worried that any one of these variables could be manipulated by the new Turkish state. Similarly, during the Cold War, the existence of the Eastern Bloc and even the nonaligned movement created the illusion that Japan might defect. As documented in Chapter 4, despite the occupation, the presence of communist sympathies among the Japanese population, for instance, remained a serious concern for both Japanese policy-makers and their American allies. However, when the Soviet Union collapsed, the only viable[20] normative alternative to the Western model also collapsed: in this post-Cold War world, where else would Russia go, if not toward the West (and to the "End of History")?

The fact that Turkey and Japan emerged from their defeats into tiered and divided international environments made them seem more likely to defect, but it is those environments which made the reconstruction efforts undertaken to gain respect from the West seem worthwhile to domestic constituencies. Strategies designed to obfuscate or correct stigmatizing attributes are much more attractive in rigidly and openly stratified societies; the pay-off is much higher.

---

[18] Such an attitude also justifies the imperial past.

[19] In addition to the comparatively friendly treatment it received after defeat as discussed above.

[20] Again, as discussed in Chapter 2, substantively, the Soviet model was never much of an alternative at all to the Western state ideal. But socially, it was.

Unlike Turkey or Japan, after the collapse of the Soviet Union, Russia faced an international environment wherein the "ideal" state norm had come to be expressed in universalized language and there seemed to be no explicit standards for picking winners and losers. Emulation under those conditions has uncertain status yields. Furthermore, lack of alternative logics in the international system made the West less willing to feign interest in Russia's overtures – an additional factor which also dampened whatever initial enthusiasm the Russian public felt about adopting Western models. As discussed in Chapter 5, all of these factors have thus far led Russia down a novel but somewhat impotent path: recently, Russia has been maintaining a stance of rhetorical hostility but is unable to reject the normative order in actuality by offering an alternative worldview. This performance is directed to some degree at capturing recognition from the East and the South.

This is where the possible shift in Turkey's and Japan's trajectory points to a convergence with Russia. Turkey and Japan increasingly have to face the reality that in today's international context, states such as Iran and China – states which are more secure in their "Asian"/"Eastern" identities – seem to have more cachet with non-Western populations increasingly disenfranchised with the hollow promises of international society than the "teacher's pets". Yet, Turkey and Japan are very much constrained by trajectories they followed in the twentieth century – and cannot put up the rhetorical performance Russia is offering without risking their hard-earned semi-Western position (especially considering the reaction even little protestations are getting). It is not surprising, therefore, that both countries have latched onto the discourse of the "Clash of Civilizations" as a way out of this conundrum – both Turkey and Japan see an opportunity in this "clash" to turn what used to be an afterthought, i.e. relations with the East, into an explicit strategy to redefine their importance for the West. To that end, both Turkey and Japan are actively sponsoring conferences and workshops[21] devoted to exploring civilizational issues. From a systemic perspective, there is not that much

---

[21] Turkey hosted its most recent "Alliance of Civilizations" conference on April 6, 2009, with high-profile names such as US President Obama, the UN Secretary General Ban Ki-moon, and many prime ministers from around the world in attendance. See Leheny, "The Samurai Ride to Huntington's Rescue," for a discussion of Japan's similar efforts to capitalize on "the clash of civilizations."

difference between this strategy and that favored by Russia at the moment. Without a substantial ideology of rejection to back it up, the Eastward-looking Eurasianist policies differ from the "bridging" efforts primarily in their rhetorical tone.

Given that conclusion, this might strike the reader as an inopportune moment to call for more attention to be paid to the social nature of the international system. It could be further argued that the international system, however socially stratified it had been in the past, has, over time, come to resemble more or less the world realists have described – one in which social constraints and stigmas play an increasingly diminished role. If that is true, perhaps mainstream IR theories are wrong about their projections into the past, but are not so problematic if we want to make sense of the present or predict the future.

I am willing to concede that the international system, very much like its liberal domestic cousin, has moved from patterns of overt stratification and stigmatization toward formal equality and discourses of cultural tolerance.[22] Overall, this has been a positive development. I do not have a problem with the argument that the system of sovereign equality created after World War II *is* preferable to the nineteenth-century Standard of Civilization. It is also plausible that as a result of these trends, more states in the international system have come to resemble (or resemble to a greater degree than before) the ideal-typical agents they were always assumed to be by IR theory. However, neither of those arguments should lead us to conclude that social stratification is a thing of the past in international relations. There are still "established" and "outsiders," "natives" and "strangers" in the international society. What is more, the make-up of those groups has changed very little in the intervening century between the Standard of Civilization and the present day. If anything, that fact should give us serious pause for thought.

For the majority of states in the international system, their placement along the historical established-outsider divide has been most formative and path-determinative. We know that social stratification persists in domestic systems even in the face of legal equality, and we

---

[22] "Emancipated from modern hubris, the postmodern mind has less need for cruelty and humiliating the Other; it can afford Richard Rorty's 'kindness.'" Bauman, *Modernity and Ambivalence*, p. 257.

also know how much of an obstacle social inequality may be for individuals to fully exercise their autonomy – how is that lesson so easily forgotten in international relations? In this book, I have analyzed the behavior of those most "fortunate" among the outsiders: states that had enough of an ontological coherence, bureaucratic tradition, material base, and institutional framework to cope with the stigmatization that accompanies being on the wrong side of the social divide in a relatively autonomous manner. Even such states were traumatized by their manner of incorporation into the modern international order, and their state identities have evolved around that experience. Most states in the periphery were absorbed in a much more violent manner; *and* they face the international normative order with fewer resources, even fewer choices, and greater stigma burdens.

The theoretical neglect of the social divisions that dominated international relations for the duration of the modern states system was and is a serious problem. My analysis above, as I am sure astute readers have recognized, leads to the rather twisted conclusion that withholding equal recognition from defeated outsider states makes them more willing to emulate the dominant international norms domestically and play nice internationally. However, we should not forget that societal models that did not deliver on their upward mobility promise proved rather unstable in modernity. There may be a limit to how long the majority of the world's population will tolerate living under an international system whose rules they have very little input in, and one in which even the most successful of outsiders (e.g. Japan) are never accorded the full respect that their material success entitles them to. There is a reason why the *schadenfreude* felt at the expense of Western powers over a wide-ranging scale of phenomena, from the 9/11 attacks to the verbal dressings-down delivered by Putin, is not confined to the immediate supporters of the perpetrators, but rather is widespread throughout what is now called "the Global South."

As I pointed out in the Introduction, with reference to Orhan Pamuk's remarks, what people want most of all is to matter, and what keeps their faith in any system is the hope that they may matter some day, even if they do not today. This is also why, for instance, people all around the world were enthusiastic about the election of Barack Obama as the President of the United States – in his person, he symbolized the hope that "others" and "outsiders," too, can be acknowledged one day. I do not want to overstate the importance of emotions in foreign policy, but I do want to offer a humble correction to a vast literature that, for the last 50 years, has largely pretended that they cease to exist once one crosses the imaginary threshold of the "international." To deny the existence of an international society with its own logic of stratification is not a neutral act – it is an act of power which perpetuates those very dynamics.

Acknowledging that people need hope and a modicum of real recognition in order to keep trudging along is not romanticism. It is the height of rationality. As Hegel pointed out, mankind's eternal quest for recognition is intimately connected with our drive toward rationality. The rational solution for long-term systemic stability is in striking the right balance between upward mobility and privilege distribution. Simply put, we need a more meritocratic international system, instead of one that is only described as such. In domestic societies, the social inequalities created by historical injustices make meritocracy a difficult ideal to achieve. However, in the IR discipline, we have barely even begun to accept that such social inequalities exist. It is about time we remembered.

There is also something that "outsiders" can do about their situation. As I noted at the outset of this chapter, the choice between Herodianism and Zeolotry is really no choice at all because both choices reaffirm the privileged position of the West, of modernity, as *the* center to react to and to order one's behavior around. Both the Zealots and the Herodians live under the imagined gaze of the West. Iran is no more free of the trappings of modernity, of the trauma of Westernization, than Turkey is. The only way out of the impasse is to truly make no choice at all, and resign oneself to living in a condition of ambivalence. True manifestation of agency, of sovereignty, of positive freedom can only be attained by facing one's own ontological insecurity, by realizing that self-construction is an inevitable part of existence. The master, the natives, the established do not ever address the tentativeness of their ontological condition – they side-step the issue by reveling in the simulated dynamics of mastery, agency, and domination. Furthermore, because of the seeming naturalness of their condition, they are most likely oblivious to the fact that their self-image is an illusion. This is why in Kojève's reading of the Hegelian master–slave dynamic, the "slave" is the only party with real hope of attaining true freedom.[23] Not having the protective cushion of

---

[23] Kojève, *Introduction*, pp. 20–2.

normativity means being forced to face the world every day in its uncertainty, to be forced to be an agent every day, to not have the ability to take anything for granted, to have to consider every action as a potentially constitutive performance – and that is very frightening (not to mention tiring). This is perhaps why in the world of outsiders, those who are best suited to grasp the full implications of such a condition have been the worst offenders in perpetuating the hierarchies of modernity. Both auto-Orientalism and its mirror image, the escape into strangerhood, have the same limited redeeming value of fixing one's place in the world. If only outsiders could realize that they do not have to settle for that and accept that an ordered world with a fixed center is itself a sham, they may perhaps be able to liberate themselves.

I opened the book by talking about Orhan Pamuk, so let me close with him as well – he made the point I am trying to make here much more eloquently in his Nobel Lecture:

This means that my father was not the only one, that *we all give too much importance to the idea of a world with a centre.* Whereas the thing that compels us to shut ourselves up to write in our rooms for years on end is a faith in the opposite; the belief that one day our writings will be read and understood, because people all the world over resemble each other. But this, as I know from my own and my father's writing, is a troubled optimism, scarred by the anger of being consigned to the margins, of being left outside. The love and hate that Dostoyevsky felt towards the West all his life – I have felt this too, on many occasions. But if I have grasped an essential truth, if I have cause for optimism, it is because I have travelled with this great writer through his love–hate relationship with the West, to behold the other world he has built on the other side.

It is my humble hope that this book will be one of the many stepping stones to that other side, the side without a center.

Bibliography

Abbott, Andrew, *Time Matters: On Theory and Method* (Chicago: University of Chicago Press, 2001).

Abizadeh, Arash, "Does Collective Identity Presuppose an Other? On the Alleged Incoherence of Global Sovereignty," *The American Political Science Review* 99, no.1 (2005), 45–60.

Abramowitz, M. and H. Barkey, "Turkey's Transformers," *Foreign Affairs* 88, no.6 (2009), 118–28.

Acharya, Amitav, "How Ideas Spread: Whose Norms Matter? Norm Localization and Institutional Change in Asian Regionalism," *International Organization* 58, no.2 (2004), 239–75.

Adomeit, Hannes, "Russia as a 'Great Power' in World Affairs: Images and Reality," *International Affairs* 71, no.1 (1995), 35–68.

Akçam, Taner, *Türkiye'yi Yeniden Düşünmek* (Istanbul: Birikim Yayınları, 1995).

Alderson, Kai, "Making Sense of State Socialization," *Review of International Studies* 27, no.3 (2001), 415–33.

Allinson, Gary D., *Japan's Postwar History* (Ithaca, NY: Cornell University Press, 1997).

Andersen, Heine and Lars Bo Kaspersen, eds., *Classical and Modern Social Theory* (Oxford: Blackwell, 2000).

Anderson, Benedict, *Imagined Communities*, 2nd edn. (London: Verso, 1991).

Anderson, Perry, *Lineages of the Absolutist State* (London: Verso, 1996).

Aras, Tevfik Rüştü, *Atatürk'ün Dış Politikası* (Istanbul: Kaynak Yayınları, 2003 [1945]).

Arbatov, Alexei G., "Russia's Foreign Policy Alternatives," *International Security* 18, no.2 (1993), 5–43.

Aristotle, *Politics*, R. F. Stalley, ed., Ernest Barker, trans. (Oxford: Oxford University Press, 2009).

Armağan, Mustafa, *Osmanlının Kayıp Atlası* (Istanbul: Ufuk Kitap, 2005).

Ashley, Richard, "The Poverty of Neorealism," in Robert O. Keohane, ed., *Neorealism and Its Critics*, pp. 255–300.

Atatürk, Mustafa Kemal, *Söylev*, H. V. Velidedeoğlu, ed., 9th edn., vols. I–II (Istanbul: Çağdaş Yayınları, 1981 [1927]).

Atatürk'ün Bütün Eserleri, A. B. E. D. Kurulu, vols. I–XX (Istanbul: Kaynak Yayınları, 2005).

Nutuk (Söylev): Belgeler, H. V. Velidedeoğlu, ed., 9th edn., vol. III (Istanbul: Cumhuriyet Kitapları, 2005 [1927]).

Atay, Falih Rıfkı, *Çankaya (1881–1939)* (Istanbul: Doğan Kardeş, 1969 [1961]).

Zeytindağı (Istanbul: Pozitif, 2004 [1932]).

Austin, Greg and Stuart Harris, *Japan and Greater China: Political Economy and Military Power in the Asian Century* (London: Hurst & Company, 2001).

Aydemir, Sevket Süreyya, *Tek Adam: Mustafa Kemal* (Istanbul: Remzi Kitabevi, 1969).

Aydın, Cemil, *Politics of Anti-Westernism in Asia* (New York: Columbia University, 2007).

Ayoob, Mohammed, "The Third World in the System of States: Acute Schizophrenia or Growing Pains?" *International Studies Quarterly* 33, no.1 (1989), 67–79.

Badgley, John H., "Necessity and Choice in Japan's Relations with Southeast Asia," in Inoki, ed., *Japan's Future in Southeast Asia*, pp. 133–66.

"Japan's Nonmilitary Road to Power," in Iriye, ed., *Japan and the New Asia*, pp. 45–65.

Bailey, Paul J., *Postwar Japan* (Cambridge: Blackwell, 1996).

Bankoff, Greg, "Regions of Risk: Western Discourses on Terrorism and the Significance of Islam," *Studies in Conflict and Terrorism* 26, no.6 (2003), 413–28.

Baranovsky, Vladimir, "Russia: A Part of Europe or Apart from Europe?" *International Affairs* 76, no.3 (2000), 443–58.

Barnett, Michael N., *Dialogues in Arab Politics: Negotiations in Regional Order* (New York: Columbia University Press, 1998).

Bauman, Zygmunt, *Legislators and Interpreters* (Cambridge: Polity Press, 1989).

Modernity and Ambivalence (Cambridge: Polity Press, 1993).

Modernity and the Holocaust (Ithaca, NY: Cornell University Press, 2001).

Befu, Harumi, "Geopolitics, Geoeconomics, and the Japanese Identity," in Peter Nosco, ed., *Japanese Identity: Cultural Analyses* (Berkeley: University of California Press, 1997), pp. 10–32.

Beinin, Joel, *Workers and Peasants in the Middle East* (Cambridge: Cambridge University Press, 2001).

Bengio, O., "Altercating Interests and Orientations between Israel and Turkey," *Insight Turkey* 11, no.2 (2009), 43–55.

Bergesen, Albert, ed., *Studies of the Modern World-System* (New York: Academic Press, 1980).

Berkes, Niyazi, *Türkiye'de Çağdaşlaşma* (Ankara: Bilgi Yayınevi, 1973).

Berlin, Isaiah, "Two Concepts of Liberty," in Isaiah Berlin, ed., *Four Essays on Liberty* (London: Oxford University Press, 1969), pp. 118–72.

Best, Shaun, "Review: Zygmunt Bauman: Personal Reflections within the Mainstream of Modernity," *The British Journal of Sociology* 49, no.2 (1998), 311–20.

Betts, Richard K., "Wealth, Power and Instability: East Asia and the United States after the Cold War," *International Security* 18, no.3 (1993/94), 34–77.

Bhagwati, Jagdish, ed., *The New International Economic Order* (Boston: MIT Press, 1977).

Bhaskar, Roy, *Reclaiming Reality: A Critical Approach to Contemporary Philosophy* (New York: Verso, 1989).

Billington, James H., *Russia in Search of Itself* (Washington, DC: Woodrow Wilson Press, 2004).

Blaney, David and Naeem Inayatullah, "The Westphalian Deferral," *International Studies Review* 2, no.2 (2000), 29–64.

  International Relations and the Problem of Difference (New York: Routledge, 2004).

Blasi, Joseph R., Maya Kroumova, and Douglas Kruse, *Kremlin Capitalism: Privatizing the Russian Economy* (Ithaca, NY: Cornell University Press, 1997).

Boli, John, "World Polity Sources of Expanding State Authority and Organizations, 1870–1970," in G. M. Thomas, J. W. Meyer, F. O. Ramirez, and J. Boli, eds., *Institutional Structure* (Thousand Oaks, CA: Sage, 1987), pp. 71–91.

Bolluk, Hadiye, *Kurtuluş Savaşı'nın İdeolojisi/ Hakimiyeti Milliye* (Istanbul: Kaynak Yayınları, 2003).

Bourdieu, Pierre, *Outline of a Theory of Practice* (Cambridge: Cambridge University Press, 1977).

  Distinction (London: Routledge, 1984).

Boxer, C. R., *Jan Compagnie in Japan, 1600–1850*, 2nd rev. edn. (The Hague: Nijhoff, 1950).

Bozdağlıoğlu, Yücel, *Turkish Foreign Policy and Turkish Identity* (London: Routledge, 2003).

Bozkurt, Gülnihâl, *Azınlık Imtiyazları-Kapitülasyonlardan Tek Hukuk Sistemine Geçiş* (Ankara: Atatürk Araştırma Merkezi, 1998).

Bracken, Paul, *Fire in the East: The Rise of Asian Military Power and the Second Nuclear Age* (New York: HarperCollins, 1999).

Brady, H. E. and D. Collier, eds., *Rethinking Social Inquiry: Diverse Tools, Shared Standards* (Lanham, MD: Rowman & Littlefield, 2004).

Braude, Benjamin and Bernard Lewis, *Christians and Jews in the Ottoman Empire: The Functioning of a Plural Society* (New York: Holmes & Meier Publishers, 1982).

Braudel, Fernand, *The Mediterranean and the Mediterranean World in the Age of Philip II* (Berkeley: University of California Press, 1995).

Brines, Russell, *MacArthur's Japan*, 1st edn. (Philadelphia: J. B. Lippincott Co., 1948).

Broido, Vera, *Apostles into Terrorists: Women and the Revolutionary Movement in the Russia of Alexander II* (New York: Viking Press, 1977).

Brooks, Stephen G. and William C. Wohlforth, "Power, Globalization, and the End of the Cold War: Reevaluating a Landmark Case for Ideas," *International Security* 25, no.3 (2000/1), 5–53.

Brown, Archie, *The Gorbachev Factor* (Oxford: Oxford University Press, 1996).

Brubaker, Rogers, "Rethinking Classical Theory: The Sociological Vision of Pierre Bourdieu," *Theory and Society* 14, no.6 (1985), 745–75.

Bukovansky, Mlada, "The Altered State and the State of Nature: The French Revolution and International Politics," *Review of International Studies* 25, no.2 (1999), 197–216.

Bull, Hedley, *The Anarchical Society: A Study of Order in World Politics*, 3rd edn. (New York: Palgrave, 2002 [1977]).

"Emergence of a Universal International Society," in Bull and Watson, eds., *The Expansion of International Society*, pp. 117–41.

Bull, Hedley and Adam Watson, eds., *The Expansion of International Society* (New York: Oxford University Press, 1984).

Bunce, Valerie, "Domestic Reform and International Change: The Gorbachev Reforms in Historical Perspective," *International Organization* 47, no.1 (1993), 107–38.

Burke, Edmund, *Reflections on the Revolution in France* (Oxford: Oxford University Press, 1999 [1790]).

Buruma, Ian, *Inventing Japan, 1853–1964* (New York: The Modern Library, 2003).

Buruma, Ian and Avishai Margalit, *Occidentalism: The West in the Eyes of Its Enemies* (New York: Penguin, 2004).

Buzan, Barry, "From International System to International Society: Structural Realism and Regime Theory Meet the English School," *International Organization* 47, no.3 (1993), 327–52.

From International to World Society?: English School Theory and the Social Structure of Globalisation (New York: Cambridge University Press, 2004).

Buzan, Barry and Richard Little, "Why International Relations Has Failed as an Intellectual Project and What to Do about It," *Millennium* 30, no.1 (2001), 19–39.

Byman, Daniel and Kenneth M. Pollack, "Let Us Now Praise Great Men," *International Security* 25, no.4 (2001), 107–46.

Çalışlar, İpek, *Latife Hanım* (Istanbul: Doğan Kitapçılık, 2006).

Cardoso, Fernando Henrique and Enzo Faletto, *Dependency and Development in Latin America*, M. M. Urquidi, trans. (New York: Columbia University Press, 1979).

Carr, Edward Hallett, *The Twenty Years' Crisis, 1919–1939* (New York: Palgrave, 2001).

Castles, Stephen, "Nation and Empire: Hierarchies of Citizenship in the New Global Order," *International Politics* 42, no.2 (2005), 203–24.

Chai, Sun-Ki, "Entrenching the Yoshida Defense Doctrine: Three Techniques for Institutionalization," *International Organization* 51, no.3 (1997), 389–412.

Chase-Dunn, Christopher and Eugene N. Anderson, *The Historical Evolution of World-Systems* (New York: Palgrave Macmillan, 2005).

Chase-Dunn, Christopher and Thomas D. Hall, "The Historical Evolution of World-Systems," *Sociological Inquiry* 64, no.3 (1994), 257–80.

Chaturvedi, Vinayak, ed., *Mapping Subaltern Studies and the Postcolonial* (New York: Verso, 2000).

Checkel, Jeffrey, "Ideas, Institutions, and the Gorbachev Foreign Policy Revolution," *World Politics* 45, no.2 (1993), 271–300.

Ideas and International Political Change: Soviet/Russian Behavior and the End of the Cold War (New Haven: Yale University Press, 1997).

"Norms, Institutions and National Identity in Contemporary Europe," *International Studies Quarterly* 43, no.1 (1999), 83–114.

"Why Comply? Social Learning and European Identity Change," *International Organization* 55, no.3 (2001), 553–88.

Chernyaev, Anatoly, *My Six Years with Gorbachev* (University Park: Pennsylvania State University Press, 2000).

Churchill, Winston, *Memoirs of the Second World War* (London: Houghton Mifflin Company, 1959).

Clapham, Christopher, *Third World Politics* (London: Routledge, 1985).

Clark, Bruce, *Twice a Stranger: the Mass Expulsions that Forged Modern Greece and Turkey* (Cambridge, MA: Harvard University Press, 2006)

Clark, Ian, "Another 'Double Movement': The Great Transformation after the Cold War?" in M. Cox, T. Dunne, and K. Booth, eds., *Empires,*

Systems and States (Cambridge: Cambridge University Press, 2001), 237–56.

"Legitimacy in a Global Order," *Review of International Studies* 29, Special Supplement 1 (2003), 75–95.

Clesse, Armand, *The Vitality of Japan: Sources of National Strength and Weakness* (New York: St. Martin's Press, 1997).

Collier, Andrew, *Critical Realism: An Introduction to Roy Bhaskar's Philosophy* (London: Verso, 1994).

Collins, Randall, "A Sociological Guilt-Trip: Comment on Connell," *The American Journal of Sociology* 102, no.6 (1997), 1558–64.

"An Asian Route to Capitalism," in *Macrohistory*, pp. 209–38.

Macrohistory: Essays in Sociology of the Long Run (Stanford: Stanford University Press, 1999).

Collins, Stephen L., *From Divine Cosmos to Sovereign State: An Intellectual History of Consciousness and the Idea of Order in Renaissance England* (Oxford: Oxford University Press, 1989).

Connell, R. W., "Why the 'Political Socialization' Paradigm Failed and What Should Replace It," *International Political Science Review* 8, no.3 (1987), 215–23.

Connor, Walker, "Illusions of Homogeneity," in *Ethnonationalism: The Quest for Understanding* (Princeton: Princeton University Press, 1994), pp. 118–43.

Cooley, Charles H., *Human Nature and the Social Order* (New York: Scribner's, 1922).

Copeland, Dale C., "Trade Expectations and the Outbreak of Peace: Détente 1970–1974 and the End of the Cold War, 1985–1991," *Security Studies* 9, no.1–2 (1999/2000), 15–58.

Cortell, Andrew P. and James W. Davis, Jr., "Understanding the Domestic Impact of International Norms: A Research Agenda," *International Studies Review* 2, no.1 (2000), 65–87.

Cox, Robert W., "Ideologies and the NIEO: Reflections on Some Recent Literature," *International Organization* 33, no.2 (1979), 257–302.

"Social Forces, States and World Orders: Beyond International Relations Theory," Robert O. Keohane, ed., *Neorealism and Its Critics*, pp. 204–54.

Crossley, Nick, "The Phenomenological Habitus and Its Construction," *Theory and Society*, 30, no.1 (2001), 81–120.

Crowdy, Rachel E., "Humanitarian Activities of the League of Nations," *Journal of the Royal Institute of International Affairs* 6, no.3 (1927), 153–169.

Dallmayr, Fred, *Beyond Orientalism: Essays on Cross-Cultural Encounter* (Albany, NY: SUNY Press, 1996).

Darling, Linda T., "The Finance Scribes and Ottoman Politics," in Caeser
    E. Farah, ed., *Decision Making and Change in the Ottoman Empire*
    (Thomas Jefferson University Press, 1993), pp. 89–100.
Davison, Roderic H., *Essays in Ottoman and Turkish History, 1774–
    1923: The Impact of the West*, 1st edn. (Austin: University of Texas
    Press, 1990).
    "Turkish Attitudes Concerning Christian/Muslim Equality in the Nineteenth
    Century," *American Historical Review* 59, no.4 (1953/4), 844–64.
Debo, Richard, *Survival and Consolidation: The Foreign Policy of Soviet
    Russia, 1918–1921* (Montreal: McGill-Queen's University Press,
    1992).
Demirel, Ahmet, *Birinci Meclis'te Muhalefet: İkinci Grup*, 3rd edn.
    (Istanbul: İletisim Yayinlari, 2003).
Derluguian, Georgi, "Terrorism, the Weapon of the Organizationally
    Weak," in R. Stemplowski, ed., *Transnational Terrorism in the World-
    System Perspective* (Warsaw: The Polish Institute of International
    Affairs, 2002), pp. 23–46.
    "A Cyclical Theory of Russia's Historical Change," in C. Canales,
    L. A. Lo Manto, and S. Plekhanov, eds., *Russie: Le défi d'une meta-
    morphose* (Toronto: York University, 2004), pp. 45–60.
    Bourdieu's Secret Admirer in the Caucasus (Chicago: University of
    Chicago Press, 2005).
    "O Mundo Que o Portugues (o Russo, o Turco) Criou: Empires on
    Europe's Periphery," paper delivered at the Conference on "Colonial
    Experiences and Colonial Legacies: Comparing Eastern Europe and
    Sub-Saharan Africa," Cornell University, May 2005.
Deudney, Daniel and John G. Ikenberry, "The International Sources of
    Soviet Change," *International Security* 16, no.3 (1991/2), 74–118.
Dilan, Hasan Berke, *Türkiye'nin Dış Politikası* (Istanbul: Alfa Basım
    Yayım Dağıtım, 1998).
Dostoyevsky, Fyodor, *Winter Notes on Summer Impressions*, David Patterson,
    trans. (Chicago: Northwestern University Press, 1997 [1863]).
Doyle, Michael, *Ways of War and Peace: Realism, Liberalism and Socialism*
    (New York: Norton, 1997).
Dunning, Eric and Stephen Mennell, "Preface," in Elias, *The Germans*,
    pp. vii–xvi.
Durkheim, Emile, *The Division of Labor in Society* (Glencoe, IL: Free
    Press, 1949).
    Suicide: A Study in Sociology, George Simpson, ed., John A. Spaulding
    and George Simpson, trans. (London: Routledge & Kegan Paul, 1952).
Eisenstadt, Shmuel, *The Origins and Diversity of Axial Age Civilizations*
    (Albany: State University of New York Press, 1986).

European Civilization in a Comparative Perspective (Oslo: Norwegian University Press, 1987).

Elias, Norbert, "Introduction: A Theoretical Essay on Established and Outsiders," in Elias and Scotson, *The Established and Outsiders*, pp. xv–lii.

The Germans (New York: Columbia University Press, 1996).

The Civilizing Process (Oxford: Wiley-Blackwell, 2000).

Elias, Norbert and John L. Scotson, *The Established and Outsiders* (London: Sage Publications, 1994).

Elias, Norbert, Robert van Krieken, and Eric Dunning, "Toward a Theory of Social Processes: A Translation," *The British Journal of Sociology*, 48, no.3 (1997), 355–83.

Ellison, Herbert, ed., *Japan and the Pacific Quadrille* (London: Westview, 1987).

Engelhardt, Ed and Reşat Ali, *Türkiye ve Tanzimat: Devlet-i Osmaniyenin Tarih-i Islâhati, 1826–1882* (Istanbul: Mürettibîn-i Osmanî Matbaası, 1912).

English, Robert, *Russia and the Idea of the West* (New York: Columbia University Press, 2000).

Erdem, Suna, "Disappointment as Michelle Obama skips trip to Turkey," *Times Online* April 7, 2009 (www.timesonline.co.uk/tol/news/world/europe/article6046656.ece).

Erickson, John, *The Soviet High Command: A Military-Political History, 1918–1941* (London: Macmillan, 1962).

Erüreten, Bahır Mazhar, *Türkiye Cumhuriyeti Devrim Yasaları* (Istanbul: Töre Yayın Grubu, 2004).

Evangelista, Matthew, "The Paradox of State Strength: Transnational Relations, Domestic Structures, and Security Policy in Russia and the Soviet Union," *International Organization* 49, no.1 (1995), 1–38.

"Norms, Heresthetics, and the End of the Cold War," *Journal of Cold War Studies* 3, no.1 (2001), 5–35.

Evans, Laurence, *United States Policy and the Partition of Turkey, 1914–1924* (Baltimore: Johns Hopkins Press, 1965).

Eyre, Dana and Mark Suchman, "Status, Norms, and the Proliferation of Conventional Weapons," in Peter J. Katzenstein, ed., *Culture and Security* (New York: Columbia University Press, 1996), pp. 79–113.

Farbman, Michael S., "The Present Situation in Russia," *Journal of the British Institute of International Affairs* 3, no.2 (1924), 83–102.

Faroqhi, Suraiya, "Crisis and Change, 1590–1699," in Halil İnalcık with Donald Quatert, eds., *An Economic and Social History of the Ottoman Empire 1300–1914* (Cambridge: Cambridge University Press, 1994), pp. 411–636.

Finnemore, Martha, *National Interests in International Society* (Ithaca, NY: Cornell University Press, 1996).
"Norms, Culture, and World Politics: Insights from Sociology's Institutionalism," *International Organization* 50, no.2 (1996), 325–47.
Finnemore, Martha and Kathryn Sikkink, "International Norm Dynamics and Political Change," *International Organization* 52, no.4 (1998), 887–917.
Fisk, Gloria, "Orhan Pamuk and the Turks," *N+1* (www.nplusonemag.com/node/66).
Flockhart, Trine, "Complex Socialization: A Framework for the Study of State Socialization," *European Journal of International Relations* 12, no.1 (2006), 89–106.
Florini, Ann, "The Evolution of International Norms," *International Studies Quarterly* 40, no.3 (1996), 363–89.
Fontaine, Stanislas, "The Civilizing Process Revisited: Interview with Norbert Elias," *Theory and Society* 5, no.2 (1978), 243–53.
Forsberg, Tuomas, "Power, Interests and Trust: Explaining Gorbachev's Choices at the End of the Cold War," *Review of International Studies* 25, no.5 (1999), 603–21.
Francis, David R., *Russia from the American Embassy, 1916–1918* (New York: Arno, 1970 [1921]).
Frank, Andre Gunder, *ReORIENT: Global Economy in the Asian Age* (Berkeley: University of California Press, 1998).
Frank, David, Ann Hironaka, John W. Meyer, Evan Schofer, and Nancy Tuma, "The Rationalization and Organization of Nature in World Culture," in J. Boli and G. M. Thomas, eds., *Constructing World Culture: International Non-Governmental Organizations since 1875* (Stanford: Stanford University Press, 1999), pp. 81–99.
Frank, David John, Ann Hironaka, and Evan Schofer, "The Nation-State and the Natural Environment over the Twentieth Century," *American Sociological Review* 65, no.1 (2000), 96–116.
Freedman, Robert O., "Russia and Israel under Yeltsin," *Israel Studies* 3, no.1 (1998), 140–56.
Friedberg, Aaron L., "Ripe for Rivalry: Prospects for Peace in Multipolar Asia," *International Security* 18, no.3 (Winter 1993/4), 5–33.
Friedman, Thomas, "Keep Rootin' for Putin," *The New York Times* December 27, 2001.
Fritz, Paul, "Prudence in Victory: The Management of Defeated Great Powers" (dissertation, Ohio-State University, 2007).
Fry, Greg and Jacinta O'Hagan, *Contending Images of World Politics* (New York: Macmillan Press, 2000).
Fukuchi, Takao, "Political Tension versus Economic Growth: The Case of Indonesia," in Inoki, ed., *Japan's Future in Southeast Asia*, pp. 57–74.

Fukuyama, Francis, *The End of History and the Last Man* (New York: Free Press, 1992).

Galtung, Johan, "Japan and Future World Politics," *Journal of Peace Research* 10, no.4 (1973), 355–85.

Gaonkar, Dilip Parameshwar, ed., *Alternative Modernities* (London: Duke University Press, 2001).

Gellner, Ernest, *Nations and Nationalism* (Ithaca, NY: Cornell University Press, 1983).

 Plough, Sword and the Book: The Structure of Human History (Chicago: University of Chicago Press, 1989).

Giddens, Anthony, *Politics and Sociology in the Thought of Max Weber* (London: Macmillan, 1972).

 Consequences of Modernity (Cambridge: Polity Press, 1990).

 Modernity and Self-identity: Self and Society in the Late Modern Age (Cambridge: Polity Press, 1991).

Gilman, Sander, *Jewish Self-Hatred: Anti-Semitism and the Hidden Language of the Jews* (Baltimore: Johns Hopkins University Press, 1986).

Gilpin, Robert, *War and Change in World Politics* (New York: Cambridge University Press, 1981).

Glass, Leon and Michael C. Mackey, *From Clocks to Chaos: The Rhythms of Life* (Princeton: Princeton University Press, 1988).

Glassner, Barry, "Where Meanings Get Constructed," *Contemporary Sociology* 29, no.4 (2000), 590–4.

Goble, Paul A., "Russia and Its Neighbors," *Foreign Policy* 90 (1993), 79–88.

Göçek, Fatma Müge, *Rise of the Bourgeoisie, Demise of Empire: Ottoman Westernization and Social Change* (Oxford: Oxford University Press, 1996).

 Social Constructions of Nationalism in the Middle East (Albany: State University of New York Press, 2002).

Goffman, Erving, *Stigma: Notes on the Management of Spoiled Identity* (New York: Simon & Schuster, 1963).

 Interaction Ritual (New York: Anchor, 1967).

 The Presentation of Self in Everyday Life (New York: Doubleday Anchor, 1969).

Goldgeier, James M. and Michael McFaul, "A Tale of Two Worlds: Core and Periphery in the Post-Cold War Era," *International Organization* 46, no.2 (1992), 467–91.

Goldstone, Jack, "Cultural Orthodoxy, Risk, and Innovation: The Divergence of East and West in the Early Modern World," *Sociological Theory* 5, no.2 (1987), 119–35.

 Revolution and Rebellion in the Early Modern World (Berkeley: University of California Press, 1991).

Revolutions: Theoretical, Comparative, and Historical Studies, 2nd edn. (Fort Worth: Harcourt Brace College Publishers, 1994).

"The Problem of the 'Early Modern' World," *Journal of the Economic and Social History of the Orient* 41, no.3 (1998), 249–84.

"The Rise of the West – Or Not? A Revision to Socio-Economic History," *Sociological Theory* 18, no.2 (2000), 175–94.

Gong, Gerrit, *The Standard of "Civilisation" in International Society* (Oxford: Clarendon Press, 1984).

Gorbachev, Mikhail, "Time of Perestroika Speech at the Ministry of Foreign Affairs, 23 May 1986," *Vestnik Ministerstva innostrannykh del SSR [Bulletin of the Ministry of Foreign Affairs of the USSR]*, August 5 1987, 4–6.

Perestroika: New Thinking for Our Country and the World (New York: Harper and Row, 1987).

"Political Report of the CPSU Central Committee at the 27th CPSU Congress, February 25, 1986," in Mikhail Gorbachev, ed., *Mikhail Gorbachev: Selected Speeches and Articles* (Moscow: Progress Publishers, 1987).

The August Coup: The Truth and the Lessons (New York: HarperCollins, 1991).

Memoirs (New York: Doubleday, 1996).

Grande, Julian, *Japan's Place in the World* (London: Herbert Jenkins Limited, 1934).

Gray, Asa, "Review of Darwin's *Evolution of the Species*," *The Atlantic* July (1860) reproduced online at www.theatlantic.com/doc/186007/gray.

Greenfeld, Liah, *Nationalism: Five Roads to Modernity* (Cambridge, MA: Harvard University Press, 1992).

Grew, Joseph C., *Turbulent Era; A Diplomatic Record of Forty Years, 1904–1945* (Boston: Houghton Mifflin, 1952).

Lozan Günlüğü, K. M. Orağlı, trans. (Istanbul: Multilingual, 2001).

Griffin, Larry J., "Causal Interpretation in Historical Sociology," *The American Journal of Sociology* 98, no.5 (1993), 1094–133.

Grigoriadis, I. "Friends No More? The Rise of Anti-American Nationalism in Turkey," *The Middle East Journal* 64, no.1 (2010), 51–66.

Grovin, J. H., "Soviet Russia: Some Observations," *Journal of the British Institute of International Affairs* 5, no.2 (1926), 61–78.

Guins, George C., "Russia's Place in World History," *Russian Review* 22, no.4 (1963), 355–68.

Güçlü, Yücel, "Turkey's Entrance into League of Nations," *Middle Eastern Studies* 39, no.1 (2003), 186–206.

Haggard, Stephan, *Developing Nations and the Politics of Global Integration* (Washington, DC: Brookings Institution, 1995).

Hall, Peter, ed., *The Political Power of Economic Ideas* (Princeton: Princeton University Press, 1989).

Hall, Rodney Bruce and Friedrich V. Kratochwil, "Medieval Tales; Neorealist 'Science' and the Abuse of History," *International Organization* 47, no.3 (1993), 479–91.

Hall, Todd, "Getting Emotional: Towards a Theory of Emotions for International Relations" (MA Thesis, University of Chicago, 2003).

Halliday, Fred, "International Society as Homogeneity: Burke, Marx, Fukuyama," *Millennium* 21, no.3 (1992), 435–61.

Handelman, Stephen, *Comrade Criminal: Russia's New Mafia* (New Haven: Yale University Press, 1995).

Haugaard, Mark, "Power, Modernity and Liberal Democracy," in Malesevic and Haugaard, eds., *Ernest Gellner and Contemporary Social Thought*, pp. 75–102.

Hayes, Louis D., *Japan and the Security of Asia* (Lanham, MD: Lexington Books, 2001).

Hazan, Barukh, *Olympic Sports and Propaganda Games: Moscow 1980* (New Brunswick, NJ: Transaction Books, 1982).

Hegel, Georg Wilhelm Friedrich, *The Phenomenology of the Spirit*, A. V. Miller, trans. (Oxford: Oxford University Press, 1977 [1807]).

Elements of the Philosophy of Right, Allen W. Wood, ed., H. B. Nisbet, trans. (Cambridge: Cambridge University Press, 1991 [1820]).

"The German Constitution," in *Political Writings*, Laurence Dickey, ed., H. B. Nisbet, trans. (Cambridge: Cambridge University Press, 1999 [1802]), pp. 6–101.

Hellmann, Donald C., *Japanese Foreign Policy and Domestic Politics: The Peace Agreement with the Soviet Union* (Berkeley: University of California Press, 1969).

Japan and East Asia: The New International Order (New York: Praeger, 1972).

China and Japan: A New Balance of Power (Lexington, MA: Lexington Books, 1976).

Herman, Robert G., "Identity, Norms, and National Security: The Soviet Foreign Policy Revolution and the End of the Cold War," in P. J. Katzenstein, ed., *The Culture of National Security* (New York: Columbia University Press, 1996), pp. 271–316.

Hiroshi, Minami, *Nihonjinron: Meiji kara Ima Made* (Tokyo: Iwanami, 1995).

Hishida, Seiji, *Japan Among the Great Powers* (New York: Longmans, Green and Co., 1940).

Position of Japan as a Great Power (New York: AMS Press, 1968).

Hobbes, Thomas, *Leviathan* (Oxford: Oxford University Press, 2009).

Hobsbawn, Eric, *The Age of Revolution: 1789–1848* (London: Abacus, 2003).

The Age of Capital: 1848–1875 (London: Abacus, 2003).

The Age of Empire: 1875–1914 (London: Abacus, 2003).

Hobson, John M., *The Eastern Origins of Western Civilisation* (Cambridge: Cambridge University Press, 2004).

Hobson, John M. and J. C. Sharman, "The Enduring Place of Hierarchy in World Politics: Tracing the Social Logics of Hierarchy and Political Change," *European Journal of International Relations* 11, no.1 (2005), 63–98.

Hollis, Martin and Steve Smith, *Explaining and Understanding International Relations* (Oxford: Oxford University Press, 1990).

Holsti, Kal J., "Politics in Command: Foreign Trade as National Security Policy," *International Organization* 40, no.3 (1986), 643–71.

Hosking, Geoffrey, *Russia and the Russians: A History* (Cambridge, MA: Harvard University Press, 2001).

Hosoya, Chihiro, "Characteristics of the Foreign Policy Decision-Making System in Japan," *World Politics* 26, no.3 (1974), 353–69.

Hume, David, *A Treatise of Human Nature* (New York: Dover, 2003 [1888/1739]).

Huntington, Samuel P., "Political Modernization: America vs. Europe," *World Politics* 18, no.3 (1966), 378–414.

Political Order in Changing Societies (New Haven: Yale University Press, 1968).

"The Change to Change: Modernization, Development, and Politics," *Comparative Politics* 3, no.3 (1971), 283–322.

"The Clash of Civilizations," *Foreign Affairs* 72, no.3 (1993), 22–49.

Hurrell, Andrew and Ngaire Woods, eds., *Inequality, Globalization, and World Politics* (Oxford: Oxford University Press, 1999).

Huysmans, Jef, "Security! What Do You Mean?" *European Journal of International Relations* 4, no.2 (1998), 226–55.

Ikenberry, John G., *After Victory: Institutions, Strategic Restraint, and the Rebuilding of Order after Major Wars* (Princeton: Princeton University Press, 2001).

Ikenberry, John G. and Charles A. Kupchan, "Socialization and Hegemonic Power," *International Organization* 44, no.3 (2001), 487–515.

Inoguchi, Takashi, "Asia and the Pacific Since 1945: A Japanese Perspective," in Robert H. Taylor, ed., *Handbooks to the Modern World: Asia and the Pacific* (New York: Facts on File, 1990), pp. 903–20.

"Japan's Foreign Policy in Asia," *Current History*, (December 1992), 407–12.

"Japan's Role in International Affairs," *Survival* (Summer 1992) 34, no.2, 71–106.

"Japan: Reassessing the Relationship between Power and Wealth," in N. Woods, ed., *Explaining International Relations Since 1945* (New York: Oxford University Press, 1996), pp. 241–58.

Japanese Politics (Melbourne: Trans Pacific Press, 2005).

Inoguchi, Takashi and Kinhide Mushakoji, "The Japanese Image of the Future," in H. Ornauer, H. Wiberg, A. Sicinski, and J. Galtung, eds., *Images of the World in the Year 2000* (Atlantic Highlands, NJ: Humanities Press, 1976), pp. 217–36.

Inoki, Masamichi, ed., *Japan's Future in Southeast Asia* (Kyoto: Kyoto University, 1966).

Iriye, Akira, ed., *Japan and the New Asia* (Chicago: The Council, 1976).

Islam, Shafiqul, *Yen for Development: Japanese Foreign Aid and the Politics of Burden-sharing* (New York: Council on Foreign Relations Press, 1991).

Jackson, Patrick Thaddeus, "Hegel's House, or 'People are States too'," *Review of International Studies* 30 (2004), 281–7.

Civilizing the Enemy: German Reconstruction and the Invention of the West (Ann Arbor: University of Michigan Press, 2006).

Jansen, Marius B., *The Emergence of Meiji Japan* (New York: Cambridge University Press, 1995).

The Making of Modern Japan (London: Belknap Press of Harvard University Press, 2000).

Jansen, Marius B. and Gilbert Rozman, *Japan in Transition, from Tokugawa to Meiji* (Princeton: Princeton University Press, 1986).

Johnston, Alastair Iain, "Treating International Institutions as Social Environments," *International Studies Quarterly* 45, no.4 (2001), 487–515.

Jones, Eric L., *The European Miracle: Environments, Economics, and Geopolitics in the History of Europe and Asia* (Cambridge: Cambridge University Press, 1981).

Kahler, Miles, "External Ambition and Economic Performance," *World Politics* 40, no.4 (1988), 419–51.

Kang, David C., "Getting Asia Wrong: The Need for New Analytical Frameworks," *International Security* 27, no.4 (2003), 57–85.

Kantemir, Dimitri, *Osmanlı İmparatorluğunun Yükseliş ve Çöküş Tarihi*, Özdemir Çobanoğlu, trans. (Ankara: Kültür Bakanlığı Yayınları, 1979 [1716]).

Karacan, Ali Naci, *Lozan* (Istanbul: Nokta Kitap, 2006 [1943]).

Kassianova, Allia, "Russia: Still Open to the West? Evolution of the State Identity in the Foreign Policy and Security Discourse," *Europe-Asia Studies* 53, no.6 (2001), 821–39.

Katzenstein, Peter J., *Cultural Norms and National Security: Police and Military in Postwar Japan* (Ithaca, NY: Cornell University Press, 1996).

ed., *Civilizations in World Politics* (New York: Routledge, 2010).

Katzenstein, Peter J., Robert O. Keohane, and Stephen D. Krasner, eds., *Exploration and Contestation in the Study of World Politics* (Cambridge, MA: MIT Press, 2002).

Katzenstein, Peter J. and Okawara Nobuo, *Japan's National Security: Structures, Norms and Policy Responses in a Changing World* (Ithaca, NY: Cornell University Press, 1993).

"Japan, Asian-Pacific Security, and the Case for Analytical Eclecticism," *International Security* 26, no.3 (2001/02), 153–85.

Katzenstein, Peter J. and Rudra Sil, "Rethinking Asian Security," in J. J. Suh, Peter J. Katzenstein, and Allen Carlson, eds., *Rethinking Security in East Asia* (Stanford: Stanford University Press, 2004), pp. 1–33.

Keene, Edward, *Beyond Anarchical Society* (Cambridge: Cambridge University Press, 2002).

Kennedy-Pipe, Caroline, *Russia and the World, 1917–1991* (New York: Arnold, 1998).

Keohane, Robert O., *After Hegemony: Cooperation and Discord in World Political Economy* (Princeton: Princeton University Press, 1984).

ed., *Neorealism and Its Critics* (New York: Columbia University Press, 1986).

"Theory of World Politics: Structural Realism and Beyond," in R. O. Keohane, ed., *Neorealism and Its Critics*, pp. 158–203.

Kerr, David, "The New Eurasianism: The Rise of Geopolitics in Russia's Foreign Policy," *Europe-Asia Studies* 47, no.6 (1995), 977–88.

Khalid, Adeeb, "Backwardness and the Quest for Civilization: Early Soviet Central Asia in Comparative Perspective," *Slavic Review* 65, no.2 (2006), 231–51.

Kingsbury, Benedict, "Sovereignty and Inequality," in A. Hurrell and N. Woods, eds., *Inequality, Globalization, and World Politics* (Oxford: Oxford University Press, 1999), pp. 66–94.

Kinnvall, Catarina, *Globalization and Religious Nationalism in India* (New York: Routledge, 2006).

Kissinger, Henry, "The New Russian Question," *Newsweek* 119, no. 6 (1992) 119, no.6 (1992), 34-5.

Klien, Susanne, *Rethinking Japan's Identity and International Role: An Intercultural Perspective* (New York: Routledge, 2002).

Klotz, Audie, "Norms Reconstituting Interests: Global Racial Equality and U.S. Sanctions Against South Africa," *International Organization* 49, no.3 (1995), 451–78.

"Norms and Sanctions: Lessons from the Socialization of South Africa," *Review of International Studies* 22, no.2 (1996), 173–90.

Kojève, Alexandre, *Introduction to the Reading of Hegel*, Allan Bloom, ed., James H. Nichols, trans. (Ithaca, NY: Cornell University Press, 1980).

Konrad, Sebastian, "Entangled Memories: Versions of the Past in Germany and Japan, 1945–2001," *Journal of Contemporary History* 38, no.1 (2003), 85–99.

Koslowski, Rey and Friedrich V. Kratochwil, "Understanding Change in International Politics: The Soviet Empire's Demise and the International System," *International Organization* 48, no.2 (1994), 215–47.

Krasner, Stephen D., ed., *International Regimes* (Ithaca, NY: Cornell University Press, 1983).

"Structural Causes and Regime Consequences: Regimes as Intervening Variables," in Krasner, ed., *International Regimes*, pp. 1–21.

Structural Conflict: The Third World against Global Liberalism (Berkeley: University of California Press, 1985).

Krastev, Ivan, "What Russia Wants," *Foreign Policy* no.166 (2008), 48–51.

Kropotkin, Petr Alekseevich, *Memoirs of a Revolutionist* (New York: Houghton Mifflin and Co., 1899).

Fields, Factories and Workshops: Industry Combined with Agriculture and Brain Work with Manual Work, new, rev., and enlarged edn. (New York: G. P. Putnam's Sons, 1913).

Kubálková, V. and A. A. Cruickshank, *Thinking New About Soviet "New Thinking"* (Berkeley: Institute of International Studies, University of California, 1989).

Laing, R. D., *The Divided Self* (Harmondsworth: Penguin, 1969).

Larson, Deborah Welch and Alexei Shevchenko, "Shortcut to Greatness: The New Thinking and the Revolution in Soviet Foreign Policy," *International Organization* 57, no.1 (2003), 77–109.

Laue, Theodore von, "Soviet Diplomacy: G.V. Chicherin, People's Commissar for Foreign Affairs, 1918–1930," in G. A. Craig and F. Gilbert, eds., *The Diplomats, 1919–1939* (New York: Athenaeum, 1963), pp. 234–81.

Lavoy, Peter, "Nuclear Myths and the Causes of Nuclear Proliferation," *Security Studies* 2, no.3/4 (1993), 192–212.

Lawrence, Philip K., *Modernity and War: The Creed of Absolute Violence* (New York: Macmillan, 1997).

Lebow, Richard Ned, "The Long Peace, the End of the Cold War, and the Failure of Realism," *International Organization* 48, no.2 (1994), 249–77.

A Cultural Theory of International Relations (Cambridge: Cambridge University Press, 2008).

Legro, Jeffrey, *Rethinking the World: Great Power Strategies and International Order* (Ithaca, NY: Cornell University Press, 2005).

Leheny, David, *The Rules of Play* (Ithaca, NY: Cornell University Press, 2003).

"The Samurai Ride to Huntington's Rescue," in Peter J. Katzenstein, ed., *Civilizations in World Politics* (New York: Routledge, 2009), ch. 5.

Levy, Jack S., "Historical Trends in Great Power War, 1495–1975," *International Studies Quarterly* 26, no.2 (1982), 278–300.

Lewis, Bernard, *The Emergence of Modern Turkey* (New York: Oxford University Press, 1961).

Little, Richard and John Williams, *The Anarchical Society in a Globalized World* (New York: Palgrave Macmillan, 2006).

Ludwig, Gerhard, *A World at Arms: A Global History of World War II* (Cambridge: Cambridge University Press, 1994).

Lustick, Ian S., "The Absence of Middle Eastern Great Powers: Political 'Backwardness' in Historical Perspective," *International Organization* 51, no.4 (1997), 653–83.

Lynch, Allen C., "The Realism of Russia's Foreign Policy," *Europe-Asia Studies* 53, no.1 (2001), 7–31.

Mahoney, James, "Comparative-Historical Methodology," *Annual Review of Sociology* 30, August (2004), 81–101.

Maines, David R., "The Social Construction of Meaning," *Contemporary Sociology* 29, no.4 (2000), 577–84.

Malcolm, Neil and Alex Pravda, "Democratization and Russian Foreign Policy," *International Affairs* 72, no.3 (1996), 537–52.

Malesevic, Sinisa and Mark Haugaard, eds., *Ernest Gellner and Contemporary Social Thought* (Cambridge: Cambridge University Press, 2007).

"Introduction: An Intellectual Rebel with a Cause," in Malesevic and Haugaard, eds., *Ernest Gellner and Contemporary Social Thought*, pp. 1–28.

Mann, Michael, *States, War, and Capitalism: Studies in Political Sociology* (New York: Basil Blackwell, 1988).

"Predation and Production in European Imperialism," in Malesevic and Haugaard, eds., *Ernest Gellner and Contemporary Social Thought*, pp. 50–74.

March, James and Johan P. Olsen, *Rediscovering Institutions* (New York: Free Press, 1989).

Markell, Patchen, *Bound by Recognition* (Princeton: Princeton University Press, 2003).

Marshall, T. H., "Citizenship and Social Class," in Thomas Humphrey Marshall, ed., *Sociology at the Crossroads* (London: Heinemann, 1963), pp. 67–127.

Martin, Lisa, *Coercive Cooperation: Explaining Multilateral Economic Sanctions* (Princeton: Princeton University Press, 1992).

Marx, Karl, *Capital: A Critique of Political Economy* (Harmondsworth: Penguin Books, 1976 [1867]).

Matsuda, Takeshi, *Soft Power and Its Perils: U.S. Cultural Policy in Early Postwar Japan and Permanent Dependency* (Washington, DC: Woodrow Wilson Press, 2007).

Matsuyama, Yukio, "The Outlook for U.S.–Japan Relations," in Iriye, ed., *Japan and the New Asia*, pp. 42–61.

Maull, Hanns W., "Germany and Japan: The New Civilian Powers," *Foreign Affairs* 69, no.5 (1990/91), 91–106.

McFaul, Michael, *Russia's 1996 Presidential Election: The End of Polarized Politics* (Stanford: Hoover Institution Press, 1997).

"Getting Russia Right," *Foreign Policy* 117, Winter (1999–2000), 58–73.

McNeill, William Hardy, *The Rise of the West: A History of the Human Community* (New York: The New American Library, 1965).

"A Defence of World History: The Prothero Lecture," *Transactions of the Royal Historical Society* 32 (1982), 75–89.

Pursuit of Power (Chicago: University of Chicago Press, 1984).

The Age of Gunpowder Empires, 1450–1800 (Washington, DC: American Historical Association, 1989).

McSweeney, Bill, *Security, Identity and Interests* (Cambridge: Cambridge University Press, 1999).

Melson, Robert, "Paradigms of Genocide: The Holocaust, the Armenian Genocide and Contemporary Mass Destructions," *Annals of the American Academy of Political and Social Science* 548, no.1 (1996), 156–68.

Mendelson, Sarah E., "Internal Battles and External Wars: Politics, Learning, and the Soviet Withdrawal from Afghanistan," *World Politics* 45, no.3 (1993), 327–60.

Changing Course: Ideas, Politics, and the Soviet Withdrawal from Afghanistan (Princeton: Princeton University Press, 1998).

"Democracy Assistance and Political Transition in Russia: Between Success and Failure," *International Security* 25, no.4 (2001), 68–106.

Mendl, Wolf, *Japan's Asia Policy: Regional Security and Global Interests* (London: Routledge, 1995).

Mercer, Jonathan, *Reputation and International Politics* (Ithaca, NY: Cornell University Press, 1996).

Meyer, John W., "The World Polity and the Authority of the Nation-state," in A. J. Bergesen, ed., *Studies of the Modern World-System* (New York: Academic Press, 1980), pp. 109–37.

Meyer, John W., John Boli, George M. Thomas, and Francisco O. Ramirez, "World Society and the Nation-State," *The American Journal of Sociology* 103, no.1 (1997), 144–81.

Meyer, John W. and Ronald L. Jepperson, "The 'Actors' of Modern Society: The Cultural Construction of Social Agency," *Sociological Theory* 18, no.1 (2000), 100–20.

Meyer, John W., Joanne Nagel, and Conrad W. Snyder, "The Expansion of Mass Education in Botswana: Local and World Society Perspectives," *Comparative Education Review* 37, no.4 (1993), 454–75.

Mikhailov, M. I. and N. V. Shelgunov, *The Proclamation to the Younger Generation* [*K molodomu pokoleniiu*] (St. Petersburg, 1861).

Mill, John Stuart, *On Liberty* (New York: Penguin, 2007 [1869]).

Mitchell, Tim, *Colonising Egypt* (Cambridge: Cambridge University Press, 1988).

Rule of Experts (Berkeley: University of California Press, 2002).

Mitzen, Jennifer, "Ontological Security in World Politics: State Identity and the Security Dilemma," *European Journal of International Relations* 12, no.3 (2006), 341–70.

Miwa, Kimitada, "Japanese Policies and Concepts for Regional Order in Asia, 1938–1940," in James W. White, Michio Umegaki, and Thomas R. H. Havens, eds., *The Ambivalence of Nationalism: Modern Japan between East and West* (New York: University Press of America, 1990), pp. 133–56.

Moore, Barrington, *Social Origins of Dictatorship and Democracy* (Boston: Beacon Press, 1966).

Morelli, Elizabeth, "Ressentiment and Rationality," unpublished draft accessible at http://bu.edu/wcp/Papers/Anth/AnthMore.htm.

Morgenthau, Hans J., *Politics among Nations: The Struggle for Power and Peace*, 5th edn. (New York: Knopf, 1978).

Morley, James W., "Between Two Eras," in Iriye, ed., *Japan and the New Asia*, pp. 1–31.

Motyl, Alexander J., "Structural Constraints and Starting Points: The Logic of Systemic Change in Ukraine and Russia," *Comparative Politics* 29, no.4 (1997), 433–47.

"Why Empires Reemerge: Imperial Collapse and Imperial Revival in Comparative Perspective," *Comparative Politics* 31, no.2 (1999), 127–45.

Mouzelis, Nicos, "Nationalism: Restructuring Gellner's Theory," in Malesevic and Haugaard, eds., *Ernest Gellner and Contemporary Social Thought*, pp. 125–39.

Mukae, Ryuji, "Japan's Diet Resolution on World War Two: Keeping History at Bay," *Asian Survey* 36, no.10 (1996), 1011–30.

Murphy, Raymond, "The Structure of Closure: A Critique and Development of the Theories of Weber, Collins, and Parkin," *The British Journal of Sociology* 35, no.4 (1984), 547–67.

"Weberian Closure Theory: A Contribution to the Ongoing Assessment," *The British Journal of Sociology* 37, no.1 (1986), 21–41.

Myint, Hla, "The Inward and Outward Looking Countries of Southeast Asia and the Economic Future of the Region," in Inoki, ed., *Japan's Future in Southeast Asia*, pp. 1–29.

Naff, Thomas, "Ottoman Empire," in Bull and Watson, eds., *The Expansion of International Society*, pp. 143–69.

Nettl, J. P. and Roland Robertson, "Industrialization, Development and Modernization," *The British Journal of Sociology* 17, no.3 (1966), 274–91.

Neumann, Iver B., "Review: International Relations Theory and the New World Order," *Mershon International Studies Review* 40, no.2 (1996), 349–51.

Russia and the Idea of Europe (New York: Routledge, 1996).

Russia as Europe's Other (San Domenico, Italy: EUI Working Paper, 1996).

"Self and Other in International Relations," *European Journal of International Relations* 2, no.2 (1996), 139–74.

Uses of the Other: "The East" in European Identity Formation (Minneapolis: University of Minnesota Press, 1998).

"Beware of Organicism: The Narrative Self of the State," *Review of International Studies* 30, no.2 (2004), 259–67.

Neumann, Iver B. and Jennifer M. Welsh, "The Other in European Self-Definition: An Addendum to the Literature on International Society," *Review of International Studies* 17 (1991), 327–48.

Nicholson, Martin, "Putin's Russia: Slowing the Pendulum without Stopping the Clock," *International Affairs* 77, no.4 (2001), 867–84.

Nietzsche, Friedrich, *On the Genealogy of Morals* (New York: Vintage Books, 1989 [1887]).

Beyond Good and Evil, Walter Kaufmann, trans. (New York: Vintage Books, 1989 [1886]).

North, Douglass C. and Robert Paul Thomas, *The Rise of the Western World: A New Economic History* (Cambridge: Cambridge University Press, 1973).

O'Hagan, Jacinta, *Conceptualizing the West in International Relations: From Spengler to Said* (New York: Palgrave, 2002).

O'Loughlin, John, Gearóid Ó Tuathail, and Vladimir Kolossov, "A 'Risky Westward Turn'? Putin's 9–11 Script and Ordinary Russians," *Europe-Asia Studies* 56, no.1 (2004), 3–34.

O'Neill, Barry, *Honor, Symbols and War* (Ann Arbor: University of Michigan Press, 1999).

Olofsson, Gunnar, "Norbert Elias," in Heine Andersen and Lars Bo Kaspersen, eds., *Classical and Modern Social Theory* (Malden, MA: Blackwell Publishing, 2000), pp. 361–75.

Olson, Mancur, *Power and Prosperity: Outgrowing Communist and Capitalist Dictatorships* (New York: Basic Books, 2000).

Orbay, Rauf, *Siyasi Hatıralar (1914–1939)*, A. Uğurlu, ed. (Istanbul: Örgün Yayınevi, 2005).

Osgood, Robert E., "Japan and the United States in Asia," in *Japan and the United States in Asia* (Baltimore: The Johns Hopkins Press, 1968), pp. 1–30.

Ottoman Archives, Yıldız Collection, The Armenian Question (Istanbul: Tarihi Araştirmalar ve Dokumentasyon Merkezleri Kurma ve Geliştirme Vakfı, 1989).

Owen, IV, John M., "Transnational Liberalism and U.S. Primacy," *International Security* 26, no.3 (2001/02), 117–52.

Oye, Kenneth, ed., *Cooperation Under Anarchy* (Princeton: Princeton University Press, 1986).

Özer, Ahmet, *Osmanlıdan Cumhuriyete* (Istanbul: Sis Yayıncılık, 2002).

Özer, İlbeyi, *Avrupa Yolunda Batılaşma ya da Batılılaşma* (Istanbul: Truva, 2005).

Özyürek, Esra, *Nostalgia for the Modern: State Secularism and Everyday Politics in Turkey* (Durham: Duke University Press, 2006).

Packard III, George R., "Living with the Real Japan," in R. E. Osgood, ed., *Japan and the Real Asia* (Baltimore: Johns Hopkins Press, 1968), pp. 31–47.

Paige, Jeffery M., "Theory in Macrosocial Inquiry," *The American Journal of Sociology* 105, no.3 (1999), 781–800.

Pamuk, Orhan, *Snow* (New York: Knopf, 2004).

"My Father's Suitcase," Nobel Lecture, given on December 7, 2006 (http://nobelprize.org/nobel_prizes/literature/laureates/2006/pamuk-lecture_en.html).

Patman, Robert G., "Reagan, Gorbachev and the Emergence of 'New Political Thinking'," *Review of International Studies* 25, no.4 (1999), 577–601.

Patomaki, Heikki, "How to Tell Better Stories about World Politics," *European Journal of International Relations* 2, no.1 (1996), 105–33.

Pempel, T. J., *Policymaking in Contemporary Japan* (Ithaca, NY: Cornell University Press, 1977).

"Japanese Foreign Economic Policy: The Domestic Bases for International Behavior," *International Organization* 31, no.4 (1977), 723–74.

Perinçek, Mehmet, *Atatürk'ün Sovyetlerle Görüşmeleri* (Istanbul: Kaynak Yayınları, 2005).

Perlmutter, Amos, "Who Lost Russia … Our New Rival? Neither Ally nor Partner," *Washington Times* February 18 (1998), A17.

Plato, *The Republic of Plato*, 2nd edn., Allan Bloom, trans. (New York: Basic Books, 1991).

Polanyi, Karl, *The Great Transformation: The Political and Economic Origins of Our Time*, 2nd edn. (Boston: Beacon Press, 2001).

Polunov, Alexander, *Russia in the Nineteenth Century*, Thomas C. Owen and Larissa G. Zakharova, eds., Marshall S. Shatz, trans. (Armonk, NY: M. E. Sharpe, 2005).

Rachman, Giedon, "America is Losing the Free World," *Financial Times* January 5, 2010, p. 9.

Ramirez, Francisco O., "Global Changes, World Myths, and the Demise of Cultural Gender," in T. Boswell and A. J. Bergesen, eds., *America's Changing Role in the World-System* (New York: Praeger, 1987), pp. 257–74.

Ramirez, Francisco O. and John Boli, "The Political Construction of Mass Schooling: European Origins and Worldwide Institutionalization," *Sociology of Education* 60, no.1 (1987), 2–17.

Reginster, Bernard, "Nietzsche on Ressentiment and Valuation," *Philosophy and Phenomenological Research* 57, no.2 (1997), 281–305.

Reisch, George A., "Chaos, History, and Narrative," *History and Theory* 30, no.1 (1991) 1–20.

Reus-Smit, Christian, *The Moral Purpose of the State: Culture, Social Identity, and Institutional Rationality in International Relations* (Princeton: Princeton University Press, 1999).

Rhee, Syngman, *Japan Inside Out: The Challenge of Today*, 2nd edn. (New York: Revell, 1941).

Ringmar, Erik, "On the Ontological Status of the State," *European Journal of International Relations* 2, no.4 (1996), 439–66.

  "The Recognition Game: Soviet Russia against the West," *Cooperation and Conflict* 37, no.2 (2002), 115–36.

Risse-Kappen, Thomas, "Ideas Do Not Float Freely: Transnational Coalitions, Domestic Structures, and the End of the Cold War," *International Organization* 48, March (1994), 185–214.

Roberts, Cynthia and Thomas Sherlock, "Bringing the Russian State Back in: Explanations of the Derailed Transition to Market Democracy," *Comparative Politics* 31, no.4 (1999), 477–98.

Rockingham, Alexandra, "Interview with Orhan Pamuk," *The Believer* May (2006), 74–8.

Rodríguez, Ileana, ed., *The Latin American Subaltern Studies Reader* (Durham, NC: Duke University Press, 2001).

Rousseau, Jean Jacques, *The Social Contract or Principles of Right* (Kessinger Publishing, 1994 [1776]) .

Ruggie, John Gerard, "Continuity and Transformation in the World Polity: Toward a Neorealist Synthesis," in Keohane, ed., *Neorealism and Its Critics*, pp. 131–57.

"Territoriality and Beyond: Problematizing Modernity in International Relations," *International Organization* 47, no.1 (1993), 139–74.

"What Makes the World Hang Together? Neo-Utilitarianism and the Social Constructivist Challenge," *International Organization* 52, no.4 (1998), 855–85.

Russett, Bruce, *Controlling the Sword: The Democratic Governance of National Security* (Cambridge, MA: Harvard University Press, 1990).

Said, Edward, *Orientalism* (New York: Vintage Books, 1979).

Saint-Exupéry, Antoine de, *The Little Prince*, K. Woods, trans. (New York: Reynal & Hitchcock, 1943).

Salter, Mark B., *Barbarians and Civilization in International Relations* (Sterling, VA: Pluto Press, 2002).

Scheff, Thomas J., "Shame and the Social Bond: A Sociological Theory," *Sociological Theory* 18, no.1 (2000), 84–99.

Schmitt, Richard, *Alienation and Class* (Cambridge, MA: Schenkman, 1983).

Schofer, Evan, "Science Associations in the International Sphere 1875–1990: The Rationalization of Science and the Scientization of Society," in J. Boli and G. M. Thomas, eds., *Constructing World Culture: International Non-Governmental Organizations since 1875* (Stanford: Stanford University Press, 1999), pp. 249–66.

Schweller, Randall L. and William C. Wohlforth, "Power Test: Evaluating Realism in Response to the End of the Cold War," *Security Studies* 9, no.3 (2000), 60–107.

Scott, W. Richard and John W. Meyer, eds., *Institutional Environment and Organizations: Structural Complexity and Individualism* (Thousand Oaks, CA: Sage Publications, 1994).

Sergeev, Viktor, *The Wild East: Crime and Lawlessness in Post-Communist Russia* (New York: M. E. Sharpe, 1998).

Service, Robert, *A History of Twentieth-Century Russia* (Cambridge, MA: Harvard University Press, 1998).

The Russian Revolution, 1900–1927, 3rd edn. (New York: St. Martin's Press, 1999).

A History of Modern Russia: From Nicholas II to Vladimir Putin (Cambridge, MA: Harvard University Press, 2005).

Sewell, William Hamilton, "Three Temporalities: Toward an Eventful Sociology," in T. J. McDonald, ed., *The Historic Turn in the Human Sciences* (Ann Arbor: University of Michigan Press, 1996).

Shaw, Stanford J., "The Financial and Administrative Organization and Development of Ottoman Egypt (1517–1798)" (PhD Thesis, Princeton University, 1959).

Between Old and New: The Ottoman Empire under Sultan Selim III, 1789–1807 (Cambridge, MA: Harvard University Press, 1971).

The Jews of the Ottoman Empire and the Turkish Republic (Basingstoke: Macmillan, 1991).

Shermer, Michael, "Exorcising Laplace's Demon: Chaos and Antichaos, History and Metahistory," *Historical Theory* 34, no.1 (1995), 59–83.

Shevtsova, L., "Vladimir Putin," *Foreign Policy* 164 (2008), 34–6, 38, 40.

Shigeru, Yoshida, *The Yoshida Memoirs: The Story of Japan in Crisis* (London: Heinemann, 1961).

Last Meiji Man, Hiroshi Nara and Yoshida Ken-Ichi, eds. (Lanham, MA: Rowman & Littlefield, 2007).

Shulman, Marshall D., "Japan's Changing Relations with the Soviet Union," in Iriye, ed., *Japan and the New Asia*, pp. 32–42.

Sikkink, Kathryn, "Transnational Politics, International Relations Theory, and Human Rights," *PS: Political Science and Politics* 31, no.3 (1998), 516–23.

Sil, Rudra and Eileen M. Doherty, *Beyond Boundaries?: Disciplines, Paradigms, and Theoretical Integration in International Studies* (Albany: State University of New York Press, 2000).

Silan, Necmettin Şahir, *İlk Meclis Anketi: Birinci Dönem TBMM Milletvekillerinin Gelecekten Bekledikleri* (Ankara: TBMM Kültür, Sanat ve Yayın Kurulu, 2004 [1923]).

Simmel, George, "The Stranger," in H. K. Wolff, ed., *The Sociology of George Simmel* (New York: Free Press, 1950), pp. 402–9.

Simpson, Gerry, *Great Powers and Outlaw States: Unequal Sovereigns in the International Legal Order* (Cambridge: Cambridge University Press, 2004).

Şimşir, Bilâl N., *İngiliz Belgelerinde Atatürk, 1919–1938* (*British Documents on Atatürk, 1919–1938*) (Ankara: Türk Tarih Kurumu Basımevi, 1973).

Homage to Mustafa Kemal Atatürk; Hero of the East: Documents from the Turkish Archives, with Additions from the Pakistan Archives (Islamabad: Institute of Islamic History Culture and Civilization Islamic University, 1981).

Singer, Max and Aaron Wildavsky, *The Real World Order: Zones of Peace/Zones of Turmoil* (Chatham, NJ: Chatham House, 1996).

Skocpol, Theda, "Review: Wallerstein's World Capitalist System: A Theoretical and Historical Critique," *The American Journal of Sociology* 82, no.5 (1977), 1075–90.

    States and Social Revolutions: A Comparative Analysis of France, Russia, and China (Cambridge: Cambridge University Press, 1979).

Slaughter, Ann Marie, "International Law in a World of Liberal States," *European Journal of International Law* 6, no.1 (1995), 503–38.

Slevin, Peter and Peter Baker, "Bush Changing Views on Putin; Administration That Hailed Russian Leader Alters Course," *The Washington Post*, December 14 (2003), p. 26.

Smith, Steve, "Wendt's World," *Review of International Studies* 26, no.1 (2000), 151–63.

Smuts, J. C., "The British Empire and World Peace," *Journal of the Royal Institute of Royal Affairs* 9, no.2 (1930), 141–53.

Snyder, Jack L., *Myths of Empire: Domestic Politics and International Ambition* (Ithaca, NY: Cornell University Press, 1991).

    "Russia: Responses to Relative Decline," in T. V. Paul and J. A. Hall, eds., *International Order and the Future of World Politics* (Cambridge: Cambridge University Press, 1999).

Soroos, Marvin S., "Global Interdependence and the Responsibilities of States: Learning from the Japanese Experience," *Journal of Peace Research* 25, no.1 (1988), 17–29.

Spruyt, Hendrik, "Institutional Selection in International Relations: State Anarchy as Order," *International Organization* 48, no.4 (1994), 527–57.

    The Sovereign State and its Competitors (Princeton: Princeton University Press, 1994).

    Ending Empire: Contested Sovereignty and Territorial Partition (Ithaca, NY: Cornell University Press, 2005).

Stavrianos, Leften Stavros, *The Ottoman Empire: Was It the Sick Man of Europe?* (New York: Rinehart, 1957).

    Global Rift: The Third World Comes of Age, 1st edn. (New York: William Morrow & Co., 1981).

Steele, Brent J., *Ontological Security in International Relations* (New York: Routledge, 2008).

Stein, Janice Gross, "Political Learning by Doing: Gorbachev as Uncommitted Thinker and Motivated Learner," *International Organization* 48, no.2 (1994), 155–83.

Steinmetz, George, "Odious Comparisons: Incommensurability, the Case Study, and 'Small N's' in Sociology," *Sociological Theory* 22, no.3 (2004), 371–400.

Steven, Rob, *Japan's New Imperialism* (Houndmills: Macmillan, 1990).

Stinchcombe, Arthur L., *Constructing Social Theories* (New York: Harcourt Brace & World, 1968).

The Logic of Social Research (Chicago: University of Chicago Press, 2005).

Stokes, Bruce, "Divergent Paths: US–Japan Relations towards the Twenty-First Century," *International Affairs* 72, no.2 (1996), 281–91.

Strang, David, "From Dependency to Sovereignty: An Event History Analysis of Decolonization, 1870–1987," *American Sociological Review* 55, no.6 (1990), 346–60.

"Global Patterns of Decolonization, 1500–1987," *International Studies Quarterly* 35, no.4 (1991), 429–54.

Stryker, R., "Beyond History versus Theory: Strategic Narrative and Sociological Explanation," *Sociological Methods Research* 24, no.3 (1996), 304–52.

Suganami, Hidemi, "Japan's Entry into International Society," in Bull and Watson, eds., *The Expansion of International Society*, pp. 185–99.

Suphi, Hamdullah, "Irk ve Milliyet," *Yeni Mecmua* 67, no.1 (1923 [1339-lunar]), 7.

Suzuki, Shogo, "Japan's Socialisation into Janus-Faced European International Society," *European Journal of International Relations* 11, no.1 (2005), 137–64.

Civilization and Empire: China and Japan's Encounter with European International Society (New York: Routledge, 2008).

"Seeking 'Legitimate' Great Power Status in Post-Cold War International Society: China's and Japan's Participation in UNPKO," *International Relations* 22, no.1 (2008), 45–63.

"The Strange Masochism of the Japanese Right: Redrawing Moral Boundaries in Sino-Japanese Relations," draft (2008), pp. 1–21.

Tajfel, Henri, *Human Groups and Social Categories* (Cambridge: Cambridge University Press, 1981).

Tanaka, Stefan, *Japan's Orient* (Berkeley: University of California Press, 1995).

Taylor, Robert H., ed., *Asia and the Pacific* (New York: Facts on File, 1991).

Tekeli, İlhan and Selim İlkin, eds., *Köktenci Modernitenin Doğuşu* (Istanbul: Istanbul Bilgi Üniversitesi, 2004).

eds., *Modernitenin Altyapisi Olusurken* (Istanbul: Istanbul Bilgi Üniversitesi, 2004).

Thies, Cameron G., "A Social Psychological Approach to Enduring Rivalries," *Political Psychology* 22, no.4 (2001), 693–725.

Thomas, George M., John W. Meyer, Francisco O. Ramirez, and John Boli, eds., *Institutional Structure: Constituting State, Society, and the Individual* (Beverly Hills, CA: Sage, 1987).

Tilly, Charles, *Coercion, Capital, and European States, AD 990–1990* (Cambridge, MA: Blackwell, 1990).

  European Revolutions, 1492–1992 (Cambridge, MA: Blackwell, 1993).

  Identities, Boundaries, and Social Ties (Boulder, CO: Paradigm Publishers, 2005).

Tilly, Charles and Gabriel Ardant, *The Formation of National States in Western Europe* (Princeton: Princeton University Press, 1975).

Tipps, D.C. "Modernization Theory and the Comparative Study of Societies," *Comparative Studies in Society and History* 15, no.2 (1973), 196–226.

Tocqueville, Alexis de, *Democracy in America* (New York: Penguin, 2003).

Tönnies, Ferdinand, *Gemeinschaft and Gesellschaft* (Devon, UK: Dover, 2002 [1887]).

Totman, Conrad D., *A History of Japan*, 2nd edn. (Malden, MA: Blackwell, 2004).

Toynbee, Arnold, *The Western Question in Greece and Turkey* (New York: Houghton Mifflin Co., 1923).

  Turkey, with Kenneth Kirkwood (New York: Charles Scribner's Sons, 1927).

Toynbee, Arnold and Denison Ross, "The Modernisation of the Middle East," *Journal of the Royal Institute of International Affairs* 8, no.4 (1929) 344–66.

Trimberger, Ellen Kay, *Revolution from Above: Military Bureaucrats and Development in Japan, Turkey, Egypt, and Peru* (New Brunswick, NJ: Transaction Books, 1978).

Trotsky, Leon, *The Revolution Betrayed* (London: New Park, 1972 [1937]).

  History of the Russian Revolution, Max Eastman, trans. (New York: Pathfinder Press, 1980).

Tsunoda, Ryusaku, *Sources of the Japanese Tradition* (New York: Columbia University Press, 1958).

Tsygankov, Andrei, "From International Institutionalism to Revolutionary Expansionism: The Foreign Policy Discourse of Contemporary Russia," *Mershon International Studies Review* 41, no.2 (1997), 247–68.

Tunaya, Tarık Zafer, *Türkiye'de Siyasal Gelişmeler [1876–1938]* (Istanbul: Istanbul University Press, 2004).

Türkiye'nin Siyasi Hayatında Batılılaşma Hareketleri (Istanbul: Istanbul Bilgi Üniversitesi, 2004).

"The Turkish Temptation," *The Wall Street Journal*, October 30 (2009), p. A24.

Turner, Jonathan H. and Robert A. Hanneman, "Some Theoretical Principles of Societal Stratification," *Sociological Theory* 2 (1984), 21–2.

Ubicini, Abdolonyme, *Lettres sur la Turquie* (Paris, 1854: Eng. trans. (by Lady Easthope) London, 1856).

Uğurlu, Andaç, ed., *Yabancı Gözüyle Cumhuriyet Türkiyesi (1928–1938)* (Istanbul: Örgün Yayınevi, 2003).

ed., *Türkiye'nin Parçalanması ve İngiliz Politikasi (1900–1920)* (Istanbul: Örgün Yayınevi, 2005).

Uldricks, Teddy J., *Diplomacy and Ideology: The Origins of Soviet Foreign Relations, 1917–1930* (London: Sage, 1979).

Üstel, Füsun, *Türk Ocakları (1912–1931)* (Istanbul: İletişim Yayınları, 2004).

Van der Vat, Dan *The Pacific Campaign: The Second World War: The US–Japanese Naval War (1941–1945)* (New York: Simon & Schuster, 1991).

Vincent, R. J., "Racial Equality," in Bull and Watson, eds., *The Expansion of International Society*, pp. 239–54.

Wallerstein, Immanuel Maurice, *The Modern World-System* (New York: Academic Press, 1974).

World Inequality: Origins and Perspectives on the World System (Montreal: Black Rose Books, 1975).

The Capitalist World-Economy: Essays (New York: Cambridge University Press, 1979).

"The Development of the Concept of Development," *Sociological Theory* 2, no.1 (1984), 102–16.

"The World-System after the Cold War," *Journal of Peace Research* 30, no.1 (1993), 1–6.

Waltz, Kenneth Neal, *Theory of International Politics* (Reading, MA: Addison-Wesley, 1979).

Man, State and the War (New York: Columbia University Press, 2001).

Wang, Hongying, "Multilateralism in Chinese Foreign Policy: The Limits of Socialization," *Asian Survey* 40, no.3 (2000), 475–91.

Watson, Adam, "Introduction," in Bull and Watson, eds., *The Expansion of International Society*, pp. 1–12.

"European International Society and Its Expansion," in Bull and Watson, eds., *The Expansion of International Society*, pp. 13–32.

"Russia and the European States System," in Bull and Watson, eds., *The Expansion of International Society*, pp. 61–74.

The Evolution of International Society: A Comparative Historical Analysis (New York: Routledge, 1992).

Weber, Max, *The Theory of Social and Economic Organization*, A. M. Henderson and Talcott Parsons, eds. (New York: Oxford University Press, 1947).

Basic Concepts in Sociology, H. P. Secher, ed. (Secaucus, NJ: Citadel Press, 1962).

Economy and Society: An Outline of Interpretive Sociology (Berkeley: University of California Press, 1978).

Max Weber on Capitalism, Bureaucracy, and Religion: A Selection of Text, Stanislav Andreski, ed. (Boston: Allen & Unwin, 1983).

"Politics as a Vocation," in *The Vocation Lectures*, Rodney Livingstone, trans. (Indianapolis: Hackett, 2004).

Weinstein, Martin, *Japan's Postwar Defense Policy, 1947–1968* (New York: Columbia University Press, 1971).

Weldes, Jutta, Mark Laffey, Hugh Gusterson, and Raymond Duvall, eds., *Cultures of Insecurity* (Minneapolis: University of Minnesota Press, 1999).

Wendt, Alexander, "Collective Identity Formation and the International State," *American Political Science Review* 88, no.2 (1994), 384–96.

"Constructing International Politics," *International Security* 20, no.1 (1995), 71–81.

Social Theory of International Politics (Cambridge: Cambridge University Press, 1999).

"Why a World State is Inevitable," *European Journal of International Relations* 9, no.4 (2003), 491–542.

"State as a Person," *Review of International Studies* 30, no.2 (2004), 289–316.

White, Stephen, *The Origins of Détente: The Genoa Conference and Soviet–Western Relations, 1921–1922* (Cambridge: Cambridge University Press, 1985).

White, Stephen and Ian McAllister, "Putin and His Supporters," *Europe-Asia Studies* 55, no.3 (2003), 383–99.

Wight, Colin, "State Agency: Social Action without Human Activity?" *Review of International Studies* 30, no.2 (2004), 269–80.

Agents, Structures and International Relations: Politics as Ontology (Cambridge: Cambridge University Press, 2006).

Wight, Martin, "Western Values in International Relations," in Herbert Butterfield and Martin Wight, eds., *Diplomatic Investigations: Essays in the Theory of International Politics* (London: Allen & Unwin, 1966), pp. 89–131.

Systems of States, Hedley Bull, ed. (Leicester: Leicester University Press, 1977).

Willetts, Peter, *The Non-Aligned Movement: The Origins of a Third World Alliance* (London: F. Pinter, 1978).

Wittfogel, Karl A., "Russia and Asia: Problems of Contemporary Area Studies and International Relations," *World Politics* 2, no.4 (1950), 445–62.

"Russia and the East: A Comparison and Contrast," *Slavic Review* 22, no.4 (1963), 627–43.

Wohlforth, William C., "Realism and the End of the Cold War," *International Security* 19, no.3 (1994/5), 91–129.

Woods, Ngaire, *Explaining International Relations since 1945* (Oxford: Oxford University Press, 1996).

Worringer, Renee, "'Sick Man of Europe' or 'Japan of the Near East'?: Constructing the Ottoman Modernity in the Hamidian and Young Turk Eras," *International Journal of Middle East Studies* 36, no.2 (2004), 207–30.

Wuthnow, Robert, "The World Economy and the Institutionalization of Science in Seventeenth-Century Europe," in A. Bergesen, ed., *Studies of the Modern World-System* (New York: Academic Press, 1980), pp. 25–55.

Yack, Bernard, "Review: Reconciling Liberalism and Nationalism," *Political Theory* 23, no.1 (1995), 166–82.

Yılmaz, Mustafa, *İngiliz Basını ve Atatürk'ün Türkiye'si* (Ankara: Phoenix, 2002).

Zaionchkovsky, Petr Andreevich and Susan Wobst, *The Abolition of Serfdom in Russia* (Gulf Breeze, FL: Academic International Press, 1978).

Zarakol, Ayşe, "Ontological (In)security and State Denial of Historical Crimes: Turkey and Japan," *International Relations* 24, no.1 (2010), 3–23.

Zeldin, Mary-Barbara, *Peter Yakovlevich Chaadayev, Philosophical Letters & Apology of a Madman*, trans. Mary-Barbara Zeldin (Knoxville: University of Tennessee Press, 1970).

Zolberg, Aristide R., "Review: Origins of the Modern World System: A Missing Link," *World Politics* 33, no.2 (1981), 253–81.

Index

Cambridge Studies in International Relations